SO-BBG-452

What do sex, contraceptives, marriage, divorce, alcohol, religion, politics, crime, and punishment have in common with inflation, monopoly, and exchange rates? The answer given in this book is that the former are all aspects of human behavior, which, like the latter, can be analyzed and modeled using conventional economic methods.

The application of economic reasoning to human behavior, which was until recently considered to be beyond the scope of economic analysis, was pioneered by Gary Becker, the 1992 Nobel Laureate in Economics. Becker's excursions into sociology, anthropology, and political science led him to think about issues such as marriage, religion, and crime in an entirely new way, and eventually to assert that all actions, whether working, playing, dating, or mating, have economic motivations and consequences.

This book is an accessible introduction to Becker's work and ideas. It explains to students the ways in which the standard tools of economics can be used to understand a wide range of human activities, and in doing so, offer provocative insights into a wide range of social issues.

The new economics of human behavior

FRANKLIN PIERCE
COLLEGE LIBRARY
RINDGE, N.H. 03461

The new economics of
human behavior

Edited by
Mariano Tommasi
and
Kathryn Ierulli

CAMBRIDGE
UNIVERSITY PRESS

FRANKLIN PIERCE
COLLEGE LIBRARY
RINDGE, N.H. 03461

Published by the Press Syndicate of the University of Cambridge
The Pitt Building, Trumpington Street, Cambridge CB2 1RP
40 West 20th Street, New York, NY 10011–4211, USA
10 Stamford Road, Oakleigh, Melbourne 3166, Australia

© Cambridge University Press 1995

First published 1995

Printed in Great Britain at the University Press, Cambridge

A catalogue record for this book is available from the British Library

Library of Congress cataloguing in publication data

The new economics of human behavior / edited by Mariano Tommasi and
Kathryn Ierulli.
    p.   cm.
ISBN 0 521 47420 5. – ISBN 0 521 47949 5 (pbk.)
1. Economics–Psychological aspects.   2. Economics–Sociological
aspects.   I. Tommasi, Mariano, 1964– . II. Ierulli, Kathryn.
HB74.P8N484   1995
330'.01'9–dc20   94-19809   CIP

ISBN 0 521 47420 5 hardback
ISBN 0 521 47949 5 paperback

HB
74
.P8
N
4r4
1995

Contents

Notes on contributors

George J. Borjas is Professor of Economics at the University of California, San Diego, and a Research Associate at the National Bureau of Economic Research. He obtained his Ph.D. from Columbia University in 1975. He has published widely in the area of immigration, including his 1990 book *Friends or Strangers: The Impact of Immigrants on the US Economy* (Basic Books). He was a member of the National Academy of Sciences Panel on Immigration Statistics, and is currently a member of the Governor's Council of Economic Advisers in California.

Barry R. Chiswick is Research Professor and Head, Department of Economics, University of Illinois at Chicago. Professor Chiswick's research has been primarily in the areas of income distribution, immigration, and racial and ethnic differences. His publications include "Education and the Distribution of Earnings" (co-author Gary S. Becker), *American Economic Review* (1967), "Racial Discrimination in the Labor Market: A Test of Alternative Hypotheses," *Journal of Political Economy* (1973), *Income Inequality* (NBER, 1974), "The Effect of Americanization on the Earnings of Foreign-Born Men," *Journal of Political Economy* (1978), "Differences in Education and Earnings Among Racial and Ethnic Groups: Tastes, Discrimination and Investment in Child Quality," *Quarterly Journal of Economics* (1988), and "The Impact of Immigrants on the Macroeconomy" (with C.U. Chiswick and G. Karras), *Carnegie–Rochester Conference Series on Public Policy*. Professor Chiswick has been on the Senior Staff of the Council of Economic Advisers (1973–7) and Fulbright Research Fellow (1992).

James S. Coleman was born in Bedford, Indiana, on May 12, 1926. He received his bachelor's degree in Chemical Engineering from Purdue University in 1949, and was awarded a Ph.D. in Sociology from Columbia University in 1955. From 1959 to 1973 he was an Associate Professor in the Department of Social Relations at Johns Hopkins University. Since 1973 he has been a Professor of Sociology and Education at the University of Chicago. His publications include *The Adolescent Society* (1961), *Introduction to Mathematical Sociology* (1964), *Public and Private High Schools: The Impact of Communities* (1987), *Foundations of Social Theory* (1990), *Equality and Achievement in Education* (1990), *Social Theory for a Changing Society* (1991). His current interests are in the social theory of norm formation, and in the functioning of schools.

Kermit Daniel is the Ken Ruby Assistant Professor of Public Policy and Management at the Wharton School of the University of Pennsylvania. He received his Ph.D. in Economics from the University of Chicago, where Gary Becker supervised his dissertation. His research interests include the economics of family structure, education, and immigration.

David Friedman is Visiting Professor at Cornell Law School. He has a Ph.D. in Physics from the University of Chicago. His research interests center on applications of economic theory to areas traditionally considered outside of economics, especially law and political institutions. He has taught at the University of Pennsylvania, Virginia Polytechnic Institute, UC Irvine, UCLA, Tulane Business School, University of Chicago Law School, and University of Chicago Business School. He is the author of *The Machinery of Freedom: Guide to a Radical Capitalism* and *Price Theory: an Intermediate Text*. He has published in journals such as *Journal of Political Economy*, *Journal of Legal Studies*, *Journal of Law and Economics*, *American Economic Review*, *Bell Journal of Economics*, and *International Review of Law and Economics*.

Edward L. Glaeser is an Assistant Professor of Economics at Harvard University. He received his Ph.D. from the University of Chicago in 1992, where he had been a student of and teaching assistant for Gary Becker. He has published on cities and (more importantly) fairy tales in the *Journal of Political Economy*.

Shoshana Grossbard-Shechtman received her Ph.D. in Economics from the University of Chicago in 1978. She wrote her dissertation on the economics of polygamy under the supervision of Gary Becker. She is presently Professor of Economics at San Diego State University. She has also taught economics and sociology at Bar-Ilan University, the Claremont Colleges, Occidental College, Tel Aviv University, and the University of California (San Diego). While a fellow at Stanford's Center for Advanced Study in the Behavioral Sciences, she co-organized an interdisciplinary group studying marriage, which led to a joint book with Kingsley Davis, *Contemporary Marriage – Comparative Perspectives on a Changing Institution*. She is the author of *On the Economics of Marriage – A Theory of Marriage, Labor and Divorce*, published by Westview Press in 1993.

Michael Grossman received his Ph.D. in Economics from Columbia University in 1970. His dissertation supervisor was Gary Becker. He is Distinguished Professor of Economics at the City University of New York Graduate School, where he has taught since 1972. He has served as Executive Officer (Chairperson) of that university's Ph.D. Program in Economics since 1983. Grossman also is Research Associate and Program Director of Health Economics Research at the National Bureau of Economic Research, where he has had an affiliation since 1970. He is the author of a monograph, twenty-nine journal articles, and fifteen book chapters. His research has focused on economic models of the determinants of adult, child, and infant health in the US; economic approaches to cigarette smoking and alcohol use by teenagers and young adults; empirical applications of rational addiction theories; the demand for pediatric care; the production and cost of ambulatory medical care in community health centers; and the determinants of interest rates on tax-exempt hospital bonds. He is an associate editor of the *Journal of Health Economics* and a member of the Institute of Medicine of the National Academy of Sciences.

David Hirshleifer is an Associate Professor of Finance at University of Michigan School of Business Administration. He was a student of and teaching assistant for Gary Becker at the University of Chicago. Hirshleifer has published papers on the enforcement of cooperation in groups; imitation, fads, and fashions; managerial self interest and corporate investment decisions; strategies for bidder and target firms in corporate takeover contests; how risk can be controlled using futures markets, and how futures prices are determined; and security analysis policies and trading styles of institutional stock market investors. He is currently interested in studying how forgetting can cause excessive inertia and project escalation in organizations. He is also currently collaborating with J. Fred Weston on a revision of *Mergers, Restructuring, and Corporate Control.*

Laurence R. Iannaccone is Associate Professor of Economics at Santa Clara University. He received a masters in Mathematics and a doctorate in Economics from the University of Chicago, and wrote his doctoral thesis on rational habit formation and religious behavior under the supervision of Gary Becker. His research on the economics of religion has appeared in the *Journal of Political Economy, American Journal of Sociology, Social Forces, Journal for the Scientific Study of Religion,* and many other journals and books.

Kathryn Ierulli is Assistant Professor at the University of Illinois at Chicago. She is in the process of receiving her Ph.D at the University of Chicago in Economics, with Gary Becker as one of her advisors. Her research interests include human capital investment, education and wage growth, and the economics of personnel.

John G. Matsusaka received his B.A. in Economics from the University of Washington in 1985 and his M.A. and Ph.D. in economics from the University of Chicago in 1991. He is now Assistant Professor of Finance and Business Economics in the School of Business Administration at the University of Southern California. His research focuses on corporate organization and restructuring, voter turnout, and direct legislation. He has been published in *The Quarterly Journal of Economics, RAND Journal of Economics, Journal of Industrial Organization,* and *Public Choice.*

Tomas Philipson is Assistant Professor at the Department of Economics at the University of Chicago. He came to the Department as a postdoctoral fellow under Gary Becker and James Coleman. His research interests include public sector economics, especially public health. He has taught price theory and public economics at both the graduate and undergraduate level at the University of Chicago.

Robert Tamura is Assistant Professor of Economics at the University of Iowa. He earned his Ph.D. in Economics from the University of Chicago in 1988. Gary S. Becker was his advisor. He works on human capital investments, fertility, economic growth, and the economics of sports.

Mariano Tommasi is an Assistant Professor at the Department of Economics of the University of California, Los Angeles. He was a student of and teaching assistant for Gary Becker at the University of Chicago. His research interests are the microeconomic effects of inflation and the interaction between politics and economics, particularly in developing countries. He has taught microeconomic theory, industrial organization, managerial economics, information and uncertainty, and political economy at UCLA (Department of Economics and Anderson Graduate School of Management), Tel Aviv University, Instituto di Tella (Argentina) and Universidad Catolica Argentina. He has been a consultant to the Argentine government. He is married to Paula Boilini and, following Becker's theory of the family, they plan to have children.

Edgardo E. Zablotsky is an Assistant Professor of Economics and Finance at the Center for Macroeconomic Studies of Argentina (CEMA). He received his Ph.D. in Economics from the University of Chicago. His current research focuses on the process of government under non-democratic political regimes. He is interested in the way in which the rules of the game affect the redistributive equilibrium in a society.

Preface

Jacob Viner, the great University of Chicago and Princeton economist, apparently once defined economics as what economists "do." By this definition, the scope of a field is determined by the subject matter addressed by the theories prevailing in that field. And by this definition, economics has changed enormously during the past four decades, for what economists "do" has been revolutionized.

Someone entering the study of economics in the 1950s, when I did, would have found a modest theory of consumer spending on goods in the marketplace, a theory of profit-maximizing firms and market equilibrium under competition, monopoly, and other market structures, a theory of the demand for labor and capital based on given production functions and factor prices, and a rudimentary theory of public choice where governments tried to maximize "social welfare."

Many of the most interesting social and economic issues were left out, perhaps to be studied by sociologists, political scientists, and psychologists. Economists failed to recognize that men and women not only buy apples and cars, but they also have children, rear and educate them, marry and divorce, buy luxury goods to gain prestige, take care of elderly parents without direct compensation, smoke and drink heavily, engage in crime, and discriminate sometimes viciously against blacks, Jews, women, and others. They also ignored that governments take many actions that can hardly be said to raise social welfare, such as imposing tariffs and quotas, and nationalizing companies.

Still, economists relied on an "approach" to economic behavior that differed radically from the approaches taken by other social scientists. Their approach assumed that firms, consumers, and workers maximize profits, utility, or wages, and that conflicts over the allocation of resources to different individuals and organizations create market forces that balance these conflicting pressures.

Several economists – including Philip H. Wicksteed, Simon Newcomb,

Francis Y. Edgeworth, and Lionel Robbins – realized long before the middle of this century that the economic approach defined by maximization and market equilibrium potentially had an enormous scope, and that economics could be considerably broadened beyond the subjects traditionally discussed. But they seldom used their vision to provide detailed analyses of phenomena outside these boundaries.

What economists "do" has vastly changed during the past several decades partly because modern economists have followed up the insights of these pioneers, and began to take seriously that maximizing behavior, equilibrium, and other aspects of the economic approach have a very wide reach. Hardly a nook or cranny of behavior is now escaping their attention. Discrimination against minorities, marriage and divorce, the legal system, addictions, the underclass, suicides, tariffs and regulations, and wars and conflict are just a few of the subjects investigated.

Moreover, it is now sometimes difficult to distinguish economists from other researchers, for increasing numbers of political scientists, lawyers, sociologists, and historians are also committed to variants of the economic approach. This intrusion of the economic approach into other fields has not usually been welcomed by scholars who take a more traditional way of looking at the subject matter of these fields.

By coming of age at a ripe time, I was able to participate in this expansion in the scope of the economic approach. Ever since my undergraduate days at Princeton, I was more interested in social issues than in those traditionally considered by economists. I almost changed to sociology when a senior because economics seemed too narrow. Fortunately, I went to Chicago for graduate studies, and the stimulus from Milton Friedman, H. Gregg Lewis, T.W. Schultz, and others then at Chicago convinced me that economics could be used to study "social" problems as well.

At the end of my first year there, I wrote an economic analysis of political behavior (published in abbreviated form much later, in the first issue (1957) of the *Journal of Law and Economics*). But my doctoral dissertation on discrimination was my first major attempt to expand the boundaries of economics. I did not anticipate that my subsequent career would be mainly devoted to considering other social and political issues outside the traditional scope of economics. Nor did I expect so many others, both inside and outside of economics, to be involved in related research.

I am flattered that many former students and present colleagues prepared essays for this volume on subjects I have studied, or on closely related subjects. The quality of the essays is very high, but I am pleased that I do not agree with all the opinions and conclusions. Disagreement, even among those using related approaches, is crucial to the progress of science.

This book is at heart not a celebration of my work, but a window to the world of research on the applications of the economic way of thinking to social, political, and legal, as well as economic, questions. The subjects considered include addictions, crime, discrimination, health, economic growth, immigration, marriage and relations among family members, peer pressure and social interactions, religious behavior, and political choices. The essays demonstrate that the economic approach provides many insights into some of the most fascinating and fundamental aspects of living in the modern world.

These essays are not technical, and can be appreciated by readers with only modest backgrounds in economic analysis. I strongly recommend them to anyone who wants a better understanding of the world about them.

Gary S. Becker

Acknowledgements

Several colleagues, friends and students provided valuable suggestions and advice throughout the process of editing this book. We would like to mention Armen Alchian, Patrick Asea, Gary Becker, Lee Fischman, Shoshana Grossbard-Shechtman, David Hirshleifer, Jack Hirshleifer, Myrna Hieke, Larry Iannaccone, Mike Intriligator, Chia-Tzn Luo, John Matsusaka, and Laura Wuertz. We are particularly indebted to Paula Boilini for her direct and indirect input into this project.

Introduction

Kathryn Ierulli, Edward L. Glaeser, and Mariano Tommasi

1 Overview

Everyone knows that economists have always studied prices, trade, markets, and money. Not everyone knows that they are now also researching topics like marriage, fertility, religion, politics, fads, crime, and punishment. These areas might seem intrinsically non-economic, and so inaccessible to economists. They are part of the field, however, when we have a broad and complete understanding of what economics is.

Contemporary economists believe that economics is not defined by its subject matter but by its method. Economists try to understand and explain the world by assuming that the phenomena they observe are the outcomes of people's purposeful decisions. *Individuals* try to achieve their objectives, given their limitations – limited time, money, and energy – that is to say, they *optimize*. The interactions of individuals will determine aggregate social outcomes – that is, *market equilibrium*.

This broader approach needs a more comprehensive definition of prices, goods, and markets. Markets are places where goods are exchanged and prices for those goods are paid. For economists, goods are just things we want to obtain. They can be resources like oil, manufactures like cars, or intangibles, such as esteem of one's colleagues, peaceful relations between countries, or a quiet evening at home. Some goods cannot be "purchased" only with money. Esteem, peace, and quietude are obtained by other means. Even goods such as meat (in Eastern Europe) and football tickets (in the US) are purchased with time, queuing on a first-come first-serve basis. The full price that people pay is a composite of the time, money, and effort they must give to obtain the good.

Divorce, parenthood, revolutions, education, crime in the alleys, and dancing in the streets are all instances of people making choices and paying prices for things they value. In this context all arenas of human interaction are markets and subject to economic analysis, which is the examination of people's behavior, of their choosing between alternative uses of resources.

1

The expansion of economics to new subjects is associated primarily with Gary S. Becker. He demonstrated the degree to which economic reasoning can improve our understanding of behavior. By illustrating the effectiveness of economic analysis in areas like crime, addiction, marriage and divorce, and addiction, Becker generated new areas of study and led hundreds of social scientists in innovative, challenging directions.

Some of these directions are examined in the following chapters. This book, written by students and colleagues of Becker, contains many illustrations of economics applied beyond the conventional scope of the discipline. In the following sections of the introduction we provide an overview of Becker's work and of the subsequent chapters.

2 Discrimination

The Economics of Discrimination was Becker's dissertation at the University of Chicago. It is very unusual for a doctoral thesis in economics to have a major impact on the field, and especially in this case where the work was very new, intellectually daring, and highly controversial even among economists. The use of economics to analyze a touchy subject such as discrimination was received with hostility by many economists, who thought this was straying too far afield. However, more than thirty-five years later, the economics of discrimination is firmly established not only in economics, but in nearly all the social sciences and in policy analysis.

Aside from the societal importance of the topic, the economics of discrimination had the hallmark of all Becker's contributions: the application of the stringent analysis of economics to a major social problem. This paper opened the way for an economic approach to human behavior, which was to have an enormous impact on the profession.

The theory, described in chapter 1 by Barry Chiswick, is fairly straightforward. It begins by assuming that some people have a taste for discrimination, a preference against associating with members of some other group. As with any taste, people are willing to pay to indulge it. For instance, a consumer who dislikes purchasing goods from a minority-owned store will pay a higher price to buy goods elsewhere. This gap in willingness to pay plays a similar role to tariffs in international trade – creating a wedge between domestic and foreign prices for the same good. As is known from the theory of international trade, such tariffs can end up hurting both countries, since gains from trade cannot be realized. Becker's theory shows that not only the discriminated-against minority but also the discriminating majority can lose out. Another result is that discrimination can lead to physical or economic segregation of the two groups.

A related question, recently much debated, is whether immigrants are discriminated against, and what kind of impact immigration has on the US labor market. George Borjas's chapter 2 on immigration explores these issues by comparing the performance of the immigrants of the 1960s and 1970s. Borjas also examines the possible impact of different immigrant groups on the earnings of native-born workers, which could shed light on the policy battles over the effect of immigration, both legal and illegal.

3 Crime and punishment

Becker began to think about crime in the 1960s when driving to Columbia University for a student's oral exam. Being late, Becker had to decide whether to park his car in a lot or park illegally on the street nearer the examination hall. He calculated the odds of getting a ticket, the size of the fine, and the cost of putting the car in a lot, and decided it was better to take the risk and park on the street. (History records that he did not get a ticket.)

As he walked to the examination room, it occurred to him that the city authorities had probably made a similar analysis. The frequency of inspection of parked vehicles and the size of the fine should depend on their estimates of the calculations potential violators would make. The first question he put to the unlucky student was to describe the optimal behavior of both the offenders and the police, something Becker himself hadn't worked out yet.

Chapter 3 by David Friedman outlines Becker's main contribution to this area, the seminal 1968 paper "Crime and Punishment." The idea of this paper is that criminal actions are not aberrations outside the scope of analysis of rational behavior. Criminals, Becker postulated, respond negatively to costs and positively to benefits in the same way any economic agent does.

A full statement of the theory shows that increased probability of detection, heavier penalties, and better alternative occupations induce less crime. Careful empirical research has demonstrated the validity of this approach. Becker's line of reasoning on crime was resisted at first, but it eventually became accepted that economics has an important role to play in the design of legal penalties and enforcement schemes. This work had great influence on the US Sentencing Commission, which reviewed criminal sanctions in the US a few years ago.

In chapter 4 James Coleman discusses who should have property rights in children with regard to education: parents or the state? Coleman argues that to effectively address the issue of rights over children, the appropriate criterion is maximizing society's wealth. This is the criterion advocated in legal issues by the members of the "Law and Economics" school. Becker is a founder – both inspirationally, and directly with his 1968 paper – of the rapidly growing branch of legal theory known as Law and Economics.

4 Human capital

Becker's work on human capital is one of his earliest and best-known contributions to economic theory. It is an idea that has acquired an extremely broad scope and had hundreds of applications to real-world phenomena. It began by addressing two relatively simple questions: why do people go to school, and why do people acquire most of their training when young? The answers to these questions are the foundations of human capital theory.

How can capital – an input into production – be part of a human being? The fundamental idea is that people can invest in *themselves*, purchasing education and training in order to earn more later in life. This may sound rather mechanistic, but casual observation confirms that most high-wage, high-security jobs require a long period of education and/or training. If a worker forgoes years of wages in order to fulfill the requirements for this type of job, it must be because earnings are high enough later to compensate for the lean years. Since the skills – the means of obtaining the return on the investment – are embodied in the worker, the name *human capital* was applied.

There had been a number of prior theories that explained these issues using biological, psychological, and sociological factors. Human capital theory, in contrast, made the assumption that people attend school to enhance their lifetime well being, and that the way education accomplishes this is by raising wages after leaving school. This had the advantage of simplicity, and also generated dozens of predictions, many of which have been confirmed in the enormous empirical literature spawned by Becker's book *Human Capital*. (For a recent survey of this literature by the other father of the field, see Jacob Mincer's "Human Capital: A Review.")

Human capital theory predicts that the longer an individual goes to school (i.e., invests in skills) the higher his earnings afterwards. The wage increases are steeper over time for people with more schooling. Becker's theory also explained the observed relationship between hours of work (say, per year) and wages earned – both rise over time, with hours rising faster, and both decline toward the end of the career. The reason for this pattern is that investment and reward for valuable job skills is directly related to time spent on the job. In this framework the worker's investment in human capital, hours worked on the job, and earnings over time are tied together in one compact theory. Earnings differentials between jobs are thus explained by differing levels of investment by the worker, both in education and on-the-job training. Chapter 5 by Robert Tamura explains this theory and gives examples from different occupations.

Becker also introduced a distinction between *general* and *specific* human capital to explain a firm's motives for investing in its employees' human capital. If the firm expects to receive a large enough benefit from the increased productivity of its workers, it has an economic incentive to educate and train them. An example is teaching a worker to run a complicated machine that is particular to a firm's production process. On the other hand, if a firm bears the cost of teaching a clerk to type, and then pays a lower wage to recoup its investment, the worker will leave and take another job, since typing is valuable at many firms and another job will pay the enhanced productivity. This explains why *general* training will be paid for by the worker in the form of lower wages while training, but the costs and benefits of *specific* training will be split between the worker and the firm. The worker is effectively "tied" to the firm once the specific training is complete – the skill is useful and rewarded in the current job, but not in another, so there is no incentive to quit.

Human capital theory also has implications for the changing composition of the workforce. It predicts that women who have interrupted labor-force participation (usually by leaving to have children) will have lower wages, fewer promotions, and less reason to acquire high levels of education or on-the-job training. It also predicts that highly educated, high-wage parents will have a high cost of time spent in raising children, and so answers several demographic puzzles, such as why the birth rate of wealthy nations has been slowing in the last century. Tamura's article on human capital, fertility, and growth expands on the connections between individuals' decisions about their own human capital, and international trends in population and economic growth.

Human capital, then, claims that people acquire stocks of knowledge and skill, and that the risks and rewards for these actions are similar in many ways to the risks and rewards of any other financial decision. The advantages of human capital over previous theories are its parsimony and flexibility – it is a useful tool for explaining several decisions of firms and individuals, and does so with the moderate assumption of rational responses to rewards in the labor market. Becker and his students have used the idea of "building stocks of human capital" to study addiction, fashion, occupational and religious choice, division of labor between spouses, and immigration, all of which are examined in this book.

5 Household production

Human capital theory is general enough to accommodate several types of capital accumulation. One of the types of capital people can invest in is *household capital*, to use in *household production*.

It may be useful here to try to understand what households produce.

After all, a household is not a business or a factory; family members do not punch timecards or get paychecks when they come home. Or do they? There are some important similarities between households and firms. Becker's framework is that every household has the task of producing the goods it cares about – home-cooked or take-out meals, many, few, or no children, neat or messy surroundings. How it produces these goods is an *economic* decision, and can be analyzed using economic methods.

The fields of household production, marriage, the family, altruism, and the allocation of time are all areas of economic inquiry that are closely related to the main tenets of human capital theory. They are related both because they are subject to the same constraints as human capital acquisition – money, time, and energy spent in the household is not available to spend in the market – and because the concept of stocks of human capital for use in the production of goods is the same for both market and household capital. In other words, individuals invest rationally, and may invest either in labor market capital or household capital, depending on where their talents will bring the highest return.

We can call a household any group of persons who engage in joint (non-market) decision making. They divide their resources into market, household, and leisure uses. If they decide to invest in household capital, how would they go about it? Household capital can be the purchase of a machine, such as a dishwasher or a microwave oven, that produces household goods or provides a household service, or it can be the ability of a family member to accomplish household tasks. This can be summarized by a household production function, which sets out the possible combinations of goods, time, and effort that will produce the desired result – in the same way that economists speak of a "production function" for firms. The household production function is extremely useful in thinking about who stays at home, who works in the market, and what the household's real income (the sum of the benefits of market production and household production) is. Different production plans will yield different incomes.

Using these concepts, Becker explained many well-known trends, such as rising divorce rates, smaller families, and women's increased labor market participation, as logical outcomes of changes in conditions in the "marriage market," in the same way that economists explain firms' decisions as responding to changing market conditions. The "marriage market" is affected by anything that alters the gains from marriage – how easy it is to divorce, whether tax law benefits married couples, or what types of careers are available to women, to name some contemporary examples.

Becker's theory of marriage is reviewed and extended in chapter 6 by Shoshana Grossbard-Shechtman. She shows how factors such as changing divorce laws and the number of men relative to the number of women affect couples' work and household decisions, as well as the way in which household members split their joint income. The theory of marriage also sheds light on time allocation of husbands and wives. Suppose for example that a married couple is deciding how to maximize their joint utility. Even if both spouses were employed prior to marriage, if there are *gains to specialization* – if one spouse spending all their time in the labor market and the other all their time at home yields a greater return than each spending some time in both sectors – then one spouse may work in the household full time and the other in the market full time. Similarly, if the returns to market labor are high for both, they may both work for wages and purchase household goods (eating out instead of cooking, and so on).

Kermit Daniel's chapter 7 on the "marriage premium" extends this theory by showing that if a wife is assisting her husband in his career – by taking responsibility for household tasks, by moving when he needs to move, or by giving advice and encouragement – she, as well as he, has invested in his wages and career. This implies that there are large economic consequences to this type of investment, and suggests that the idea of human capital is even broader than was previously thought. It includes not only the worker's investment, but the investment of the worker's family (and friends).

To summarize, the way in which a household accomplishes its goals is inextricably related to the members' abilities in the market and household, and whether specialization in either of these sectors is profitable. This area of economics also lends insight to the issue of who benefits most from marriage, and how the structure of families will respond to outside forces, such as rising wages or changing divorce laws.

6 A theory of public policy

Economists in general have been more concerned with telling governments what they should do than with explaining what they actually do. There has been a recent revival in the study of how the political system actually works, and, in particular, of the interaction of political and economic factors. Research in this area is based on the same principles as other economic analyses: individuals and groups rationally pursuing their self-interest. This leads to a number of ideas about the public sector that conflict with the naive economics textbook view of government as a purely benevolent institution.

Becker has contributed a theory of the behavior of interest (or pressure) groups based on the idea that most government actions are largely redistributions of income across groups in society. Edgardo Zablotsky provides a detailed account of Becker's model in chapter 8, along with the model's historical roots in Arthur Bentley's work at the beginning of this century. One of the virtues of this model is its generality: it applies to dictatorships as well as democracies.

Chapter 9 by John Matsusaka provides an economic perspective on the workings of democracy. He argues that actual democracies are quite different from the democracies taught in high school civics classes – an ideal world in which fully informed citizens elect their representatives, who faithfully serve the people's mandate. Matsusaka describes the real-world democratic process as one in which political actors behave in such a way as to maximize their private benefit in a world with imperfect information. Interestingly, he concludes that the "political market" ends up delivering outcomes that are somewhat efficient and not that different from the civics text's ideal. This is consistent with Becker's view that redistribution is achieved by fairly efficient means.

7 Opium and masses

Part V of the book contains articles that are related to Becker's more recent work. As such, this section is more exploratory in nature, both in its topics and in its methodology. All of these chapters represent attempts to push the boundaries of economics even further. The method is first outlined in Stigler and Becker's article "De Gustibus Non Est Disputandum." This paper sets out a method for examining the evolution of tastes at the individual level in response to economic variables like prices, incomes, and information. This is useful in analyzing several issues including habit, addiction, fashion, and advertising.

Methodologically, this work expands the domain of individual preferences to include intertemporal components (consumption of a good today may affect the utility of that good tomorrow) and interpersonal components (one person's consumption may affect the benefits another receives from that same good – for example, fax machines are more useful if many other people own them).

Addictive behavior

The economic analysis of addiction, pioneered by Becker in his work with Kevin M. Murphy and Michael Grossman (author of chapter 10), is an application of the tools of economics to study a pressing social and personal issue. Using economic concepts like elasticities, addiction capital, and price and income effects, a theory has been developed to understand the impact of alternative policies ("sin" taxes, legalization) on the consumption of drugs, cigarettes, and alcohol by different demographic groups.

A similar structure – aided by the household production approach – is used by Larry Iannaccone in chapter 11 to develop an economic theory of religious choice. He finds systematic patterns of church attendance, contributions, interfaith marriage, and religious conversion, consistent with economic models of social behavior. He speaks of a "religious production function," which uses the time and money of members as inputs, and shows that the choice of whether to contribute time or money responds predictably to prices. People with a high value of time (busy professionals) spend more on contributions and less time in church than people with a lower value of time, typically young and old people.

Social interactions

An ironic comment heard in New York or California is that a restaurant's long lines are only made up for by its bad, overpriced food. Traditional economics has a hard time explaining why people queue for hours for an "in" restaurant when a similar place across the street has no queue at all. Even more puzzling is why the fashionable place doesn't raise prices to the point where tables demanded equals tables supplied.

Recent work by Becker and others has shed some light on these not-uncommon cases. Becker looks at situations where people like things more, the more other people like them. This relationship across people's demands can come from several sources. It may be that we enjoy crowds, seeing others, and being seen. It may also be due to the information implicit in other people's actions. This latter possibility is studied at length in chapter 12 by David Hirshleifer. Using the concept of "informational cascades," Hirshleifer extends this reasoning to stock markets, urban development, book sales, politics, medical practices, scientific theories, and even zoology.

This analysis has several interesting implications. The success of restaurants will tend to be unpredictable. When a crowd focuses on a single eating place, that place may well remain popular for a long time *despite* high prices and bad food. People will keep coming because they enjoy being with the rest of the "in" crowd. It also predicts that essentially any place could serve as a focus; hence the sudden switching when switching does occur. Therefore the declines in popularity will not be smooth, but drastic. The entire popularity depended on the crowd, so a decrease in the crowd will make patrons disappear even faster. This snowballs until the restaurant vanishes.

Becker's model explains why the restaurant cannot raise prices. If it did, demand would fall, and then fall still further with the thinning of the crowd. A small price increase does not lower demand slightly until demand equals supply; instead a drop in demand spirals till the restaurant goes bust.

Other predictions are that the crowds will be in busy areas visible to passers-by, and restaurants may not expand capacity, because of the dire cost of a seemingly empty restaurant.

The crowds in the hot spots of Los Angeles are not a conventional topic of economic analysis, but why shouldn't they be? The crowds are a result of social interactions, and so interesting to economists. They also yield insights into other areas of economic analysis where information is a crucial issue, as explained by Hirshleifer's chapter.

Contagious diseases are another timely example of how individual decisions are influenced by the behavior of others. Chapter 13 by Tomas Philipson outlines the first recent attempt to contrast economic analysis with epidemiological analysis. He explains the economics of sexually transmitted diseases, such as AIDS, and, more generally, infectious diseases. He concludes that actual epidemics look more "economic" than "biological," that individuals may want to be sick when sickness leads to immunity, and that less common diseases should receive more research funding from government.

8 Methodology

Becker's program has been called (mostly by critics) "economic imperialism": the economic approach applied outside the home field. According to Becker, the economic approach consists of:

1 optimizing behavior by individuals,
2 market equilibrium, and
3 stable preferences.

1 The assumption of *optimizing behavior* gives economics its strength and structure by hypothesizing that people make the best choices they can subject to limitations on their resources, most particularly time and money, but also information, energy, and ability. Therefore analysis of behavior is possible without assuming humans are crazy or stupid or have decisions totally determined by their environment. We assume, instead, that people are doing their best to make themselves happy with whatever means are available to them. Environments affect tastes and cost–benefit analyses, but that does not weaken the case that human behavior is the outcome of individuals making choices to improve their lives.

It is important to clarify that optimizing behavior is a method of analysis and not an assumption about particular motivations. It does not mean that people are only interested in money, are narrow-mindedly selfish, or that decisions are unaffected by limited information, social considerations, or accidents of time and place. Optimization does not mean that people are cash registers with legs. It does not mean that we should not incorporate effects of families, schools, jobs, and governments on an individual's decisions. In fact, economists are including these elements more and more, and this is due at least in part to Becker's example.

2 The concept of *market equilibrium* can be understood narrowly or broadly. Narrowly defined, it is associated with some notion of perfectly competitive equilibrium, in which the anonymous interactions of large numbers of participants without individual market power leads in general to beneficial social outcomes (the "invisible hand" of Adam Smith). Although Becker as a member of the Chicago School is somewhat sympathetic to this view, its truth is not something that can be assessed a priori, and is not part of a methodology. The broader methodological definition of equilibrium refers to the aggregation of the choices of individuals in order to derive implications at the group or macro level. For this definition, a system is said to be in equilibrium when the behavior of all individual agents is consistent.

Equilibrium is the usual mode of analysis in economics, and it does not imply that everything is perfect, since not all equilibria exhibit socially desirable properties. An example can be found in Becker's work on pressure groups. If we look at a case with two groups identical in influence, the result is that there are no winners or losers, because there is no redistribution in favor of any group. But both parties have spent valuable resources in order to get their way – lobbying for lower taxes, for example – and the outcome is an equilibrium, even though the social outcome is worse than if the groups had never fought at all.

3 *Stable preferences* are used to avoid the *reductio ad absurdum* that people's behavior varies because their tastes are continually changing. Stigler and Becker argue in "De Gustibus Non Est Disputandum" that people have stocks of experience that affect their enjoyment of goods (the more exposure I had to classical music in the past, the more I enjoy it today) and that these stocks of "consumption capital" are what change over time, not the underlying tastes themselves.

In this view, stocks of consumption capital are accumulated by individuals (to some extent by choice) having future implications in mind. Much of Becker's work has relied on the idea that people realize that their preferences are in part a function of what they allow themselves to experience. Reformed alcoholics use this concept when avoiding places that serve alcohol, for example.

Economics has been widened, deepened and energized by Becker's writings and teachings. It has been long referred to as the dismal science; we (and he) prefer to call it the science of human behavior.

References

Becker, Gary S. 1976. *The Economic Approach to Human Behavior*, Chicago, IL: University of Chicago Press.
    1993. "Nobel Lecture: The Economic Way of Looking at Behavior," *Journal of Political Economy*, 101(3) (June): 385–409.
Mincer, Jacob. 1993. *Human Capital: A Review*, Hants: Edward Elgar.
Rosen, Sherwin. 1993. "Risks and Rewards: Gary Becker's Contributions to Economics," *The Scandinavian Journal of Economics*, 95(1): 25–36.
Sandmo, Agnar. 1993. "Gary Becker's Contributions to Economics," *The Scandinavian Journal of Economics*, 95(1): 7–23.
Shackleton, J.R. 1981. "Gary S. Becker: The Economist as Empire-Builder," in J.R. Shackleton and Gareth Locksley (eds.), *Twelve Contemporary Economists*, London: Macmillan, pp. 12–32.
Stigler, George J., and Gary S. Becker. 1977. "De Gustibus Non Est Disputandum," *American Economic Review*, 67: 76–90.

I

Discrimination and immigration

1   The economics of discrimination: a primer

Barry R. Chiswick

Introduction

The application of the tools of economic theory to discrimination began with the publication in 1957 of the now classic study by Gary S. Becker, *The Economics of Discrimination* (University of Chicago Press, 1957, second edition, 1971), which was based on his doctoral dissertation.[1]

Becker's analysis of discrimination foreshadowed his research contribution to the social sciences. The essential element in his analysis of discrimination is the role played by the individual who is maximizing his or her own well-being (utility) in a non-conventional market, given the person's resources and preferences. Individuals receive the benefits and pay the consequences of their own actions, although government policy and institutions influence the parameters within which they operate. This theme is to be found in his later research on human capital, the value of time, crime, the family, addictive behavior, etc.

Until Becker's pioneering study, discrimination in labor markets had been considered to be outside the realm of economic theory. Economics, it was said, might explain the price of butter or the rate of inflation, but could not provide insights into such "social" and "psychological" matters as labor market discrimination. Becker's study, which was quite controversial for many years after its publication, provided a very fruitful framework for looking at the consequences of discrimination in labor markets, and has directly or indirectly served as the basis of all future studies of the economic dimensions of discrimination. Understanding the consequences of discrimination is crucial for designing policies that are constructive rather than counter-productive in attaining the nation's goal of ending "unwarranted" labor market discrimination.[2]

The intent of this chapter is to provide an introductory understanding of the model of discrimination developed in Becker's classic study. It will have served its purpose if it demystifies Becker's original analysis. It will have

15

served a greater purpose if it encourages the reading of the original which has a richness of insights that cannot be developed in this chapter.

One frequent misconception about Becker's model of discrimination, and of labor market discrimination in general, is that it applies only to employers. On the contrary, in separate chapters he demonstrates the power of the approach for understanding discrimination by many agents – employers, consumers, co-workers, and the government. In his analysis, he emphasizes the distinction between the two channels through which discriminatory behavior affects the labor market, namely, through wage discrimination and employment segregation. Wage discrimination refers to the payment of different wages to workers of the same level of skill who are experiencing the same working conditions but who differ by gender, race, ethnicity, attractiveness, or some other ascriptive characteristic not directly related to performance on the job. Employment segregation, on the other hand, refers to the separation of the employment of individuals of comparable productivity based on an ascriptive characteristic. This separation may be by industry, occupation, location, firm, establishment (plant), or status within the enterprise.

Becker's model of discrimination showed that when labor markets and markets for goods and services are competitive and the government protects property rights and personal safety, market forces tend to drive discriminatory wage differentials to zero; that is, wages tend to be equal for workers with the same level of skill and experiencing the same working conditions. Recent research does indeed show that much of the observed differences in wages among racial and ethnic groups, and between men and women, are attributable to the different skills that they bring to the labor market. The model, however, also has important implications for employment segregation. It is shown that even in competitive markets discrimination can result in segregated employment. Moreover, competitive forces that may tend to eliminate wage discrimination may increase employment segregation.

"Tastes" for discrimination

Economists approach human behavior by assuming that, given their "preferences" or "tastes," people act rationally and are willing to pay (i.e., give up something of value) to have something pleasant or to avoid something unpleasant. However, the more they must pay the less likely they are to buy the pleasant or to avoid the unpleasant. People are willing to pay to eat good food, obtain new clothing, or put gasoline in their gas tank. They are also willing to pay to have their garbage removed, their car washed, and their broken limbs mended. To say that people have a "taste for discrimination," a concept developed in Becker's study, is to say that they have a preference for or against associating with someone or some group. That tastes for discrimination can influence behavior is crucial to understanding the impact of discrimination in the labor market.

The concept of "tastes for discrimination" can be applied to any of the three roles that people play in the market: consumers, employers, and employees. We are all consumers, buying some things and not others, from some people and not others. Driving into a new community we may prefer to buy pizza from an Italian restaurant rather than a Korean restaurant. If so, we are engaging in discrimination on the basis of expectations regarding the quality of the product (i.e., Italians are "better" at making pizza than Koreans).

Many people are also employers, even if it only involves hiring the services of babysitters, domestics, gardeners, and dog walkers. If we prefer to hire teenage boys to cut our grass rather than teenage girls, even though both may do an equally good job, we are engaging in labor market sex discrimination.

Finally, most people, at some time in their adult life, are employees. In this role they may believe that they get more satisfaction from their job if they work with some co-workers rather than others. Discrimination arises, for example, if a person is willing to take a lower wage to work with a clean, cheerful colleague, rather than the colleague's messy, boring identical twin, if male workers prefer working with other men, or if white workers prefer working with other whites.

An application: Chinese restaurants

The implications of Becker's analysis of discrimination are easiest to discern through example. Many find it difficult to discuss models of discrimination because they feel that it is morally repugnant. It is, therefore, useful to take an example from everyday life to which most people can relate.

Let us assume that *all* consumers perceive a difference between Chinese food served in a restaurant with a Chinese atmosphere and the same food lacking this ambience. The atmosphere may include the restaurant's decor, but also the racial characteristics of the service workers visible to the customer, including the maitre d', waiter or waitress, and busboy. Consumers prefer a meal served by a Chinese waiter to an otherwise identical meal served by a white, black, or Hispanic waiter. Put differently, they would be willing to pay more for a Chinese meal served by a Chinese waiter than for an identical meal served by a non-Chinese. This difference in the price they are willing to pay measures the intensity of the consumer's taste for discrimination.

As a result of consumers' tastes for discrimination, Chinese waiters are more valuable to employers in Chinese restaurants than are waiters of other racial backgrounds. If they are otherwise equally efficient, employers would be willing to offer Chinese waiters higher wages than other waiters. Non-Chinese waiters would be employed in these jobs only if they accepted a sufficiently lower wage to offset their negative effect on business.

As long as consumers either do not know or do not care who is preparing the food in the kitchen, Chinese cooks would have no particular advantage over other cooks who are otherwise equally skilled in preparing Chinese food. If consumers do care who prepares the food and they can check the identity of the chef (e.g., by looking through the kitchen door), Chinese cooks are more likely to be hired by the employer if the wages are the same.

Consumers do not know who makes the noodles or grows the vegetables used in a Chinese restaurant, and even if they did, they might not care. Then Chinese noodle makers and Chinese growers of Chinese vegetables would have no particular advantage, assuming others can be equally productive in making noodles and raising Chinese vegetables.

Suppose the Chinese community in an area, say Provincial City, is relatively small. Also suppose that the non-Chinese people in Provincial City have a high demand for Chinese food and a strong "taste for discrimination." The wages of Chinese waiters and cooks will be bid up by Chinese restaurant owners *above* those for similar jobs in other restaurants. Restaurant workers who look Chinese will gravitate to Chinese restaurants and will avoid other types of restaurants where they are not at an economic advantage.

In addition, because the taste for discrimination results in high wages in this sector, Chinese workers who otherwise would have worked elsewhere, or not worked at all, would be more likely to become Chinese restaurant employees. If the Chinese community is sufficiently small, segregation in employment results, with the Chinese concentrated in visible Chinese restaurant jobs and underrepresented in non-visible Chinese restaurant jobs (e.g., the restaurant's accountant) and elsewhere in the economy.

Wage differentials may be created. Within the Chinese restaurant sector, any firm that hired non-Chinese workers would have to charge lower prices and offer a lower wage for the restaurant to survive the competition because it is offering an "inferior" (less-valued) product as far as the consumers are concerned. And Chinese workers, having a scarce characteristic prized in the Chinese restaurant market, would command higher wages than otherwise identical non-Chinese workers in other sectors of the economy.

Cosmopolitan City, on the other hand, has a large Chinese community relative to the population and the number of Chinese restaurants. So many Chinese are enticed by the high wages in the restaurant sector that their entry lowers the wages in these occupations. Wages fall until they are the same as those received by non-Chinese restaurant workers in non-Chinese restaurants, and the same as what Chinese workers could earn in other parts of the economy.

As a result, in Cosmopolitan City there are no differences in wages among workers of the same skill, regardless of the race of the workers or the sector of employment. Although all workers in visible Chinese restaurant jobs are Chinese, many Chinese work elsewhere in the economy. There is occupational segregation but it is less intense than in Provincial City.

In these examples wage discrimination, defined as the payment of different wages to workers with the same "objective" level of productivity, existed in Provincial City but not in Cosmopolitan City. Yet, would wage discrimination persist in Provincial City in the long run?

The wage premiums received by Chinese workers in Provincial City because of their scarcity value would be difficult to maintain over time. The supply of Chinese workers would grow until the premium disappeared. If there are no artificial barriers to job mobility, such as restrictions on geographic mobility (migration), union regulations, or occupational licensing that limit job choices, Chinese workers would migrate to Chinese restaurant jobs in Provincial City. The movement from low-wage to higher-wage jobs will continue until the rise in wages in the lower-wage sector and the fall in wages in the higher-wage sector eliminate the wage differential.

Suppose that a significant proportion of the population of Provincial City concludes that Peking Duck is Peking Duck, whether or not it is served by a Chinese or non-Chinese waiter. They, of course, will patronize Chinese restaurants with *non*-Chinese waiters. Indeed, because these restaurants charge lower prices, non-discriminating consumers who would otherwise eat Greek food or eat at home would now patronize the cheaper "non-Chinese" Chinese restaurants. That is, since consumers differ in their discriminatory preferences they will allocate themselves among types of Chinese restaurants depending on the intensity of their preferences. If there are a sufficiently large number of non-discriminating consumers, the scarcity value of Chinese waiters (even in Provincial City) disappears. While the Chinese may still work disproportionately in the restaurant sector, there is no wage differential among restaurant workers by race, or between restaurant jobs and other jobs for the Chinese.

Note that the analysis implies that under certain circumstances discrimination will result in wage differences ("wage discrimination") but that in other instances, and particularly in the long run, wage differences tend to disappear for workers of the same skill level. Thus, discriminatory behavior does not necessarily result in wage discrimination. On the other hand, in each of the situations described employment *segregation* results. For example, in the scenarios presented above the employer/occupational/industrial distribution of Chinese and non-Chinese workers differ. Indeed, the discrimination model can be characterized as having stronger implications for employment segregation than for differences in wages.

Equal pay regulations

Suppose wages for Chinese waiters are higher in Chinese restaurants and the government institutes a policy to end what it perceives to be wage discrimination. Wages for restaurant workers have to be the same in all restaurants. Either the wages of Chinese waiters in Chinese restaurants would have to be lowered, or the wages in other restaurants would have to be raised. If Chinese restaurant wages were lowered it would be harder for restaurant owners to hire Chinese waiters (some would work elsewhere, others may leave the labor force). There would be fewer Chinese restaurants providing the preferred service. Consumer satisfaction would fall as the remaining Chinese restaurants would be more crowded, meals would be rushed, and lines would be longer. Illegal behavior would be encouraged as it would be in the interests of the consumers and employers to make "under the table" payments to Chinese waiters in Chinese restaurants.

Raising wages for *other* restaurant workers through the equivalent of a minimum wage or the adoption of the concept of "comparable worth" to end the wage discrimination in favor of the Chinese also creates problems. Compelling other restaurants to pay artificially higher wages would raise their prices; some would go out of business and others would reduce the ratio of waiters to customers, perhaps by substituting other labor (e.g., busboys) or by adopting alternative means of providing service (e.g., self-service salad bars). Working conditions would deteriorate or side payments would be made by non-Chinese workers seeking to obtain the smaller number of "high paying" jobs. Again, there is a divergence between actual practice and what would have been optimal if there were no equal pay or comparable worth legislation.

A broader model – consumer, employer, and co-worker discrimination

The Chinese restaurant example considers consumer discrimination in *favor* of a minority racial/ethnic group. It is, however, perhaps no less prejudicial in essence than other forms of differentiation, such as avoiding members of particular racial and ethnic groups or a particular gender. The implications for labor market behavior of other forms of consumer discrimination, such as aversion to blacks or females, is essentially the converse of what was developed above.

Assume, for example, all patients have the same "taste for discrimination" against female dentists.[3] Patients would be willing to pay more for equally good dental care, up to a point, if it is provided by a male dentist. Female dentists would have to charge lower fees and would receive lower incomes. If, however, some patients no longer perceive women as inferior providers of dental care (either because their "consciousness" has been raised or for some other reason), they will perceive the fee differential as too costly. The newly non-discriminating patients will flock to female dentists as they charge lower fees. This movement will tend to reduce the gender differences in fees. As long as there are a sufficient number of non-discriminating patients, their behavior in seeking lower-cost dental care, and changes in the supply of male and female dentists, will tend to eliminate the fee and income differential by gender among dentists. The non-discriminating (or low-discriminating) patients will be seen in the offices of female dentists, while those with strong discriminatory preferences will seek care from male dentists.

Employer and employee (co-worker) discrimination can also be understood in a similar manner. Under employer discrimination, for example, discriminating white employers would hire black workers only if they worked at a lower wage than white workers. Non-discriminating employers would clearly have an advantage in hiring workers, and hence a cost advantage in selling their product. On the other hand, suppose there was no competition in the market for the final goods or services. Under a monopoly situation a discriminating employer could, to a greater extent, exercise discriminatory preferences in hiring, promotion, and pay, and incur higher labor costs without fear that the higher costs of production would put the firm at a competitive disadvantage in selling the product.

If there is competition in the market for buying firms, entrepreneurs who perceive they can make larger profits will tend to buy the enterprises of those who for whatever reason make lower profits. Less-discriminating or non-discriminating entrepreneurs would have lower labor costs and would therefore tend to buy firms from those with stronger tastes for discrimination. Competitive forces result in less-discriminating entrepreneurs having an advantage over more-discriminating ones, but these forces are muted if the discriminating firm has monopoly power in the marketplace or if the non-discriminating entrepreneur cannot benefit if the enterprise generates larger profits. Profit limitations may arise from profit ceilings imposed on regulated industries or because the enterprise is a not-for-profit organization or government agency. Thus, competition in the market for goods and services, competition in the capital market for funds to buy businesses, and the ability of entrepreneurs to benefit if their firms can generate greater profits tend to result in the least-discriminating entrepreneurs surviving as employers.

Under employee discrimination discriminating white workers would have to be paid a higher wage to work with black workers, that is, in an integrated workforce. Unless there are productivity gains from having white and black workers working together, workforce segregation would result, but there would not necessarily be wage differences between white and black workers. Integrated employment would involve the least discriminating whites working with blacks. Employee discrimination can result in segregated employment even if there are no wage differentials.

One important implication of Becker's model of discrimination is that it is the least-discriminating consumers, employers, and workers who are most likely to be buying from, hiring, and working with groups subject to discrimination. Another is that the structure of industry matters. Although competition does not change "tastes for discrimination" it does change outcomes, with discrimination being least in the most competitive environments.

Estimating wage discrimination

In the nearly four decades since the publication of *The Economics of Discrimination* there has emerged a voluminous literature estimating the size and number of changes over time in the differences in wages among racial and ethnic groups (primarily studies of blacks and whites) and between men and women.

There is no explicit measure of discrimination and there are no direct measures of the effect of discrimination on wages. To estimate the effect on wages of labor market discrimination one needs to isolate the magnitude of wage differences due to differences in skills and other characteristics brought to the labor market. This turns out to be very difficult to do with precision. There are some readily measurable dimensions of skill, such as years of schooling and years of labor market experience. The earnings differences that persist after taking account of measurable characteristics may be due to a combination of discrimination and other unmeasured (and perhaps unmeasurable) characteristics that vary systematically across groups. These characteristics may include quality of schooling, hours worked per year in the past, educational enrichment received at home, tradeoffs between money and non-money incomes, labor market effort, cultural traits, etc. There have been valiant attempts to refine the measures of skill and other characteristics and, in particular, to refine measures of schooling quality in studies of black–white differences and of past work experience in male–female comparisons. Yet even with improved measurement, estimating the wage differential that arises solely from discrimination eludes researchers.

There is, unfortunately, a tendency to assume that the wage differences that exist after best efforts have been made at adjusting the data for measurable characteristics are the result of discrimination in the labor market. That this approach is fraught with danger can be seen in the following examples. Both overall and when other measured variables are the same there are some minority groups that earn more than the majority population. Among men, Asian Americans, American Jews, and long-duration immigrants tend to earn more than, say, US-born white men who are not Jewish.[4] These three minority groups have not been the beneficiaries of favorable discrimination in the US (even given the Chinese restaurant example). If anything, on balance, they have been the victims of discrimination. Nor could discrimination by these groups for or against the majority population enhance their earnings position. Indeed, in his *The Economics of Discrimination* Becker shows that discrimination against the majority by a small economic minority would lower the income of the minority. What must be happening is that whatever disadvantages in wages, if any, that these groups experience because of discrimination are more than offset by other unmeasured factors that enhance their earnings capacity. This suggests that because of unmeasured differences that may exist, estimated earnings differentials for other groups, even when measurable differences in characteristics are taken into account, may be either overestimates or underestimates of the true differential due to discrimination. To call the remaining earnings differentials a measure of discrimination is to place an unwarranted label on our ignorance.

There is, however, an additional complicating factor. The skills workers bring to the labor market may be a consequence of labor market discrimination. Even if wage differences for workers with similar skills are small, these small differences may generate large differences in investments in skills. If so, estimates of wage differences due to discrimination would underestimate the total impact on wages of labor market discrimination.

An example may be helpful for understanding this point. Suppose there is labor market discrimination (by employers, co-workers, or consumers) against women in the labor market which lowers their wages relative to men. Men and women who anticipate marriage perceive these differences. If men and women are equally productive in the home sector, it is to a married couple's advantage for the husband to devote relatively more hours to the labor market and the wife to devote relatively more hours to home production activities. The husband would have an incentive to make greater investments in schooling and on-the-job training that are specific to the labor market and the wife would have made fewer of these investments. As a result, women would be observed working less and bringing fewer relevant skills to the labor market, and having even lower earnings on average relative to men.

Similar processes may be operative for other groups. Expectations of low returns to skill, whether due to discrimination or other factors, have feedback effects on skill formation. Groups with lower rates of return on human capital tend to make smaller investments, thereby widening even further the observed differences in earnings.

Government discrimination – explicit and implicit

Becker's analysis of discrimination explicitly considers the role of government. Disenfranchised groups are shown to be vulnerable to discrimination through the medium of the government by those who are enfranchised, particularly in the provision of publicly provided goods and services. Even enfranchised groups that are not creditable partners for a winning (or potentially winning) coalition can be subject to government discrimination. The long sorry history of discrimination in publicly funded education in the United States demonstrates both the vulnerability of minorities to discrimination (e.g., inferior schooling) and the consequences for disadvantaged groups of limited choice due to government monopolization.

The greatest threat to those with strong tastes for discrimination are those with weaker tastes or no such preferences. Competitive forces penalize those with strong discriminatory preferences. Cartels formed to enforce discrimination can be effective only if they can bar (or co-opt) the entry of non-discriminators and prevent cheating by cartel members with weaker discriminatory preferences. As a result, the government has at times been used as an agent for legally enforcing discriminatory cartel agreements through regulation (e.g., licensing) and government protected monopolies.

It was not uncommon in the past in some jurisdictions for the government authorities to permit (and sometimes actively participate in) illegal means to enforce discriminatory behavior against minorities or to impose one group's discriminatory behavior on the behavior of others with smaller or no tastes for discrimination. Terrorism or violence, direct or implied, against the property or persons of those who choose not to discriminate or against those who sought relief from discrimination through changing their residence or employer was not uncommon in American history. Continued vigilance in preserving property rights and protecting personal safety is a prime function of the government, if not its *raison d'etre*. The benefits of eliminating any remaining wage discrimination are also obvious.

Where do discriminatory "tastes" come from?

Becker's analysis of the consequences of "tastes for discriminating" is superb. Yet, the model takes these "preferences" as given. What is not clear is where these "preferences" come from, why they appear both to exist and to vary in intensity across time, across space, and across groups.

Perhaps the need to differentiate between the small group "us" and all others ("them") was an important survival trait in the emergence of the primate that evolved into modern people. If so, discrimination may be imprinted in our genes. Alternatively, perhaps it evolved as a protective cultural trait as civilizations arose around the world. And, perhaps in some complex way that is not well understood it is itself endogenous – that discriminatory attitudes and behavior are a consequence of current (or recent) social, political, and economic forces. Nor need there be a single answer as different forms of discriminatory attitudes in different times and places may have different origins. Although the determinants of these attitudes may be elusive, *The Economics of Discrimination* provides a framework for analyzing their consequences.

Policy implications

Becker's approach to analyzing labor market discrimination offers an effective way to combat wage discrimination, whether caused by consumers, employers, or employees. Unhindered competition in labor markets encourages the flow of resources, including workers, from where they are less well rewarded to where they are most highly rewarded. No government agency or court, regardless of the best of intentions, can be as effective as the impersonal market forces in determining who "should" work where and at what wages and working conditions. Policies that limit labor mobility can perpetuate, or at least lengthen, the period until the unwarranted wage effects of discrimination are dissipated by competition. Thus, minimum wage laws, union restrictions on hiring (e.g., *de facto* requirements of union membership), occupational licensing, and other hindrances to labor mobility serve to slow the effect of market forces in reducing discrimination. Similarly, restrictions on the entry of new firms through reduced competition in product markets or capital markets (including licensing or granting of *de facto* or *de jure* monopoly power to existing firms) also shields discriminators from the economic consequences of their actions. There is much to be gained from removing the remaining barriers to free competition, and one among many benefits would be the further reduction or elimination of whatever wage discrimination may persist among workers who bring the same skills to the labor market.

Becker's model provides another important insight. Unhindered competition combined with the preservation of property rights and personal safety also mean those with the strongest "tastes for discrimination" pay the heaviest cost in terms of paying higher prices for goods and services (consumer discrimination), receiving lower profits (employer discrimination), and receiving lower wages (employee discrimination). This is perhaps as it should be.

Notes

1 Although it has been thirty-seven years since its publication, the book is still frequently cited. For example, the *Social Science Citation Index* indicates that in 1992 it was cited in an impressive thirty-one different articles published in English language social science journals on economics, sociology, organizational behavior, industrial relations, ethics, and law (*Social Science Citation Index, 1992*, columns 1,297–9). Nearly all textbooks of labor economics cite it as the foundation for their analysis of discrimination.

2 "Unwarranted discrimination" refers to forms of discrimination that violate the law. Discrimination in the labor market against persons because of their race, ethnicity, national origin, religion, gender, or disability violates federal law.

3 In 1991 only 10.1 percent of dentists in the US were female, in contrast to 20.1 percent females among physicians and 48.1 percent among all professionals, including teachers (US Bureau of the Census, *Statistical Abstract of the United States, 1992*, Washington, table 629, p. 392).

4 See, for example, Barry R. Chiswick. 1983. "An Analysis of the Earnings and Employment of Asian-American Men," *Journal of Labor Economics* (April): 197–214, Barry R. Chiswick. 1993. "The Skills and Economic Status of American Jewry: Trends Over the Last Half Century," *Journal of Labor Economics*, I (January): 229–42 and Barry R. Chiswick. 1986. "Is the New Immigration Less Skilled than the Old?" *Journal of Labor Economics* (April): 168–92.

2 The economic analysis of immigration

George J. Borjas

1 Introduction

The 1980s were turbulent years in the history of immigration to the United States. Three major events characterized the demographic and political shifts. Auspiciously enough, the decade began with the Mariel boatlift. In April 1980, Fidel Castro decided to let Cuban nationals freely migrate to the United States, and over 125,000 people quickly took advantage of this offer. The Marielitos, as they came to be known, were responsible for substantial social disruptions in the Miami area, and the uncontrolled flow rekindled the debate over the type of refugee policy that a humanitarian and democratic welfare state should have.

The 1980s also witnessed an unsuccessful resolution to the political concern over illegal aliens that had been simmering over the past two decades. Fueled by charges that perhaps ten to twenty million illegal aliens were overrunning the country, Congress enacted the 1986 Immigration Reform and Control Act (IRCA). This legislation had two key provisions. The first gave amnesty to about three million illegal aliens, while the second introduced a system of employer sanctions that would presumably stem the flow of additional illegal workers. It is fair to conclude that the legislation is already a failure. Although the number of illegal aliens apprehended declined immediately following IRCA, apprehensions are now back up to about 1.2 million per year, roughly the same number of apprehensions observed in 1983.

Finally, the decade witnessed the continuation and acceleration of historic trends in both the size and composition of legal immigrant flows. During the 1950s, for instance, approximately 250 thousand legal immigrants entered the United States annually, and about 53 percent of these immigrants originated in European countries. By the 1980s, the annual flow had increased to 600 thousand, with only 11 percent originating in Europe. These changes renewed the debate over how many visa applicants

27

the US should admit and how these visas should be allocated. To some extent, the debate was motivated by the growing consensus that the economic benefits from immigration would increase if the immigrant flow were more skilled. This concern led to the 1990 Immigration Act, which raised the number of persons that could be legally admitted by about 145,000 persons per year, with half of these additional visas being awarded to skilled workers.

These historic shifts in the "immigration market" were accompanied by equally important changes in our understanding of the economics of immigration. In particular, the decade witnessed the development of an economic approach to the analysis of immigration which has been greatly influenced by the Beckerian research strategy. In particular, the "new" economics of immigration uses the "combined assumptions of maximizing behavior, market equilibrium, and stable preferences ... relentlessly and unflinchingly" (Becker, 1976, p. 5). As a result of this economic approach, economists have now made substantial contributions to our understanding of the immigrant experience, to the analysis of the benefits and costs associated with immigration, and to the ongoing public debate over immigration policy.

This explosion of research activity has already established a number of important stylized facts: The (relative) skills of successive immigrant waves declined over much of the post-war period, and this decline accelerated in the 1970s; it is unlikely that recent immigrants would reach parity with, let alone overtake, the earnings of natives during their working lives; although there was only a weak negative correlation between the presence of immigrants in a local labor market and the earnings opportunities of natives in that labor market, immigration may have been partly responsible for the decline in the earnings of unskilled native workers that occurred during the 1980s; the new immigration had an adverse fiscal impact because the recent waves use the welfare system more intensively than the earlier waves; and there existed a strong intergenerational link between the skills of immigrants and the skills of second-generation Americans, so that the huge skill differentials observed among today's immigrant national origin groups would become tomorrow's differences among American-born ethnic groups.

In this chapter, I survey the methodological changes that led to such a pivotal reappraisal of the economic contribution of immigrants. The chapter is not meant to be a complete survey of the large and growing literature on the economics of immigration. Instead, the chapter focuses on the work directly motivated by the three central economic questions in the debate over immigration policy: How do immigrants perform in the US economy? What is the impact of immigrants on the economic opportunities of natives? Does the United States benefit from immigration?

2 Trends in immigration

Immigration is again becoming a major component of demographic change in the United States. The flow of legal immigrants has increased steadily since the 1930s, and is rapidly approaching the historic levels reached in the early 1900s. After reaching a low of about 500,000 immigrants admitted during the Great Depression, the flow has increased at the rate of about 1 million immigrants per decade. By the 1980s, the average annual flow was near 600,000 persons per year. In addition to these legal immigrants, there has been a steady increase in the number of illegal aliens entering the United States. A number of demographic studies (Warren and Passel, 1987) estimate the number of illegal aliens present in the United States (prior to IRCA) to be around 3–4 million persons, so that the flow of legal and illegal immigrants during the 1980s was about 8.4 million persons.

As a result of the increase in the number of legal and illegal immigrants, as well as the decline in the fertility rate of American women and the aging of the baby boom, immigrants are an increasingly important component of new population growth and new labor market entrants. By the 1980s, both legal and illegal immigration accounted for over a third of the new population in the United States, and for about a quarter of all new workers.

These changes in the size of the immigrant flow are partly attributable to shifts in US immigration policy. Prior to 1965, immigration was guided by the national-origins quota system. Under this system, which dated back to the 1920s, the United States allocated visa quotas to countries outside the Western Hemisphere, and these quotas were based on the national origin composition of the US population in 1920. As a result, two countries, the United Kingdom and Germany, received nearly two-thirds of all visas. In addition, immigration from Asia was essentially prohibited.

The 1965 Amendments to the Immigration and Nationality Act removed the national origin requirements, made family ties to US residents the key variable in the visa allocation system, and "redistributed" visas across source countries. The 1965 Amendments shifted visas away from Western European countries where income levels were reaching parity with those in the United States, and hence incentives to migrate were small, to less-developed countries with substantially lower income levels, and correspondingly higher emigration incentives. It is not surprising, therefore, that once a few family members from non-European countries could establish "beachheads" in the United States, the size of the immigrant flow increased rapidly. As a result, the national origin mix of the immigrant population changed substantially.

3 Immigrant performance in the US labor market

As noted above, a central question in the debate over immigration policy concerns the economic performance of immigrants in the United States. There exists a large literature attempting to determine how the earnings of immigrants grow over time as they adjust to the US labor market. These studies typically find that recent immigrants tend to earn less than immigrants who have resided in the United States for many years.

The original studies of Chiswick (1978) and Carliner (1980) reinterpreted the melting pot hypothesis (which interestingly was a cornerstone of the original Chicago School of Sociology) in terms of Becker's theory of specific training (1964) to explain the process of "economic assimilation." When immigrants first arrive in the United States, they lack skills valued by US employers, such as English proficiency, and are uninformed about the way the US labor market works, where and how to apply for jobs, and some key characteristics of the industrial structure. As a result, recently arrived immigrants are likely to have lower wages than native workers. Over time, immigrants make the necessary human capital investments in US-specific skills and their earnings begin to catch up with the earnings of demographically comparable natives.

More recent work has stressed the fact that there are skill differences among immigrant cohorts, and hence not all immigrant waves may experience the same type of convergence between their earnings and those of natives (Borjas, 1985, 1990). In view of the post-war changes in the size and national origin composition of the immigrant flow and in the selection mechanism that allocates visas among applicants, it is unlikely that the skill composition of the immigrant flow remained constant across cohorts.

In fact, Census data unambiguously reveal that cohort skill differentials exist. In particular, more recent cohorts are relatively less skilled than earlier waves. Immigrants who arrived in the late 1950s, for instance, had about 0.4 years more schooling than natives, and earned only 12.8 percent less than natives at the time of arrival. By 1980, immigrants who had just entered the country had about a year less schooling and earned 29.9 percent less than natives.

To illustrate the importance of these cohort effects, figure 2.1 contrasts the age/earnings profiles of two specific immigrant waves (those who arrived in the 1960–4 period and those who arrived between 1975 and 1979) with the age/earnings profile of natives. It is evident that because recent

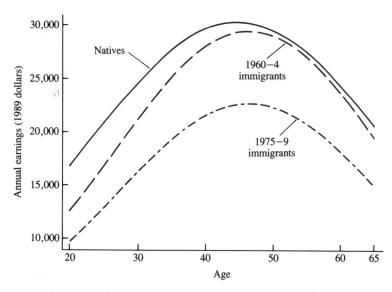

Figure 2.1 Earnings over the working life for immigrant and native men

immigrant waves have such a large initial wage disadvantage, they will not reach earnings parity with natives during their working careers. Even after thirty years in the United States, the post-1965 immigrants lag far behind natives in terms of their economic achievement.

A number of studies have tried to identify the factors responsible for the skill decline across immigrant waves (Borjas, 1992b; LaLonde and Topel, 1992). The changing national origin mix of immigrants seems to be the main variable responsible for the lagging economic performance of more recent waves. As noted earlier, post-1965 immigrants are much more likely to originate in Latin American and Asian countries. There are huge disparities in the relative wage of the various national origin groups. In 1980, for instance, the immigrants who had just arrived from Sweden or the United Kingdom were earning about 20 percent more than natives, those from India or Iran earned about 20 percent less, while those from Mexico or Haiti earned about 50 percent less.

Although Becker's theory of discrimination (1957) has sometimes been used to explain these national origin differentials, the differences are consistent with the existence of real differences in skills across these groups. For instance, by again appealing to Becker's concept of specific training, it is apparent that skills attained in advanced, industrialized economies are more easily transferable to the American labor market. After all, the industrial structure of advanced economies and the types of skills rewarded by those labor markets greatly resemble the industrial structure of the United States and the types of skills rewarded by American employers. In contrast, the industrial structures and labor markets of less-developed countries require skills that are much less useful in the American labor market. The human capital embodied in residents of those countries is, to some extent, "specific" to those countries and is not easily transferable to the US labor market.

However, because not all persons in the source countries choose to migrate to the United States there is an additional reason for the dispersion in skills among national origin groups (Borjas, 1987). Suppose that immigration to the United States is mainly motivated by the search for better economic opportunities. Which individuals find it worthwhile to migrate? If the worker originates in a country which offers relatively low returns to their skills, as is common in countries with relatively egalitarian income distributions such as the United Kingdom and Sweden, the source country in effect "taxes" able workers and "insures" the least productive against poor labor market outcomes. This situation obviously generates incentives for the most able to migrate to the United States and the immigrant flow is positively selected (i.e., a "brain drain").

Conversely, if the source country offers relatively high rates of return to skills (which is typically true in countries with substantial income inequality, such as Mexico), immigration to the United States now taxes the most able and subsidizes the least productive. Economic conditions in the US relative to those in the country of origin become a magnet for individuals with relatively low earnings capacities, and the immigrant flow is negatively selected.

This model of how immigrants are self-selected provides an interesting explanation of the decline in skills observed among successive immigrant waves. Prior to the 1965 Amendments, the allocation of visas across countries was guided by the ethnic/racial composition of the US population in 1920, and thus favored immigration from a number of Western European countries. The 1965 Amendments removed these restrictions and led to a major increase in the number of immigrants originating in Asian and Latin American countries. The "new" immigration, therefore, is more likely to originate in countries where income inequality is relatively high and where skills are less easily transferable to the United States. Economic theory thus predicts that the earnings capacities of immigrant waves will have declined as a result of the redistribution of visas initiated by the 1965 Amendments.

A major consequence of the shift toward a less skilled immigrant flow is a sizable increase in the fraction of immigrants who are welfare recipients (Borjas and Trejo, 1991). It is evident that more recent immigrant waves have higher welfare participation rates than earlier immigrant cohorts (for given length of residence in the United States). For instance, newly arrived immigrant households in the 1970 Census (those who arrived between 1965 and 1969) had an overall welfare participation rate of only 5.5 percent in 1970. In the 1980 Census, however, newly arrived immigrant households (who had migrated between 1975 and 1979) had a welfare participation rate of 8.3 percent. This 2.8 percentage point increase in the welfare participation rate across the two cohorts exceeds the corresponding increase of 1.8 percentage points experienced by native households over the decade. Moreover, for a given immigrant cohort, the welfare participation rate *increases* the longer the cohort resides in the United States. For instance, the welfare participation rate of the 1965–9 wave nearly doubled between 1970 and 1980.

The finding that more recent cohorts use the welfare system more intensively is not surprising in view of the earlier discussion on the declining quality of successive immigrant waves. What is surprising is the seemingly perverse correlation between years-since-migration and welfare participation rates. It seems that immigrants assimilate into welfare. This correlation may be related to the lifting of legal restrictions, such as permanent legal residence or citizenship, that limit the participation of recent immigrants in some welfare programs. Immigrants may also believe that their chances for naturalization (and hence for sponsoring the entry of relatives through the family preference system) are jeopardized if they receive welfare. Finally, it is also possible that immigrant assimilation involves the accumulation of information not only about the labor market, but also about the income opportunities available through the welfare system.

Although the evidence suggests that the new immigrants will not be relatively successful during their working lives, the cause for concern would be greatly diminished if there was substantial assimilation between the first and second generations. Recent studies, however, indicate that the skill differentials observed among national origin groups in the first generation are transmitted to their ethnic offspring (Borjas, 1992a, 1993). The data reveal substantial dispersion among ethnic groups in the earnings of second-generation Americans. Second-generation workers of British ancestry, for instance, earned about 9 percent more than second-generation Canadians, and about 35 percent more than second-generation Mexicans. Put differently, today's differences in skills among foreign-born national origin groups become tomorrow's skill differentials among American-born ethnic groups.

4 The impact of immigrants on native earnings

Do immigrants have an adverse effect on native earnings and employment opportunities? If so, how large is the loss in the economic welfare of natives? Finally, are all native groups equally affected by the entry of immigrants into the labor market?

These questions address some of the most important and most emotional issues in the debate over immigration policy in host countries. The fear that "immigrant hordes" displace natives from their jobs and reduce the earnings of those lucky enough to still have a job has a long (and not so honorable) history in the US immigration debate. The presumption that immigrants have an adverse impact on the labor market has been and continues to be used as a key justification for policies designed to restrict the size and composition of immigrant flows into the United States.

There are two opposing views about how immigrants affect the native labor market. One approach asserts that immigrants have a harmful effect on the employment and earnings opportunities of natives because immigrants and natives are easily substitutable by American employers. That is, immigrants and natives tend to have similar skills, and are suited for similar types of jobs. As immigrants enter the labor market, the supply of these skills to the labor market increases, and there is more competition among the workers supplying these skills to employers. Firms, therefore, can attract workers – both immigrants and natives – at lower wage rates because these skills are now abundant in the marketplace. In addition, because of the lower wages now paid to native workers, some native workers find it worthwhile to withdraw from the labor force, and hence the number of native workers employed declines.

It is possible, however, that immigrants and natives are not interchangeable types of workers, but that they complement each other in the production process. For instance, some immigrant groups may have very low skill levels and a comparative advantage in agricultural production. This frees the more skilled native workforce to perform tasks that require relatively more skills. The presence of immigrants increases native productivity because natives can now specialize in tasks where they too have a comparative advantage. This makes natives more valuable to firms, and increases the firm's demand for native labor. Since employers are now competing for native labor, native wage rates are bid up. In addition, some natives who previously did not find it profitable to work will now see the higher wage rate as an additional incentive to enter the labor market, and hence native employment also increases.

This conceptual framework suggests a simple way of establishing empirically the sign of the labor market interactions between immigrants and natives. If immigrants and natives are substitutes in production, the earnings of native workers should be lower in labor markets where immigrants are in relatively abundant supply. On the other hand, if immigrants and natives are complements in production, native earnings should be relatively lower in labor markets where the supply of immigrants is scarce.

Beginning with the early work of Grossman (1982) and Borjas (1983), practically all research takes this implication of the theory as its departure point. In particular, the studies compare native earnings in localities where immigrants are a substantial fraction of the labor force (for example, Los Angeles or New York) with native earnings in localities where immigrants are a relatively trivial fraction (for example, Pittsburgh or Nashville).

The cross-city correlations reveal that the average native wage is slightly smaller in labor markets where immigrants tend to reside. However, the decline in the native wage attributable to an increase in the supply of immigrants is numerically trivial. If one city has 10 percent more immigrants than another, the native wage in the city with the most immigrants is only 0.2 percent lower. A doubling of the number of immigrants in the local labor market, therefore, reduces the native wage rate by only 2 or 3 percent. The overwhelming consensus of the literature seems to be that immigrants and practically all native groups are, at worse, very weak substitutes in production.

These area-based studies indicate that the impact of immigration on the earnings of natives is small even in labor markets that received very large immigrant flows. On April 20, 1980, Fidel Castro declared that Cuban nationals wishing to move to the United States could leave freely from the port of Mariel, Cuba. By September 1980, about 125,000 Cubans, mostly unskilled workers, had chosen to undertake the journey. The numerical impact of the Mariel flow on Miami's population and labor force was sizable. Almost overnight, Miami's labor force had unexpectedly grown by 7 percent. Yet Card's (1990) careful analysis of the data indicates that the trend of wages and employment opportunities for Miami's population, including its black population, was barely affected by the Mariel flow. The economic conditions experienced by Miami between 1980 and 1985, in terms of wage levels and unemployment rates, were similar to those experienced by such cities as Los Angeles, Houston, and Atlanta, cities which did not experience the Mariel flow.

It is fair to conclude that the cross-city correlations have not established a single instance in which the earnings of US-born workers have been strongly and adversely affected by the increase in the supply of immigrants over the last two decades. This unexpected finding raises an important question: Why is the empirical evidence so at odds with the typical presumption in the public arena?

One possible (and testable) explanation of this result is that natives attenuate the negative impact of immigration by choosing to reside in other localities. Using 1980 Census data, Filer (1992) finds a negative correlation between the in-migration rates of natives into particular cities and the presence of immigrants in those cities. This result suggests that natives respond to the increase in immigrant labor supply by moving elsewhere. In effect, the internal migration of natives dissipates the impact of immigration on particular labor markets and makes it difficult to determine the effects of immigration by looking at cross-city correlations.

It may also be the case that the local impact of immigration is dampened by capital investments flowing into (or out of) immigrant areas. This would again have the effect of dissipating the impact of immigration on a particular labor market over the entire economy. In a sense, to the extent that workers or firms respond to the entry of immigrants by moving to areas with better opportunities, there would be little reason to expect a correlation between the labor market opportunities of natives and the presence of immigrants and hence the comparison of labor markets could be masking a "macro" impact of immigration.

Circumstantial evidence for this macro effect is present in the labor market for workers with less than a high school education. The 1980s witnessed a substantial increase in the wage gap between these unskilled workers and workers with more education. From the 1970s through the 1980s, earnings differentials between more- and less-educated workers skyrocketed and inequality rose among workers in given skill categories, producing a more unequal income distribution. The relative wage of high school "dropouts" declined by 10 percentage points during the 1980s.

The recent study by Borjas, Freeman, and Katz (1992) implies that the flow of less-educated immigrants contributed substantially to the rise in earnings differentials across education groups. Although only about 13 percent of high school dropout workers were foreign born in 1980, upwards of one-quarter of American workers with fewer than twelve years of schooling were immigrants in 1988. By contrast, the effect of immigration on the supply of more educated workers was relatively modest: the fraction of immigrants among college graduates increased from 8 to 11 percent over the same period.

Given reasonable responses of wages and employment opportunities to an increase in the ratio of less-educated to more-educated workers, this massive change in relative supplies must have had a sizable adverse impact on the economic well being of less-skilled workers. Borjas, Freeman, and Katz suggest that perhaps a third of the 10 percentage point decline in the relative weekly wage of high school dropouts between 1980 and 1988 can be attributed to the less-skilled immigration flow.

This conclusion contrasts sharply with the inference drawn from the cross-city correlations. As noted above, a potential explanation for the differing implications of the results from the Borjas–Freeman–Katz study and the spatial analyses is that local labor markets adjust rapidly to the increased supply of immigrants (either through labor or capital flows). This hypothesis would imply that both the spatial correlations and the macro findings are "correct," but that the findings differ because they address very different questions. The cross-city correlations correctly tell us that immigrants have no measurable impact on particular labor markets, but are not informative about the economy-wide effects of immigration.

5 Summary

Changes in immigration policy since 1965 greatly altered the number, national origin mix, and skill composition of immigrants. The development of an economic approach to the analysis of immigration has greatly increased our understanding of the role that immigrants play in the economy. It is evident that Becker's ideas and approach pervade the immigration literature. In fact, in his *Business Week* columns Becker (1987, 1988) uses many of the research results in this literature to propose that the United States institute an open market for visas as an alternative to our current immigration policy.

In view of the sizable demographic and economic impact that immigrants have on the United States, the debate over immigration policy is sure to be reignited in the 1990s. This debate will have to address the basic cost–benefit question raised by the economics literature. There is obviously a substantial benefit associated with the immigration of unskilled workers: a relative abundance of cheap labor for American companies, and hence lower prices for consumers. It is worth asking, however, if these benefits exceed the costs associated with lost employment opportunities for unskilled native workers and the increasing tax burden.

In the end, we will have to confront head-on the difficult question of whether to keep the current family reunification system, which allocates most visas to applicants who have relatives residing in the US, or to switch to a system which awards entry visas mainly to skilled applicants, or to a Becker-type market for visas. A shift toward either a skill-based policy or a policy of selling visas to the highest bidder will obviously alter the size and national origin composition of the immigrant flow. The perceived impact of these changes on the United States is sure to be a central ingredient of the debate over immigration policy in the 1990s.

References

Becker, Gary S. 1957. *The Economics of Discrimination*, Chicago, IL: University of Chicago Press.
  1964. *Human Capital*, Chicago, IL: University of Chicago Press.
  1976. *The Economic Approach to Human Behavior*, Chicago, IL: University of Chicago Press.
  1987. "Why Not Let Immigrants Pay for Speedy Entry," *Business Week*, March 2, 1987: 20.
  1988. "Hong Kong's Best and Brightest: Ours for the Asking," *Business Week*, October 17, 1988: 20.
Borjas, George J. 1983. "The Substitutability of Black, Hispanic, and White Labor," *Economic Inquiry*, 21 (January): 93–106.
  1985. "Assimilation, Changes in Cohort Quality, and the Earnings of Immigrants," *Journal of Labor Economics*, 3 (October): 463–89.
  1987. "Self-Selection and the Earnings of Immigrants," *American Economic Review*, 77 (September): 531–53.
  1990. *Friends or Strangers: The Impact of Immigrants on the US Economy*, New York: Basic Books.
  1992a. "Ethnic Capital and Intergenerational Mobility," *Quarterly Journal of Economics*, 107 (February): 123–50.
  1992b. "National Origin and the Skills of Immigrants in the Postwar Period," in George J. Borjas and Richard B. Freeman (eds.), *Immigration and the Work Force: Economic Consequences for the United States and Source Areas*, Chicago, IL: University of Chicago Press.
  1993. "The Intergenerational Mobility of Immigrants," *Journal of Labor Economics*, 11 (January): 113–35.
Borjas, George J., Richard B. Freeman, and Lawrence F. Katz. 1992. "On the Labor Market Effects of Immigration and Trade," in George J. Borjas and Richard B. Freeman (eds.), *Immigration and the Work Force: Economic Consequences for the United States and Source Areas*, Chicago, IL: University of Chicago Press.
Borjas, George J. and Stephen J. Trejo. 1991. "Immigrant Participation in the Welfare System," *Industrial and Labor Relations Review*, 44 (January): 195–211.
Card, David. 1990. "The Impact of the Mariel Boatlift on the Miami Labor Market," *Industrial and Labor Relations Review*, 43 (January): 245–57.
Carliner, Geoffrey. 1980. "Wages, Earnings, and Hours of First, Second and Third Generation American Males," *Economic Inquiry*, 18 (January): 87–102.
Chiswick, Barry R. 1978. "The Effect of Americanization on the Earnings of Foreign-Born Men," *Journal of Political Economy*, 86 (October): 897–921.

Filer, Randall K. 1992. "The Impact of Immigrant Arrivals on Migratory Patterns of Native Workers," in George J. Borjas and Richard B. Freeman (eds.), *Immigration and the Work Force: Economic Consequences for the United States and Source Areas*, Chicago, IL: University of Chicago Press.

Grossman, Jean B. 1982. "The Substitutability of Natives and Immigrants in Production," *Review of Economics and Statistics*, 54 (November): 596–603.

LaLonde, Robert J. and Robert H. Topel. 1992. "The Assimilation of Immigrants in the US Labor Market," in George J. Borjas and Richard B. Freeman (eds.), *Immigration and the Work Force: Economic Consequences for the United States and Source Areas*, Chicago, IL: University of Chicago Press.

Warren, Robert and Jeffrey S. Passel. 1987. "A Count of the Uncountable: Estimates of Undocumented Aliens Counted in the 1980 United States Census," *Demography*, 24 (August): 375–93.

II

Crime, punishment, and rights

3 Rational criminals and profit-maximizing police
The economic analysis of law and law enforcement

David Friedman

> ... how many resources and how much punishment *should* be
> used to enforce different kinds of legislation? Put equivalently,
> although more strangely, how many offenses *should* be
> permitted and how many offenders *should* go unpunished?
>
> Gary Becker (1968)

The economic analysis of crime starts with one simple assumption: Criminals are rational. A mugger is a mugger for the same reason I am a professor – because that profession makes him better off, by his own standards, than any other alternative available to him. Here, as elsewhere in economics, the assumption of rationality does not imply that muggers (or economics professors) calculate the costs and benefits of available alternatives to seventeen decimal places – merely that they tend to choose the one that best achieves their objectives.

If muggers are rational, we do not have to make mugging impossible in order to prevent it, merely unprofitable. If the benefits of a profession decrease or its costs increase, fewer people will enter it – whether the profession is plumbing or burglary. If little old ladies start carrying pistols in their purses, so that one mugging in ten puts the mugger in the hospital or the morgue, the number of muggers will decrease drastically – not because they have all been shot but because most will have switched to safer ways of making a living. If mugging becomes sufficiently unprofitable, nobody will do it.

The assumption of rationality applies not only to criminals but to everyone included in the analysis. Judges, policemen, legislators, and potential victims are all, like criminals, rational individuals pursuing their own ends as best they can. Economic theory gives us no reason to assume that criminals are less rational than judges, or judges less self-interested than criminals.

When the analysis moves from descriptive to prescriptive, it seems

43

natural to apply a similar approach to ourselves. In designing institutions to control crime, our concern is not sin but cost. Eliminating all murders, even all muggings, would no doubt be a fine thing – but whether we ought to try to do it depends on how much it costs. If reducing the annual murder rate from ten to zero requires us to turn half the population into police, judges, and prison guards, it is probably not worth doing.

1 The theory of optimal enforcement

What I have said suggests a simple question: How can we structure laws and law enforcement so as to minimize the net costs of crime and crime prevention? The modern attempt to answer that question begins with Gary Becker's classic article "Crime and Punishment: An Economic Approach." In trying to explain the theory as it now exists, I will not distinguish Becker's own work from what has been added later by others; interested readers may wish to look at the articles cited at the end of this chapter.

It is useful to begin our analysis of optimal law enforcement with a simple, although entirely unrealistic, case. Suppose we can catch all criminals and collect fines from them, and that it costs nothing to do so. In this fortunate world, how should we set the fines?

Our first guess might be that the fine should be high enough to deter all crimes. But there may be some crimes we do not want to deter. Consider a hunter, lost and starving in the woods, who comes across a locked cabin containing food and a telephone. The benefit to him of breaking in and calling for rescue is much larger than the cost to the cabin's owner; we will, on net, be better off if that particular offense is not deterred. For a less dramatic example, consider the driver who occasionally exceeds the speed limit when he is in a hurry. We could deter all or almost all speeding if we routinely confiscated the cars of convicted speeders – but many of us would regard that as more deterrence than we want.

If a crime produces a net benefit, if the gain to the speeder or the lost hunter is more than the loss to the rest of us, we are better off not deterring it. In many cases our legal system permits such "efficient crimes" by not classifying them as crimes. Every time I breathe out I exhale carbon dioxide – regarded, in some contexts, as a pollutant. Most of us are confident that this particular offense is an efficient one – we are better off if we put up with a certain amount of extra carbon dioxide than if we all stop breathing. So exhaling, unlike some other forms of pollution, is not illegal. Similarly, the lost hunter of my example would probably be excused from criminal liability under the doctrine of necessity.

But there are other cases where a sharp line between efficient and inefficient crimes is hard to draw. By driving my car at eighty miles an hour I impose a cost, a risk of accidents, on other drivers. Often that is inefficient – if I had to take into account the risk I impose on them as well as the risk I impose on myself, I would not drive so fast. Occasionally, however, driving fast is efficient – the benefit of getting where I am going half an hour earlier more than balances the associated cost. How, in such situations, can we deter inefficient speeding while permitting efficient speeding?

The answer is simple: Set the expected punishment equal to the damage done. If exceeding the speed limit imposes on other drivers a cost in increased risk of $100, and all speeders are caught, then a driver who speeds will have to pay a $100 fine. If, to make our assumptions a little more realistic, only one speeder in ten is caught, we set the fine at $1,000, making his average cost of speeding, his "expected punishment," again equal to $100. If speeding is worth more than $100 to him, he will speed; if it is not, he will obey the limit.

Under this rule, criminal punishment functions as a probabilistic price system. Each crime has a price – a certain probability of a certain fine – set so that the average fine equals the damage done. Someone willing to pay that price will commit the crime – and, from the standpoint of economic efficiency, should. In just the same way, on an ordinary market, each good has a price. That a buyer is willing to pay that price shows that the good is worth more to him than to the seller, so the transaction produces a net gain.

While this may be a reasonable way of looking at speeding, it seems less appropriate for more serious offenses. If we are really setting our punishments in the way I have described, it follows that the offenses which still occur are ones that produce net benefits. Do we really have a legal system where the reason we do not raise the punishment for murder is the fear that we would then have too few murders?

The answer is no. So far I have been describing a world where crime control costs nothing and we therefore buy as much of it as we want. In such a world we would set the punishment for murder so high that only efficient murders occurred. While some of us may be able to think of one or two people who would improve the world by their absence, it is unlikely we would agree on who they were – so the consensus would probably be for an efficient murder rate of zero.

In the real world, that is not a practical option. In order to catch and convict criminals we must pay police, hold trials, train lawyers – pay a variety of costs which I will refer to, for convenience, as apprehension costs. Once the criminals are convicted, we must punish them – and that too is costly.

What is the net cost of punishment? In the simple case of a fine, it is zero – the criminal pays $100 and the court system collects $100. In the case of imprisonment or execution, the cost is higher. The cost of imprisonment includes not only the wages of guards but also the time of jail inmates – unlike the case of a fine, nobody gets what the prisoner loses. An execution costs more than the price of a bullet or a hangman's rope – one life more.

In controlling crime, we can get a given amount of deterrence in many different ways. We might catch half the criminals and fine them each $500, we might catch one criminal in twenty and put him in jail for a year, or we might catch one in five hundred and hang him. Suppose that all of these alternatives are equivalent from the standpoint of the criminal and thus have the same deterrent effect, just as a $100 fine was equivalent, in the earlier example, to one chance in ten of a $1,000 fine. Generalizing our earlier term, we may say that all of these alternative combinations of probability and punishment represent the same expected punishment.

In choosing among them, we are trading off one kind of cost against another. It takes fewer policemen to catch five criminals out of a hundred than fifty and fewer judges to try them, so lowering the number we catch while raising their punishment saves on apprehension costs. But, since there is a limit to how large a fine a convicted criminal can pay, raising the punishment typically means shifting from fines to imprisonment or execution – which increases punishment cost. An efficient law enforcement system would produce any given level of deterrence with whatever combination of probability and punishment minimized the sum of the two sorts of cost.

This raises an interesting puzzle – why do we imprison anyone? One answer is that we imprison people because they are judgment proof – they do not have enough money to pay a fine high enough to represent an adequate punishment. But while that explains why we cannot fine some people, it does not explain why we imprison them, since imprisonment appears to be not only less efficient than a fine but also less efficient than execution. Bullets and rope are cheap, so the total cost of an execution consists almost entirely of the cost paid by the criminal – his life. Jails and jail guards are expensive, so the total cost of imprisonment is substantially more than the cost to the criminal.

Suppose we have determined that the cost to a criminal of life imprisonment is exactly half the cost of execution – meaning that a criminal is indifferent between a certainty of a life sentence and a 50 percent chance of execution. We then make a small modification to present law. Whenever a criminal receives a life sentence, we flip a coin. Heads he goes free; tails we hang him.

On the face of it, this seems an unambiguous improvement. The criminal is no worse off, on average, since he considers a 50 percent chance of execution as equivalent to a certainty of life in prison. Potential victims are no worse off; since the two punishments are equivalent from the standpoint of criminals, they will have the same deterrent effect. The only significant effect of the change is that we can now replace a large number of prison guards with a small number of hangmen – with a substantial net savings.

Nothing in the logic of the argument limits it to criminals who have been sentenced to life terms. The same argument would apply to anyone sentenced to serve time, however short – the only difference is in the appropriate odds. If my sentence is one year, the court uses a roulette wheel instead of a coin – on a double zero they hang me, on any other number I go free.

What is wrong with the grisly conclusion of this simple and straightforward argument? One possibility is that there is nothing wrong with it – I have described an efficient system of law enforcement, and the reason our system does not work that way is that it is not efficient, either because efficiency is not our objective or because we have done a bad job of getting it.

There are at least two other possible explanations of our preference for expensive imprisonment over cheap execution. One is that execution is not really cheap – indeed is more costly than imprisonment, if the calculation is done correctly. One respect in which it is costly is that execution is irreversible; if the real murderer confesses a week after we hang someone else, there is no way of unhanging him. Irreversible error also involves costs, although ones we have so far ignored. Another is that execution offends the sensibilities of many citizens in ways in which imprisonment does not. If many of us are made unhappy by the knowledge that the legal system we support and pay for kills people in cold blood, that too is a cost. In addition, in the US legal system as it now exists, execution is very expensive because it involves a lengthy process of appeals – although one should perhaps regard that less as a reason for our reluctance to execute criminals than a result of it.

A second explanation is that we are reluctant to make too much use of execution precisely because it is efficient. So far I have applied the assumption of rationality only to criminals. I have treated courts and police as merely servants of the public, with no will of their own. That might be a dangerous mistake.

Suppose we suspect that the people running the enforcement system may sometimes, under some circumstances, have an incentive to carry their job substantially too far. An ambitious mayor, or governor, or president might decide that there is political profit to be made from a reputation as a crime fighter – enough so that it is worth ignoring the costs to those he convicts, rightly or wrongly, and punishes. If, for most crimes, punishment means imprisonment, he will be constrained by the reluctance of taxpayers to pay for an unlimited number of prisons. If he is free to execute criminals even for relatively minor offenses, that constraint vanishes. So one possible explanation of our reluctance to make more use of execution is that we wish to limit our officials to punishments that impose costs on the enforcement system as well as on the convicted criminal, as a way of limiting the risk of overpunishment in a system in which we have no guarantee that political decision makers will take all costs into account in making their decisions.

This may seem, to some readers, like a purely theoretical argument, and an implausible one at that. It becomes more plausible if we consider a real world case in which we have provided the police with the power to impose efficient punishments – and we may well be worse off as a result. The example I have in mind is civil forfeiture for drug crimes.

Under present law, police can, in a wide range of cases, seize property that they claim was used in connection with illegal drugs – without having to convict the owner of anything. It is up to the owner to go to court and prove his innocence in order to get his property back. Critics of the system argue that it results in widespread abuse. There is no reason, after all, to expect police, or the local governments that employ them, to be less rational than criminals, or less interested in serving their own objectives. It may sometimes be prudent to ban punishments that are so efficient that they produce a profit for the punisher at the expense of the punishee – at least in situations where it is the punisher who gets to determine guilt and set the punishment.

Having offered some possible solutions to the puzzle of why we prefer inefficient imprisonment to (apparently) efficient execution, let us now return to the main topic – what an efficient system of enforcement and punishment would look like.

In deciding how much deterrence we want, we must balance the costs and benefits of increasing expected punishment. It is inefficient for me to steal a television set that is worth five hundred dollars to you and only four hundred dollars to me. But it is still more inefficient to prevent me from stealing the set if the cost of doing so is two hundred dollars additional expenditure on police, courts, and prisons. The rule "prevent all inefficient offenses and only inefficient offenses" is correct only if doing so is costless. The more generally correct rule is to prevent an offense if and only if the net cost from the offense occurring is greater than the cost of preventing it.

To provide more deterrence for a particular crime, we must either catch a larger fraction of offenders or impose a more severe punishment – which means increasing either apprehension or punishment cost per offense. Increasing cost per offense, however, does not necessarily increase total cost – it depends what happens to the number of offenses. Suppose that, for some particular offense, an increase in the expected punishment from $100 to $110 reduces the number of offenses from 100 to 10. The cost per offense of catching and punishing offenders has increased, but the total cost has almost certainly decreased, since there are many fewer offenders to be apprehended and punished.

This is a situation where, in the language of economics, the demand for offenses is highly elastic; when we increase the price of committing an offense the number committed falls sharply. The result is that the marginal cost of deterrence, the extra cost of deterring one more offense, is negative – increasing deterrence lowers cost. If, on the other hand, the demand were highly inelastic, if, for example, the increased punishment only reduced the number of offenses from 100 to 99, total cost would almost certainly increase. In such a situation, increasing deterrence raises cost, so the marginal cost of deterrence is positive.

The difference between crimes for which marginal cost is positive and crimes for which it is negative is important when it comes to setting the optimal punishment. If deterrence is costly, then it is only worth deterring offenses that impose substantial net costs. If a particular offense costs the victim $100 and benefits the criminal by $99, deterring it produces a net benefit of only $1. If the marginal cost of deterrence is positive, crimes that are only slightly inefficient are not worth deterring.

Which crimes we deter is determined by how high an expected punishment we set. If, in the previous example, we set the expected punishment at $99 for a crime that does $100 worth of damage, then any criminal whose benefit is less than $99 will be deterred while any whose benefit is more than $99 will find it worth committing the crime. We will be deterring all offenses whose net harm is more than $1 and permitting, although still punishing, offenses that produce a net harm of less than one dollar, and that it is therefore worth less than a dollar to deter.

Generalizing the example gives us a simple rule. The expected punishment for a crime should equal the damage done minus the marginal cost of deterrence. A potential offender whose gain is less than that will be deterred – and should be, since the net damage of his crime (victim's loss minus criminal's gain) is more than the cost of deterring it.

This probably describes the situation for serious crimes such as murder. Catching a large enough fraction of the criminals and punishing them severely enough to make the expected punishment equal to the damage done, if possible at all, would be very expensive and provide only a moderate increase in deterrence over a lower but still substantial expected punishment. The marginal cost of punishment is positive, so we impose a punishment well below the damage done.

What about crimes for which the demand for offenses is elastic enough to make the marginal cost of deterrence negative? The same analysis applies; only the sign has changed. If raising expected punishment by enough to deter one more crime decreases apprehension and enforcement cost by $10, the efficient rule is to set punishment equal to damage plus $10. We will be deterring some slightly efficient offenses, but it is worth deterring them in order to save the cost of catching and punishing the offenders.

Our rule for punishment combines elements of two different intuitions: punishment equal to damage done and enough punishment to deter. If catching and punishing criminals is inexpensive, the optimum is about equal to damage done – enforcement and punishment costs are unimportant, so we simply design our system to deter all inefficient and only inefficient offenses. If, on the other hand, catching and punishing criminals is costly and the supply of offenses is highly elastic at some particular level of punishment, so that below that level there are many offenses and above it very few, then we set the punishment at the point where any further increase would have very little deterrent effect to balance its cost – just enough punishment to deter most offenses.

One implication is that it may sometimes be worth treating different sorts of criminals differently. An example is the insanity defense. If insane people cannot be deterred by the threat of punishment then their demand for offenses is perfectly inelastic; the marginal cost of deterring them is infinite. If they can be deterred, but a large punishment produces only a very small amount of deterrence, the marginal cost of deterrence is so high that it is probably not worth doing. We may still wish to confine insane criminals in order to prevent them from committing more crimes, or in the hope of curing them, but not as a punishment intended to deter.

A less extreme example is the imposition of a higher punishment for a premeditated murder than for a murder committed in a blind rage. Presumably the offender who plans out his murder in advance is more likely to consider consequences – including punishment – and is therefore more easily deterred. The marginal cost of deterring such murderers is lower, so the optimal punishment is higher.

Another example of the same logic is raised by a question that my students sometimes ask: should rich and poor criminals pay the same fine? A hundred dollars may be a crushing fine to a pauper but a trivial punishment to a wealthy man. In a legal system where all criminals face the same expected punishment, are we not, in effect, overpunishing the poor and underpunishing the rich?

There are two answers to this question. The first is that, in defining economic efficiency, we measure costs and benefits by willingness to pay – a criterion which weights the desires of rich people more highly than the desires of poor people. A legal system in which rich people "buy" more illegal driving than poor people may or may not be just, but it is efficient for the same reason that a system in which rich people buy more television sets than poor people is efficient. A full discussion of the reasons why I (and many other economists) do not regard unequal distribution of goods as an adequate reason to reject efficiency as a useful criterion would carry us far beyond the bounds of this chapter (Friedman, 1990, chapter 15).

A second answer, however, is that it is not clear that an efficient system will always impose the same fines on rich people and poor people. As we have seen, in a world where law enforcement is costly the correct rule for determining punishments is more complicated than simply setting expected punishment equal to the damage done. We must also take account of how much additional deterrence we can get for an additional dollar of enforcement and punishment cost. For some crimes, the deterrent effect of punishment depends on the income of the criminal.

Stealing a hundred dollars provides the same dollar benefit for rich and poor, so the same dollar punishment will deter it. The same is not true for speeding. On average, a rich person is willing to spend more dollars to save half an hour of his time than a poor person, so deterring him from speeding requires a higher fine. The same is true for a variety of other crimes. A richer person, on average, is willing to pay more dollars for the pleasure of slugging someone he is mad at, or murdering someone he is very mad at. We may generalize these examples by saying that for crimes where the payoff is in money, deterring rich people requires about the same punishment as deterring poor people, while for crimes where the payoff is in time or pleasure, it typically requires a larger fine to deter a richer victim.

Since one element in setting the punishment for a crime is how much punishment is required to deter, it will sometimes, for some crimes, be efficient to impose more severe punishments on richer criminals. For other crimes, however, an efficient system might actually set lower punishments for richer criminals – because they are so hard to deter that deterring them, like deterring lunatics, is not worth doing.

There is a second difference between rich and poor that leads to a less ambiguous conclusion. One constraint on punishment is its cost. Fines are a more efficient punishment than imprisonment, and richer people can pay larger fines. If deterring poor criminals is expensive and deterring rich criminals is cheap, an efficient system will prefer to deter rich criminals – and will do so by imposing higher punishments on them.

Before ending this part of the chapter, I would like to raise one further point that may have struck some readers. In my analysis of costs and benefits I have made no distinction between criminals, victims, and taxpayers. The cost of punishment to criminals and the benefit of crime to criminals receive the same weight as any other costs and benefits. To many non-economists, and even to a few economists, this seems wrong. Why should we care about criminals – have they not, by their acts, put themselves beyond the pale, forfeited their claim to have us take account of their welfare in our policies?

I think not – for two reasons. The first is that our analysis is intended to cover a broad range of illegal activity – speeding and illegal parking as well as murder and rape. With regard to at least the milder sorts of crimes we are all potential criminals as well as potential victims; it seems an odd form of economic accounting to include our costs and benefits in the latter role but not in the former.

A second reason is that economics does not start with assumptions about right and wrong – merely with the idea that individuals have objectives and choose means to achieve them. Economic efficiency is an attempt to define, as objectively as is practical, the degree to which each of us succeeds in achieving his own objectives – without making any ethical judgment about the objectives themselves. Part of what is exciting about the economic analysis of law is its ability to reason from the goal of economic efficiency to what look like ethical rules – "thou shalt not steal," for example. If we start out by assuming that certain acts are wicked and that benefits to people who commit wicked acts should not count in our social calculus, we are assuming our conclusions where we ought to be deriving them.

We now have a sketch of an economically efficient legal system for controlling crime. Of course, no court and no legislature has the information necessary to follow fully the program I have described – we do not know enough about how much different levels of enforcement and punishment cost, about how high a level of crime will be associated with any given level of deterrence, or about how much damage is done by each offense. The purpose of such analysis is not to provide a precise formula to be entered into a computer and used to generate a police budget and a schedule of punishments. It is rather to figure out what we would be doing if we only knew enough to do it, in order that we can use that knowledge in trying to come as close as our actual knowledge permits to constructing an efficient system of laws and law enforcement.

So far I have not distinguished between efficient deterrence as a prescriptive rule and efficient deterrence as a descriptive rule. I have not said whether I am describing what our legal system does or what it ought to do. Here as elsewhere in the economic analysis of law, economic efficiency plays a dual role. There are arguments for why creating an economically efficient system of law is desirable (Friedman, 1990, chapter 15). There are also arguments for why real-world legal institutions might be expected to be economically efficient (Posner, 1992, pp. 12–16). If one accepts the first sort of argument, the analysis I have just given is a description of what we should have; if one accepts the second, it is an explanation of what we do have.

I have also not said much about evidence in favor of the underlying assumptions of the economic approach to crime, in particular the much debated question of whether and to what degree punishment deters. Interested readers may want to look at the summary of the evidence in Nagin 1978. The author reports on more than twenty empirical studies done between 1968 and 1975; only one failed to find "some significant inverse associations between crime and sanctions." He argues, however, that the evidence for deterrence is not conclusive, since there are other possible explanations for such an association.

2 Should we abolish the criminal law?

In the first part of this chapter, I applied the assumption of rationality to criminals but not, save for one digression, to other participants in the criminal justice system. I will now try to correct that omission. What does the assumption that policemen, like criminals, are rational imply for how we ought to enforce the law?

The modern discussion of this issue owes a good deal to an article by Gary Becker and George Stigler, entitled "Law Enforcement, Malfeasance, and Compensation of Enforcers." The relevant part of their argument may be summarized quite simply:

I am a policeman, you are a criminal, and I have the evidence that will convict you. The cost to you of being convicted is $50,000 – either a fine or an equivalent jail sentence. The benefit to me of convicting you is a commendation from my superior officer and a small increase in my prospects for promotion – worth, say, $10,000 in future income.

Seen from the standpoint of Dragnet, the rest is obvious. I deliver both you and the evidence to the D.A., and the story is over. Seen from the standpoint of an economically rational police officer, it is equally obvious. I sell you the evidence for something between ten and fifty thousand dollars, and we both go home.

Of course, this is not the whole story – if it were, criminals would almost never be convicted. Real-world legal systems spend considerable time and effort trying to prevent such transactions and punishing those who engage in them. But the need to do so is a substantial cost – it means that police officers must spend part of their time watching each other instead of watching criminals. And sometimes, when one police officer eludes the vigilance of his fellows or when a whole department succeeds in conspiring together in their own interest and against the interest of the taxpayers who employ them, the economics text is a better description of the real world than the television program.

Becker and Stigler suggested a simple and radical solution to this problem – privatize the catching of criminals. Instead of paying the policeman a salary, pay him the fines collected from the criminals he brings in. If the convicted criminal will owe a $50,000 fine to the policeman, the lowest bribe the policeman will accept to let him off is $50,000. If the criminal offers that much, in order to avoid the expense of defending a hopeless case in court, there is no reason we should object – the criminal has paid his fine, the policeman has received his salary, and the taxpayers have been saved the cost of a trial.

Such a system of private enforcement raises a new issue: how to allocate crimes. Since policemen are now private bounty hunters, how do we decide which one is entitled to catch a particular criminal and collect his fine? One solution is to make the crime the property of the victim. He sells the right to solve it to a (private) policeman. This process allocates crimes to enforcers – efficiently, since the enforcer best able to catch the criminal will be willing to pay the highest price. Victims receive some reimbursement for their loss, and we need no longer worry about keeping policemen from accepting bribes.

By following out the line of argument begun by Becker and Stigler, we have reinvented civil law – the law of torts as distinguished from the law of crimes. It is the victim of a tort, not the state, who has a claim against the tortfeasor. While modern American law does not permit him to sell the entire claim to the lawyer who will go to court and collect it, he can sell part of the claim by hiring the lawyer on a contingency basis. Some earlier forms of civil law permitted the outright sale of civil claims, and some modern writers have argued that we should do the same. (Friedman, 1984; Shukaitis, 1987).

What we call bribery in the criminal context is called an out of court settlement in civil law – and is how most civil claims are collected. Since the payment is made to the person who would have collected the fine (called a "damage payment" in the civil system), an out of court settlement achieves the same result as a trial and at lower cost.

This suggests an interesting question: Should we abolish the criminal law? Would we be better off if we turned all crimes into torts, replacing enforcement by the state with enforcement by private police selected by the victims? To put the question differently, is there any logic to our present system, where if someone assaults me I call the police but if he reneges on a contract I call my lawyer?

The civil system has some obvious advantages. It replaces a centralized, government-run system for catching criminals with a decentralized market. In many other contexts, from schools to postal delivery, there seems to be evidence that markets produce a better product than governments at a lower cost. In addition, a civil system provides reimbursement to the victim. This not only appeals to our sense of justice, it also provides an incentive for victims to report crimes, even when doing so involves a certain amount of risk or inconvenience – something notably lacking in a criminal system. And it eliminates the conflict of interest between the enforcer and his employers that appears as bribery, and precautions to prevent bribery, under current institutions.

There are, however, some problems with a pure civil system. One is that under a civil system, at least our present civil system, the victim is limited to collecting a damage payment that will "make him whole." The fine, in other words, is supposed to be set equal to damage done. That may be close to the efficient level if almost all tortfeasors are identified and convicted. But suppose only one burglar in ten is caught. Nine times out of ten he steals a hundred dollars from me and keeps it, one time out of ten he is caught and gives it back – making burglary a profitable profession.

If we replace criminal law by civil law, we should probably modify the damage rule, scaling up the amount collected to compensate for the uncertainty of collection. We might, for instance, require the burglar who is caught one time in ten to pay a thousand dollars to his victim. On average the burglar pays as much in fines as he steals. He receives no net compensation for his time and effort, so finds some more attractive profession. In a more sophisticated version of such a legal system, the analysis of section 1 of this chapter could be used to calculate the optimum punishment – now a damage payment rather than a fine.

This, however, raises a further problem. The larger the damage payment, the less likely it is that the burglar can pay it. A criminal system can punish offenders unable to pay fines by putting them in jail. But a private law enforcer, whether lawyer or bounty hunter, receives no salary from the taxpayer. Hunting down a criminal who is judgment proof, unable to pay the damages the court awards, is a waste of time and effort, so if most criminals are judgment proof there will be little incentive for a civil system to catch them. For this reason, Becker has suggested that the essential distinction between civil and criminal offenses is that criminal acts are, or at least should be, those for which the offender cannot pay the appropriate fine. One solution to this problem would be to replace damage payments by bounties in the case of judgment proof criminals. The state would pay the convicted criminal's fine to the enforcer who got him convicted, then punish the criminal by putting him in jail. Criminals able to pay their own fines would do so. Such a system is more costly than a pure civil system, but not more costly than our current system, since fines paid to enforcers would replace salaries now paid to police.

An alternative approach would be to make criminals less judgment proof, by eliminating some current restrictions on what assets can be seized to satisfy a civil judgment. In an extreme version of such a system, convicted criminals might be required to work off their fines, perhaps with private prisons competing with each other on how quickly they would pay off a fine in exchange for an inmate's labor, just as private employers competed, two or three hundred years ago, on how short a period of service they would accept in exchange for paying the travel costs of immigrants who came to this country as indentured servants (Friedman, 1979).

A second problem with scaling up a damage payment to compensate for the chance that the criminal will not pay is that it gives "victims" an incentive to forge crimes. Under present law, there is very little point in my arranging for your car to run into mine under circumstances in which you appear to be responsible, since all I will get if I win my suit is enough money to fix the car. But if the law permits the victim to recover ten times the damage, on the theory that 90 percent of those responsible for such offenses are never apprehended, arranging a fake accident may be profitable. This is the same problem of overenforcement that I discussed in the previous section in the context of charging people with drug crimes in order to confiscate their property, this time in the context of private rather than public law enforcement.

It would take more space than I have here to discuss fully arguments for, and problems with, a pure civil system, in which crime is controlled by damage suits instead of criminal indictments. Readers interested in the subject may wish to read some of the more technical articles listed at the end of the chapter; they may also be interested in Friedman (1979), which describes the workings of a real world system in which killing was a civil offense, prosecuted by relatives of the victim. In fairness, I should say that while I believe a good case can be made for a pure civil system, with appropriate modifications to take account of special problems posed by the offenses that we now call crimes, that is almost certainly a minority opinion among those who have written on the subject.

3 What I have left out

In this chapter I have tried to sketch out two areas of the economic analysis of law based in part on early work by Gary Becker: the theory of optimal punishment and the analysis of the choice between civil and criminal law. In doing so, I have covered only a small part of the relevant territory, ignoring applications of the analysis outside the fields of tort and crime. One example would be patent law, which, Becker argued, could be viewed as a sort of negative punishment – a system for rewarding those who provide benefits to the rest of us. Another would be the application of the arguments that Becker and Stigler made with regard to the compensation of enforcers to the compensation of other agents facing similar conflicts between their interest and the interest of their employers.

I have also said very little about ways in which the theory ignores real-world complications, some of them important for the analysis. I have not, for example, discussed the issue of marginal deterrence, the problem of deterring someone out of one crime into another. If we make the penalty for armed robbery as high as the penalty for murder, robbers have no incentive not to kill their victims (Friedman and Sjostrom, 1993), since there is no additional punishment for doing so. I have not discussed the implications for the theory of the fact that some criminals are abler than others, and thus harder to catch, nor of the fact that courts sometimes make mistakes. Nor have I considered the issue of incapacitation – imprisoning a criminal not only to punish him for the crime but also in order to prevent him, at least for the term of his sentence, from repeating it. And I have said very little about empirical questions associated with statistical analysis of crime – as exemplified in the work of Isaac Ehrlich (1972), who found that the death penalty had a substantial effect in deterring murder, and his critics (Blumstein et al., 1978).

I hope, however, that I have given the reader some feel for how economic analysis can be applied to the problem of controlling behavior, whether labeled criminal or civil, by which one person imposes costs on others, and of how sharply our understanding of such issues is changed by the simple assumption that human beings, whether criminals or police, are rational.

References

Becker, Gary S. 1968. "Crime and Punishment: An Economic Approach," *Journal of Political Economy*, 76(2): 169–217.
Becker, Gary S. and George J. Stigler. 1974. "Law Enforcement, Malfeasance, and Compensation of Enforcers," *Journal of Legal Studies*, 3(1): 1–18.
Blumstein, Alfred, Jacqueline Cohen, and Daniel Nagin (eds.), 1978. *Deterrence and Incapacitations: Estimating the Effects of Criminal Sanctions on Crime Rates*, National Academy of Sciences, Washington, DC.
Ehrlich, Isaac. 1972. "The Deterrent Effect of Criminal Law Enforcement," *Journal of Legal Studies*. 1(2): 259–76.
Friedman, David. 1979. "Private Creation and Enforcement of Law – A Historical Case," *Journal of Legal Studies*, 8(2): 399–415.
   1981. "Reflections on Optimal Punishment or Should the Rich Pay Higher Fines?" *Research in Law and Economics*, 3: 185–205.
   1984. "Efficient Institutions for the Private Enforcement of Law," *Journal of Legal Studies*, 8(2):379–95.
   1990. *Price Theory: An Intermediate Text*, Cincinnati: South-western.
Friedman, David and William Sjostrom. 1993. "Hanged for a Sheep – The Economics of Marginal Deterrence," *Journal of Legal Studies*, 12(2): 345–66.
Landes, William M. and Richard A. Posner. 1975. "The Private Enforcement of Law," *Journal of Legal Studies*, 4(1): 1–46.

Nagin, Daniel. 1978. "General Deterrence: A Review of the Empirical Evidence," in Blumstein *et al.* (eds.).

Polinsky and Shavell. 1979. "The Optimal Tradeoff between the Probability and Magnitude of Fines," *American Economic Review*, 69: 880.

Posner, Richard A. 1992. *Economic Analysis of Law*, Boston: Little, Brown and Company.

Shukaitis, Marc J. 1987. "A Market in Personal Injury Tort Claims," *Journal of Legal Studies*, 16(2): 329–49.

4 Property rights in children[1]

James S. Coleman

In modern Western societies nearly everyone has a full set of civil rights. This contrasts greatly with earlier societies, in which most persons were lacking some portion of full civil rights. The English historians, Frederick Pollack and Frederick Maitland, writing about thirteenth-century England, describe this situation:

Of the diverse sorts and conditions of men our law of the thirteenth century has much to say; there are many classes of persons which must be regarded as legally constituted classes. Among laymen the time has indeed already come when men of one sort, free and lawful men (*liberi et legales homines*) can be treated as men of the common, the ordinary, we may perhaps say the normal sort, while men of all other sorts enjoy privileges or are subject to disabilities which can be called exceptional. The lay Englishman, free but not noble, who is of full age and who has forfeited none of his rights by crime or sin, is the law's typical man, typical person. But besides such men there are within the secular order noble men and unfree men; then there are monks and nuns who are dead to the world; then there is the clergy constituting a separate "estate"; there are Jews and there are aliens; there are excommunicates, outlaws and convicted felons who have lost some or all of their civil rights; also we may make here motion of infants and of women, both married and unmarried, even though their condition be better discussed in connection with family law. (vol. 1, p. 407)

In thirteenth-century England, the class of "free and lawful men" constituted a distinct minority of the population. Serfs constituted more than half of the population, and the other subjugated classes, of which women and children were the most numerous, constituted probably three quarters of what was left. So perhaps no more than an eighth or a tenth of the total population enjoyed full civil rights, free, independent, and responsible for their own actions. The remainder were either under the protection and authority of another party or were otherwise lacking a portion of their rights.

One by one, these classes have gained full civil rights. Protectorates and constraints have given way to freedom and equal rights. There are, however, exceptions, and one of these is the class of children. Children do not have full civil rights, nor are they held fully responsible for their actions. They remain a protected and constrained class. It is no accident that while other classes have gained full civil rights, children have not. A child needs protection of others who are stronger, as well as the guidance of others with more extensive experience. The ages at which particular rights can be acquired differs in different settings, but the principle of protection and constraint exists everywhere.

Not quite so universal is the determination of what party holds the rights that would, if children were fully free, be in their own hands. Traditionally, the holders of these rights have been the child's mother and father, or in earlier times, the father alone. In special cases when both parents are missing or otherwise unable to exercise the rights and responsibilities, a guardian takes their place. Traditionally, this has been one or more members of the extended family, for, in most societies, the extended family has been the guardian of the nuclear family itself. But increasingly in Western society, governments have taken responsibility for and authority over children whose parents are missing or are grossly unable to raise their children.

For all children, governments hold some rights concerning education. Those educational rights that are held by government are often partitioned among levels of government. The American Constitution by default places the responsibility for education, and rights to pass laws concerning education, not at the Federal level, but at the state level. The states, in turn, have delegated much of the authority over education to local education authorities, that is, counties, towns, and cities. Beginning in the 1960s, the Federal government captured from the states some of the authority over education, principally through the Civil Rights Act of 1964, the Elementary and Secondary Education Act of 1965, and subsequent acts of Congress. Also in part because of Federal intervention, states have withdrawn from localities some of the authority given to them.

Although the partitioning of rights over children, and more particularly their education, among these three levels of government is in itself of considerable interest, I will ignore this partitioning, and will lump all three together as "the state." My examination will be of rights held or claimed by the governmental levels which taken together constitute the state, and those claimed by the child's parents.

This entrance of the state into the raising of children is in part the filling of a vacuum left by the breakdown of the extended family as a unit that could act as a safety net. In part, it has been a consequence of changes in the economic and social systems more broadly. Before these changes, households themselves were nearly self-contained subsistence economies, and the child's actions, either as a child or later as an adult, rarely had consequences that went beyond the local community's bounds. Within the community, but not beyond it, there were norms that exercised authority over actions of members, and over their children, and there were safety nets at the community level to take responsibility for children and other dependents when the family broke down.

With industrialization, all that has changed – slowly at first, but then more rapidly. The larger society, beyond the local community, now experiences the consequences of individuals' actions and thus has a legitimate interest in the upbringing of the child. The extent of those interests increases as the scope of social and economic systems increases. The nation state, with ultimate authority and with taxation powers, is in a position analogous to the earlier position of the local community, which exercised its interests with respect to the raising of children through its norms.

These structural conditions create the scenario for three overlapping claims to rights: claims of the parent, claims of the state, and claims of the child itself. There are other claims that exist in certain cases, such as the competing claims by father and mother for custodial rights at time of divorce, or claims of small communities for schools of their own in opposition to higher-level policies of school consolidation. However, the central actors in this play are parents, children, and the state. In this chapter, I will indicate the status of those claims and the interdependence and conflicts among them; and, having done that, I will attempt to provide a way of looking at these rights that provides a basis for adjudicating among competing claims.

Rights of parents and rights of the state

Perhaps the best way to gain some idea of the overlaps in rights claims is to identify some of the arenas in which conflict has erupted. There are a number of these arenas in which the conflicting parties have been parents and the state.

The rights of parents to keep their child at home; the rights of a state to have its children schooled

One of the earliest arenas of conflict between parent and the state concerns compulsory attendance at school between particular ages – in most states of the US, between ages six or seven and sixteen. Associated with this are laws against or extensive restrictions upon home schooling, that is, the child being taught by parents at home. The latter laws vary from state to state, ranging from few restrictions on home schooling to its outright prohibition.

Interests of families in keeping their children out of school altogether have characteristically been one of two: interests in the labor of their children, ordinarily on the farm; and interests in not having the child "corrupted" by alien beliefs and cultural mores. The former interest can be seen as a selfish interest of parents in exploiting their children's labor, against the children's long-range interests. The latter interest often has a religious basis; and most parents who today engage in home schooling have religious grounds as at least one reason for doing so. Thus the latter interest can be seen as less selfish, more nearly a concern for the child's interests.

The states' interests also appear to be two: One is as protector of the child from parental exploitation of the child's labor, or from parental lack of diligence. The second is more nearly a selfish interest on the part of the state, an interest in strengthening itself by providing a common socialization, with a single language, a single cultural heritage, obliterating the divergent cultural heritages that different families, clans, religious, ethnic, and national groups left to themselves will transmit to their children. In the United States, these differences have largely been those brought by different immigrant streams; in many other countries, these differences are those remaining from ethnic, national, or tribal domains that do not coincide with state territorial boundaries.

One might argue, then, that one of the two major interests of parents is selfish, while the other is unselfish, in their role as guardian of the child, while one of the two major interests of the state is selfish, while the other is unselfish, as protector of the child. Thus it would be hard to give an unqualified argument for or against parents having rights for home schooling. It is likely that, in different times and places, the strength of the rights claims on the two sides would differ. For example, in the early part of this century, when in some states the proportion of subsistence farmers was still high, the child's interests were perhaps best served in such states by strict school attendance laws and by rather extensive regulation of home schooling. Today, parents' interest in the child's labor is far less frequent, while the claim that the school environment is an unmitigated benefit to the child is less tenable. Thus the parents' claim to this right is stronger now than it was fifty or seventy-five years ago.

The right to send a child to a non-state school – with or without public support

Closely related to the conflict over claims of rights concerning the child's school attendance are claims of rights concerning enrollment in schools other than those organized and run by the state, that is, "private schools."

This is, in fact, a continuum, for regulations upon "private schools" can be so extreme that these schools are no less agents of the state than are schools explicitly operated by the state – or, at the other extreme, the private schools may be totally unregulated. At that extreme, of course, the allocation of rights is indistinguishable from the case of no compulsory education at all. Ordinarily, however, schools that are operated by parties other than the state and are known as "private" or "non-public" are somewhere between these two extremes. They are probably most accurately described as agents of the sponsoring bodies (which are most often religious bodies) and of the family, subject to constraints by the state. Thus it can be said that, in the United States, parents have a limited right to enroll their child in a school which is not an agent of the state – a right subject to much the same restrictions as the right to school their child at home.

There are two directions of movement concerning this right: one toward eliminating entirely the right and requiring all children to be schooled by agents of the state, and the other toward expanding the right, so that parents not only have the right for their children to be schooled by agents of bodies other than the state, but also the right to have this schooling paid for from taxes in the same way as state-provided or "public" schooling.

Examples of eliminating the right include most prominently state socialism as it existed in the Soviet Union and Eastern Europe, in which the right to non-state schooling did not exist. The interest of parents in holding this right is evidenced in at least one country which has recently overturned state socialism. In Poland, an almost immediate development was the emergence of private schools – not run by the church, nor organized for the new capitalist elite, but organized by groups of parents, and called "social" schools to distinguish them from state schools, but also to indicate their independence from the church. It is unlikely that many of these schools will survive, because of costs, but it is significant that among the first impulses, once the overthrow of state socialism made it possible, was the recovery of the right of parents to select and shape their children's educational experiences.

There have been sporadic attempts to eliminate parents' right to private schooling in some US states, but with little success. Malaysia has made similar attempts, with the aim of eliminating the right of the Chinese and Indian populations of Malaysia to send their children to their own schools.

Attempts to expand the private school right so that it will include the use of tax revenues to pay for private schooling are much more numerous. Most of the Western world other than the United States provides public funds for private schools. Perhaps the most extensive allocation of rights to parents is in the Netherlands, where any group of parents beyond a certain minimal number can organize a school. Most schools in the Netherlands other than state schools are Protestant schools or Catholic schools, resulting in three major educational sectors in the Netherlands, all supported by public funds. But the expansion of parents' rights that this law brings about has been exemplified quite recently: Using this right, Indonesian immigrants to the Netherlands have brought a few Muslim schools into being.

One of the major current issues in American education concerns precisely this right. The policy issue is fought under several different terms, with "tuition tax credits" and "vouchers" being the most frequent. But the central issue is the question of a right: Should parents have the right to have their children's education at schools of their choice, public or private, at public expense, analogous to the state-run schools? Yet to examine this right, it is valuable first to examine the recent history of a more restricted right: The right of assignment of a child to a school, not outside the state sector, but among schools within the state sector.

Who has the right to assign a child to a school?

An important right, similar to the private-school right, concerns the assignment of a child to a particular school within the state sector. Suppose the child is attending a state school – as is true for 90 percent of American children, and for a majority of children in most countries. Then who has the right to assign a child to one state school rather than another? This question is answered differently in different countries; and, in the United States, it has been answered differently at different times and places. Traditionally in the United States, the school district has had the right of assignment. It has exercised this right primarily through the creation of school attendance zones, with children residing in a given school's attendance zone required to attend that school. Transfers have sometimes been allowed, and, in some places, there have been exceptions at the secondary level in the form of specialized high schools attended by parent and student choice. But, in spite of these exceptions, most parents in most localities have been in the position of simply having to accept the school to which their children were assigned – unless they were willing and able to pull up stakes and move. In many other countries, this right is not in the school district's hands, but in the parents' hands, although sometimes subject to passing a test. In England, for example, a child has in most places been able to attend whatever school the parent desires within the Local Education Authority. At the primary level, this right is contingent on space in the school, and at the secondary level, it was for some time contingent on passing the 11-plus examination. Entrance requirements for admission to secondary schools have been eliminated, along with different secondary school options, in those local educational authorities where comprehensive schools have been introduced – but, in general, in England as elsewhere a far larger share of the right of assignment to school has been in the parents' hands than is true in the United States.

In the US, the local school district's right of assignment has not been universal. School districts have been subject to higher authority. Prior to 1954, local school districts in the Southern states were required by the state to assign black children and white children to different schools, creating "dual school districts." After the Supreme Court ruling in the Brown decision of 1954, a lawsuit brought by a black parent demanding the right to send a child to a school legally defined to be for white children, these state laws requiring dual school districts were overturned by Federal law. This ruling required those districts (though after a long delay, extending in some cases to 1970) to replace the dual assignment with unitary assignment.

By 1970, the school desegregation actions by courts and by Federal government agency rulings had moved the right of assignment in many districts out of the district's hands into those of the court, which employed this right to carry out affirmative integration. This ordinarily meant bussing[2] to achieve racial balance, which in turn meant that not only did the district lose a right to the higher authority, but parents lost a right as well. This was a less clearly defined right, but one that was a part of the delicate implicit balance of rights between the parent and the district: the district had the right of assignment so long as it observed the right of parents to have their child assigned to school only on grounds agreed to be relevant to the child's education. It was the failure to observe this balance that led to the Brown decision in the first place. Black children were being bussed past nearby schools attended by whites, in order to achieve racial separation. By 1970, the violation of this implicit right had reversed direction: Bussing was now being used to achieve racial integration. This bussing was seen by most white parents, and over time by most black parents, not to be relevant to the child's education. White parents protested the loss of this right either by some form of collective action (demonstrations, boycotts) or more often by individual action, moving out of the school district within which bussing was mandated.

But more recently there has begun in some places a movement of the right of assignment out of the hands of school districts and of the court into the hand of parents. In many large cities, this takes the form of specialized "magnet" schools in which enrollment is not by residence in the attendance zone nor by race, but by choice. Sometimes this is constrained by the requirement of passing an admissions test, and sometimes it is constrained by racial quotas. But the right has become widespread in some cities.

Beyond magnet schools, there have come to be new forms of parents' rights to choose. For example, in Minnesota, parental choice now exists across school district boundaries, with parents having the right to send their child either to the school assigned by the school district, or to a school of their choice in another district. Similar extensions of parental rights are under consideration in a number of states of the US. In 1991, ten states passed legislation increasing parental choice, and in thirty-seven states, legislation to increase parents' rights of choice was introduced.

It is then only one further step to an extension of parental choice to private schools. This brings us back to the right discussed earlier, the right to private school choice through vouchers. The conflict over this right – a right which currently exists only for parents of about 500 black children in Milwaukee, Wisconsin – is the voucher controversy, and is probably the most heated in American education today. Since the fifty states of the United States have legal responsibility for education, and state taxes pay for over half of schooling costs (with about 40 percent paid by local real estate taxes, and 8 percent paid by the Federal government) the introduction of vouchers is a state-level decision. There have in recent years been attempts in several states to introduce vouchers – most recently in California in 1993 – but until now without success.

The principal question that arises is simple: Should parents who wish to send their child to a non-state school have the same right to free education as do parents who send their children to a state-provided school? The more general question is, where should rights over children be located?

Wealth-maximizing allocation of rights

This question is a central one for American education today and one that cannot be answered simply. How does one answer a question about where rights *should* be located? Many social scientists would argue that the question cannot be answered except by leaving positive social science to engage in normative pronouncements. There is, however, a branch of legal theory, known as law and economics, that argues otherwise. In law and economics, as laid out for example in the works of Judge Richard Posner, the question of how rights should be allocated in court cases is answered by giving rights to the party who will make most productive use of them. This is called in law and economics "wealth maximizing," because it increases the total wealth of the community.[3] It is analogous to the economists' answer to the question of which of two policies is better. The answer is, that policy which increases the total wealth of the community.

Applied to the question of how rights over children's education should be allocated, this principle gives a simple answer: Rights should be allocated in whatever way will maximize the child's value to society. Viewed in purely economic terms, this means maximizing the child's future economic productivity, which is measured by its income (since in economic markets, individuals are paid approximately the value of their product). Viewed in somewhat broader terms, this would include not only direct economic productivity, but also non-market benefits and costs the child is expected to bring to society throughout its life.

According to this principle, there is no "natural right" of parents to raise their children. Nor is there a presumption that the state has a right to determine that the child remain in school until age sixteen, or to assign a child to a particular school. This answer then leads to the question: What allocation of rights will maximize the child's value to society?

There is some evidence on this question for one of the rights, the right of assignment of the child to a school. This is evidence from research on public and private schools in the US and in other countries. Two questions can be asked: First, are the outcomes of education in general better in social systems where parents have extensive choice of the school their child will attend than in those where parents have little choice of school? This is a difficult comparison, because it involves comparison of different educational systems, and there are many differences between systems other than the extent of parent choice. If these differences are ignored, then, based solely on the very poor US performance in standardized international tests, we would have to say that outcomes of education are much worse when the right of school assignment is in the hands of the state than when it is in the hands of parents, who can make a choice among schools. The US, with the most rigid school assignment of any industrialized country, consistently scores at or near the bottom in every international comparison. But this is a very crude test, for there may be many other factors producing this difference. I know of no systematic comparison of performance of educational systems which differ in the degree of state regulation of school choice.

At the individual rather than social system level, one can ask whether students who are otherwise comparable do better in public schools or in private schools. The answer is that they consistently do better in private schools, both religious and non-religious. The first results were found in the US, where private school students from comparable backgrounds and 10th-grade achievement levels do better in a variety of ways: They are much less likely to drop out before grade 12; their achievement at grade 12 is higher in most school subjects; their initial enrollment and continued enrollment in college is higher; and they do better in jobs after school (Coleman and Hoffer, 1987). The differences are not large in some of these areas, but they are consistent. Similar results for performance on standardized tests have been found in the Netherlands, Scotland, and Australia, where comparable analyses have been carried out.

A first answer, then, to the question of how rights of assignment of children to school should be allocated is that they should *not* be allocated as they generally are in the United States, but they should be in the hands of parents. This is based solely on an empirical answer to the question of what allocation of rights will maximize the child's value to society. The answer to the current voucher controversy is a resounding one in favor of vouchers. This is based on the empirical evidence about which allocation is, in the law and economics language, wealth maximizing, that is, which results in children whose value to society is greater.

Beyond school choice

This, however, answers only the immediate policy question. It indicates which of two possible assignments of rights is better; but both might very well be suboptimal. The broader question is, what allocation of rights between parents and the state maximizes the expected value of a child to a society? The answer was at one time simple. Before the Industrial Revolution, parents held effective property rights over a portion of their children's productive activity. So long as the children were within the parents' household, those children's production was the property of the household. When the parents, in old age, became unproductive and economically dependent they held a claim, enforced by the extended family and the community, on the children's assets. Children had an obligation to provide support for their parents, and parents had the corresponding right to this support. In some societies, this obligation falls on particular children. Still today in Japan, the son has the obligation to provide for his parents in old age. As Mary Brinton (1992) points out, this creates a strong incentive for parents to see that their sons get the best education and training possible; but it creates a much less strong incentive to attend to their daughters' education.[4] In the pre-Industrial Revolution setting that I have described, it was entirely appropriate that all rights over a child's education and training be held by parents, as they in fact were; and because the local community could experience consequences of particularly bad child rearing, it was appropriate that the local community was a court of last resort for the child.

But matters have changed as a consequence of the Industrial Revolution. With social changes in the United States, such as the advent of Social Security and pension funds, the parents' need for their children to care for them as they become dependent is greatly reduced. The decline in community norms that children should care for their dependent parents in part reflects the growth of these pension and Social Security sources of support, and in part results from the overall decline in community.

A result of these changes is that parents have a sharply reduced incentive to bring their children up in such a way that they will be productive. Thus the rationale for parents holding rights to determine their children's education is weaker than it once was. There is no reason to expect that parents will be motivated to bring their child up in a way that maximizes the child's value to society. This suggests that the rationale for rights to children's education being largely in parents' hands no longer holds. Then, however, a second question can be asked: Is it appropriate for the state to hold those rights? The empirical results that I have given above, showing poorer performance of state schools than of schools chosen by parents, suggests that at least for the right of school assignment, the state is not better, but worse, than parents.

The deficiencies of the state are somewhat different than those of parents. The question is whether the state has both the incentive and the capacity to bring children up in such a way that they are of maximum value to the society. The answer is that unlike the parents, the state has a strong incentive to do so – from a child brought up to be of high value to society, the state gains in increased productivity, increased taxes, and reduced public expenditures. In fact, much of the current concern over education is a result of the state's direct interest in the productivity of the next generation.

What the state lacks is not the incentive to transform children into productive adults, but the ability to do so. Although the state has the appropriate incentives, the teacher, as the agent of the state, has quite different incentives: keeping order, keeping a happy classroom, and, as a distant third goal, bringing about high achievement. The principal has the incentive of keeping good morale among teachers, keeping order among students, keeping parents happy, and, as an even more distant goal, bringing about high achievement. Even this low-ranked goal of "achievement," measured by scores on achievement tests, is far from the goal of maximizing the potential value of the child to society. It ignores the common virtues of diligence, honesty, and other character traits that make a person an asset to society.

With changes in the rights and obligations within the family, with the decline of community, and with the perverse incentives of teachers and principals, no one who is close to the child has a strong and direct incentive to maximize the child's value to society. Parents, who are closest to the child and most able to bring about results they desire, have had the incentive cut from under them by the social changes which brought pension funds, Social Security, and reduction of strength of community norms. The state is the beneficiary of that incentive, but it is incapable of transmitting the incentive downward to those parties – principals and teachers – who directly affect the productive capacity of the next generation. In short, the shift from a society in which parents hold property rights to a portion of their children's productivity to one in which the state holds these property rights has taken away from parents a major incentive to bring into adulthood productive successors. But it has not relocated that incentive in any other party capable of carrying out that task. The problem will be solved only when those property rights are once again held by parties in a position to act on the incentive the rights create.

How can that be done? We can start with two pieces of information. One is that it is possible to calculate, over a person's lifetime, the direct monetary benefits brought to the state and the direct monetary costs imposed upon the state. These quantities show the size of the state's incentive to see that the benefits are brought into being and that the costs are avoided. If this information were calculable at the beginning of a person's life, rather than at the end, it would be available to be used toward creating incentives. This would be done by vesting property rights in some fraction of that quantity in appropriate parties. A simple example will illustrate. The old age benefits of Social Security in the United States were initially conceived to be the return of a portion of the individual's earnings throughout that person's working life, just as a private pension operates. There was of course from the beginning a redistributive component of Social Security, redistribution that has grown over time. Nevertheless, the old age benefits of Social Security were seen as a return on an investment. Suppose a different form of Social Security had been initiated instead: The parents were to get, in old age, a portion, not of the taxes they themselves had paid from earnings, but a portion of the taxes *their children* had paid, or perhaps, the average of this over their children. However crude a measure this is of their children's value to society, it is a measure that would have provided a stronger incentive to the parents than they now have to bring their children up to be assets to society. Some redistributive component would, of course, have been necessary, just as it was in the Social Security that was enacted. But the point should be clear: By giving parents property rights to some part of the value their children bring to the state, incentives are created that result in a better next generation.

It can reasonably be contended that in pre-industrial society, such incentives did exist. Caldwell (1976) who has studied such societies ethnographically, contends that there are only two fertility regimes in societies: a high-fertility regime, which is in place so long as the flow of wealth in society is from young to old, and a low-fertility regime which comes into being when the flow of wealth comes to be from old to young. The young-to-old flow of wealth creates an incentive not only to have many children (and to exploit their labor when they are young), but also to raise them to be productive over their lifetime. The old-to-young flow eliminates this incentive.

To make a parent's well-being contingent on the productivity of their children would, of course, be too simple. It would create incentives to have a large number of children, which is one of the defects of the informal property rights that parents held over their children's production in the pre-industrial world. There are much more sophisticated ways in which the state could make use of the property rights it holds. But before turning to that, we can ask if it is not more appropriate to attempt to reconstitute the family, and thus recreate both the family's property rights in its children's value to society and its interests in maximizing that value.

I believe it is inappropriate on several counts to look in this direction. First, the social structure necessary for enforcement of the family's upbringing of its children has gone, and is unlikely to return. Both the community surrounding the family and the older generations within the family have largely lost the capacity for imposing effective sanctions on parents in bearing and properly raising children, and on children (as adults) in accepting obligations for dependent parents. Secondly, that social structure had inherent biases leading to differential effectiveness of the property rights allocation, and thus to great inequalities among children from different social strata. Third, the property rights allocation which brought about investments of social capital in the young depended as much on the stick as on the carrot, as much on negative sanctions for non-performance of duty as on positive rewards for performance. In the voluntaristic social structure that increasingly characterizes society, negative sanctions for non-performance are hardly effective, because relationships can easily be broken with little cost.

A second direction that is inappropriate is suggested by a recent announcement of new books by the Committee for Economic Development (CED), a business-financed and business-oriented group concerned with educational issues. Two titles announced are *Investing in Our Children: Business and the Public Schools*, and *Children in Need: Investment Strategies for the Educationally Disadvantaged*. Both of these titles suggest what the books in full discuss: investment strategies for business firms, either for all children (the first book) or for "educationally disadvantaged" children (the second book). There is only one difficulty with the investment strategies discussed in these books: No business firm can expect a return on its investments. The authors indeed do not expect the investments to give a positive return to the business firm that makes the investment. The reason, of course, is that the firm has no property rights in the value created by its investment. If the investment is a good one, that is, if it does create value by increasing the future productive potential of the children affected, the value will accrue to all firms in the relevant labor market area, an area that is continuing to expand, and for some occupations constitutes the whole of the United States, or even the world. The value created is a public good, not a private one.

Thus the general prescription to business firms or to any other actor to invest in children has a fatal flaw, a "tragedy of the commons" flaw which will deter any reasonable firm not to make the investment, unless it expects to use the fact of the investment itself to improve its public image.

What, then, is an appropriate direction? The answer, as in most such cases, is to get the property rights right. Once this is done, it will automatically overcome the free-rider problem, and will do so by introducing the proper incentives into the system.

How can "getting the property rights right" be accomplished in this case? The following costs of non-development of human capital and benefits of its development accrue to governments: costs of schooling, costs of crime, including costs of apprehension and incarceration of criminals; costs of welfare payments; medical costs induced by style of life; costs associated with alcohol and drug use; and, finally, benefits from income taxes. Government would gain by vesting rights to a portion of the realized benefits and to a portion of the unrealized costs to any actor which undertook to reduce the costs and increase the benefits for particular children. This would necessitate use of social science methods to make a statistical prediction, on the basis of background characteristics, of the expected costs and benefits to government of a given child. The improvement on this prediction that an agent for the child could make would be the basis for a "bounty" on the head of the child, an incentive offered by the government for increasing the child's value to society. The right to the bounty would be initially held by parents, but marketable by parents to whatever agent (such as a school) undertook to develop the child in a way that would reduce the costs and increase the benefits. Since the costs and benefits occur over the lifetime of the child in question, the return on the investment made by the responsible agent (whether parent or another agent) would accrue to that actor as the young person passed the age at which the costs and benefits would be expected to occur.

This vesting of property rights in actors which would take responsibility for specific children may seem unrealistic. I contend that it is the only viable direction for the future task of bringing the young into adulthood. The case can perhaps be made more persuasive for children who are wards of the state. Here, parents' rights no longer exist, because of death, abandonment, or abuse. But the state is poorly prepared to raise these children. It farms them out to various foster homes and private agencies. But it does so without providing an incentive to make those children into productive adults. Instead, their payment depends only on feeding, housing, and clothing the children. But if introduction of an appropriate incentive for foster parents would be wise policy, then why not for all parents?

What then can we say about parents' rights and the state's rights concerning children's education? What I have argued is a short-range reallocation and a long-range allocation. The short-range reallocation is far less extensive than the other. Using the criterion from law and economics that rights should be allocated so as to maximize the social product, the reallocation should be such that it maximizes the value of the child to society. Sociological research on outcomes in public and private schools leads to the policy position that full-scale parental choice, including private schools with vouchers, is superior to school district or other governmental assignment of children to schools.

The long-range allocation involves recognizing that the loss of informal property rights in children's production has partially destroyed the incentives for parents to attend carefully to the value that their children will bring to society. The appropriate policy is one which gets the property rights right. This involves reconstituting, through actions by the state (offering to parents marketable "bounties" based on predicted costs and benefits of that child to the state) incentives loosely analogous to those parents had prior to the Industrial Revolution, when the flow of wealth was from young to old.

Notes

1 This paper was originally prepared for presentation (in April 1992) in a faculty seminar titled "Rational Choice in the Social Sciences" which Gary Becker and I have run at the University of Chicago since 1984.
2 Bussing is the transport of students to a school ordinarily more distant than their current school for the purpose of achieving racial integration.
3 One might well argue against a wealth-maximizing assignment of rights in this case, on grounds that it treats the person as nothing more than an agent of society, with no rights of its own. However, because the person gains full civil rights at a particular age such as eighteen or twenty-one, rights revert to the person at that point. If the guardian has not acted in the person's interests, the person, once having acquired civil rights, will not act to maximize its value to society.
4 As Brinton shows, this leads to far more resources being put into sons' education than into daughters', and is part of the general gender inequality in Japan.

References

Brinton, Mary. 1992. *Women and the Economic Miracle*, Berkeley, CA: University of California Press.
Caldwell, John C. 1976. "Toward a Restatement of Demographic Transition Theory," *Population and Development Review*, 2: 321–66.
Coleman, James S. and Thomas B. Hoffer. 1987. *Public and Private High Schools: The Impact of Communities*, New York: Basic Books.
Ellickson, Robert C. 1991. *Order Without Law: How Neighbors Settle Disputes*, Cambridge, MA: Harvard University Press.
Pollack, Sir Frederick and Frederick William Maitland. 1968. *The History of English Law*, vol. I, 2nd edition, Cambridge University Press.

III

All in the family

5 Human capital, fertility, and economic growth

Robert Tamura[1]

Gary Becker has combined two research areas, human capital and the economics of the family, to understand economic growth. Human capital theory (1964, 1975) examines the determinants of earnings and wealth through the accumulation of knowledge and skills. Formal education in schools is an example of skill acquisition. However, investments in job training, health care, and searching for a better job are other examples of human capital accumulation. Becker's work on human capital forms the theoretical base upon which almost all modern labor economics is built. The second area is fertility. He first wrote about the economic determinants of fertility in 1960, and his research has continued over the past three decades. The combination of human capital theory and the economics of fertility produced fundamental changes in the way social scientists view not just the workings of the family, but the entire dynamic process of social interactions.

Human capital theory states that individual differences in skills and productivity explain differences in earnings across individuals. Just as firms choose to purchase new equipment based on its contribution to increased profitability, individuals decide to increase their productivity through investments in their skills. The longer time period the skill can provide a return, the more likely an individual chooses to invest in human capital. The lower the costs of human capital investment, the more likely an individual chooses to invest in human capital. If the individual is patient, then the individual will more likely engage in human capital investment. The worse the other opportunities, the more likely the individual will choose investment.

Gary Becker's work on fertility illustrates the applicability of economic reasoning to explain family size. Rising returns to a woman's time in the marketplace induce a woman to reduce the size of her family. Fewer children allow the woman to spend more time in the workforce. Smaller families have become more educated families. Parents choose to increase

77

their investments in the human capital of the average child. Five hundred years ago large families were the rule, and one generation lived no better than preceding generations. In contrast, today the children of high human capital parents are more skilled than their parents and enjoy higher living standards than their parents.

The combination of these two fields contributes to understanding economic growth. The key is the continuous investment in human capital. As new discoveries occur, teachers translate the new ideas into something to be taught and learned, not rediscovered. This synthesis of new ideas provides education with the ability to transmit the rising level of knowledge and technology to students, without increasing substantially the years of training. Thus a college graduate in science or engineering has more knowledge of the workings of the natural world than a scientist had 100 or even fifty years ago!

Human capital

Becker's work on human capital investment shows that the determinants of college attendance are comparable to the determinants of the purchase of a new passenger jet by United Airlines. The additional skills acquired in college provide a larger flow of services that the worker can rent to employers. Just as a plane with a longer useful life makes it more likely that an airline will purchase the plane, the longer the career of the worker, the greater the return on the investment and hence the more likely the worker will choose to attend college. If United Airlines is shortsighted and does not worry about the future profits, then it is less likely to purchase a new plane. Equivalently, the more impatient the worker, the less likely the long-term investment required to acquire skills. If the customers of United Airlines prefer better meals and service to a new jet, then United Airlines is less willing to purchase a new plane. Similarly the better the opportunities without college training, the less likely an individual will forego these opportunities to invest in skills. Obviously a higher price for the plane reduces United Airlines' willingness to purchase it. The higher the direct costs of training, e.g., tuition, the cost of tools, materials, etc., the less likely an individual will accept training.

Some examples will reveal how human capital theory works. I assume all individuals are identical in their abilities and their desires. Acquiring additional education raises the worker's productivity, at the cost of tuition and foregone earnings. Suppose that a new high school graduate can earn a constant real salary of $16,000 for fifty years. Assume that the interest rate is 10 percent. The present discounted value of this income stream is $175,000.[2] Now suppose that this individual can increase his or her productivity through attendance at a public college for four years and then work at a higher constant salary for forty-six years. Assume that the real cost of tuition for college is $4,000 per year. An individual must earn a higher salary to compensate for the four years of not earning the high school graduate salary and the direct tuition costs. When the present discounted value of college net of costs is equal to the present discounted value of the high school graduate an individual does not prefer either career over the other. Competition in the labor market equalizes the returns to each career path for the marginal student, that is, the student who could flip a coin to decide whether to attend college or not. If the present discounted value of college net of costs increases (decreases) more (fewer) individuals will choose to attend college. Thus the real earnings of this college graduate must be about $25,500. This 60 percent premium over the annual earnings of a high school graduate compensates for the direct tuition costs, the lost earnings over the four years of college attendance, and a shorter working career. In the United States colleges like Harvard, Princeton, and many other private colleges charge annual tuition of $20,000, but the average student receives an annual scholarship of $10,000. Therefore the direct cost of college at a private college is about $10,000. Using this tuition cost the college graduate salary must be at least $28,000, or a premium of 75 percent. At a public school where annual tuition is closer to $4,000, average scholarships are much smaller. However, public college students take five or more years to graduate compared to private college students' four years of attendance. A public college student who graduates in five years must earn an annual salary at least $28,500 in order for the college investment to be worthwhile.

The longer the training period, the greater the returns must be. This shows that a student's foregone earnings are an important determinant of earnings differences. In this example, the present value of the direct tuition costs for the four-year public college graduate, the four-year private college graduate, and the five-year public college graduate are (approximately) $14,000, $35,000, and $16,500. Notice that while a five-year public college graduate pays less than 50 percent of the direct tuition costs of the four-year private college graduate, the additional year out of the labor force requires the five-year college graduate to earn a premium of $500 over the private college graduate!

In table 5.1, I present the results of similar calculations for a four-year private college graduate contemplating the acquisition of an MBA degree, an MD degree, a JD (lawyer) degree, and a Ph.D. I present the market salaries for the individual who does equally well by working as a college graduate or continues his or her training beyond college. Years in school describes how many years of training beyond college are required. For the medical doctor, I assume four years in medical school, three years of residency, and three years of specialization. Tuition per year describes the direct costs of additional training. For the MD, I assume that during the last six years of training, residency, and specialization, the doctor is paid $20,000 per year. For the Ph.D. student, tuition is generally negative since most students receive either fellowships, teaching assistantships, or research assistantships. Career length describes the number of years an individual works in the market. The final column lists the real salary the individual must earn to compensate for the additional years of training.

Table 5.1. *Salary required to compensate the costs of training*

Degree	Yrs in school	Tuition per year	Career length	Salary
MBA	2	$10,000	44	$36,000
MD	10	$20,000	36	$75,000
JD	3	$15,000	43	$42,500
Ph.D.	6	$8,000	40	$53,750

For the MBA a four-year private college graduate must receive an MBA salary of at least $36,000, or a 30 percent premium. The lawyer must receive a premium of at least 50 percent. A doctor who specializes beyond general practice earns at least 167 percent more than a college graduate. Finally, the Ph.D. earns at least 56 percent more than a college graduate.

Table 5.2 contains evidence from a variety of sources on the earnings of various educational graduates. Some are for new graduates; others are for all graduates in the field. The following table presents the incomes of these professions in 1991 dollars.

Table 5.2. *Actual earnings*

Degree	Salary	Sample
High school	$18,000	1986 data, all high school graduates
College	$25,000	average starting salaries
MBA	$40,500	average starting salaries of *Business Week* second 20 schools
MD	$165,000	average earnings all physicians, net of liability premiums
JD	$74,000	average earnings all lawyers, 1967–87
Ph.D.	$42,500	average salary offers to new graduates

Tables 5.1 and 5.2 indicate that the human capital model does a surprisingly good job of explaining income differences. That such a simple model of wealth maximization, that does not assume differences in ability, hours worked, or other job characteristics, can easily produce earnings

differences across professions, is testament to the power of the model. Therefore the human capital model provides convincing explanations why some workers earn more than others. As workers acquire more skills through human capital investments, they earn greater incomes through higher productivity.

Fertility

Becker is a pioneer in the economics of fertility. He married his work on human capital with his work on fertility to create the encompassing *Treatise on the Family* (1981). Surprisingly his 1960 contribution to the theory of fertility states: "Economic theory has little to say about the quantitative relationship between price and amount. There are no good substitutes for children, but there may be many poor ones."

Table 5.3. *Regional population (in millions)*

Year	North America	Latin & South America	Europe	Former Soviet Union	Asia	Africa	Oceania
1650	1	7	103	*	257	100	2
1750	1	10	144	*	437	100	2
1850	26	33	274	*	656	100	2
1900	81	63	423	*	857	141	6
1950	166	164	392	180	1,380	219	13
1970	226	283	460	244	2,091	354	19
1992	283	453	511	284	3,207	654	28

Note: * Included in Europe.

Table 5.3, from *The 1993 Information Please Almanac*, provides a historical context for population. Within the US, fertility has generally declined over the past 250 years. The regions of North America, Europe, the newly industrialized countries of East Asia, Australia, and New Zealand in Oceania and the former Soviet Union have fertility rates below population replacement. Africa, Asia, Latin and South America have substantially higher fertility rates than zero population growth. Over the last decade, these fertility rates have begun to drop in all but parts of Africa. To demographers the recent experience of this second group of regions might be signaling the second great demographic transition. The first great demographic transition occurred in Europe when sudden declines in mortality rates preceded changes in fertility rates. This led to a great surge in population. Unlike previous population changes, living standards did not fall, but rather the Industrial Revolution arrived, eventually lifting the living standards in Europe substantially. As in Europe mortality rates in Africa, Asia, Latin and South America have dropped dramatically. Perhaps this population surge will end as it did in Europe.

To capture the experience of the demographic transition in Europe, as well as the low rates of fertility in the post-World War II era in the industrialized West, in 1973 Becker and H. Gregg Lewis produced the modern economic theory of fertility and intergenerational transfers. They explain the decline in fertility as arising from the increase in real wages women receive in the labor market. The crux of their argument is that parents are concerned both about the number of children they have and the average welfare of their children. By introducing the idea that these are separate characteristics of fertility, Becker changed his view about the lack of good substitutes for children. Just as a consumer can substitute many lower-priced televisions in a house with fewer high-priced televisions, parents can choose the number of children they have in their family. Other "substitutes" are the timing of children. Parents can choose to alter the "quality" of children by having them when they are young or old. Thus holding the number of children constant, the quality of children changes by having them at different ages of the parent. A family with three children aged eight, five and three whose parents are twenty-six years old is a different family than one with the same number of children of the same ages whose parents are forty.

Great theories have the advantage of simplicity. The effects of the interaction of quality and quantity illustrate this point. Rising wages in the market sector provide an incentive for women to invest more in skills appropriate for the market, and less in home sector production. Women become more attached to the labor market through the idea of a career as opposed to a sequence of unrelated jobs. This leads to greater investments in career-specific skills, i.e., women attend college and choose majors much as men do, with regard to the value of the career. There has been a dramatic increase in the fraction of lawyers, doctors, engineers, business people, etc. that are women. Women make smaller investments in skills in the household, skills like cooking, cleaning, and child rearing. A reduction in these home sector skills reduces the gains both spouses receive from marriage. This reduction in the gains from marriage increases the likelihood of the dissolution of the marriage. This leads to a further incentive to acquire market-related skills. If each child imposes a time cost of rearing that is independent of the skill of the parent, then as the value of time increases the quantity of children becomes more expensive. These time costs, like breast-feeding an infant, attending parent-teacher conferences, attending school activities, etc., require an amount of a parent's time independent of his or her work skills. As a woman's wages rise, she faces a rising price of quantity of children, relative to quality. An increase in wages, then, provides the impetus for households to choose small families and larger capital (physical and human) investments in their children.

The possibility of divorce has impacts on investment in children. Women who believe that divorce is a significant probability invest in market skills to insure themselves against the possibility of divorce. These women face a higher market wage for their time, and hence are likely to choose smaller families and greater investment in each child. Divorce settlements require financial support for children. Does no-fault divorce reduce these payments, thereby reducing the investments in each child? (See Shoshana Grossbard–Shechtman, chapter 6 in this volume.)

Courts intervene on behalf of children when parents are unable or unwilling to provide for their well-being. Child support payments, educational support for minority and disabled students, child labor regulations, adoptions, etc. are issues that the courts routinely rule upon. Many of these have strong implications for families' level of investment in human capital (see James Coleman, chapter 4 in this volume).

Growth

Economic growth is the rising standard of living across generations. Thus our children enjoy better living standards than we did, often for the same number of years of schooling. This requires that the technology that workers use to produce goods and services constantly improves. Human capital theory provides an explanation for the continuous improvement in technology.

In the economics literature there exist two theories of economic growth, the neoclassical growth model and the Malthusian model. In the neoclassical growth model physical capital (buildings, machines, etc.) and labor work together using existing technology to produce output. As physical capital accumulates with a fixed amount of workers and a given technology, output rises. However, output rises at a decreasing rate. Living standards approach a limit. For living standards to rise forever, the technology must improve forever. In the neoclassical growth model population grows at a constant rate. Technology improves at a constant rate. This constant technological improvement induces individuals to accumulate more capital. However, since population growth and technological improvements are unexplained, the increase in living standards over the last 200 years remains a mystery.

In the Malthusian model there exists a stable constant standard of living. When living standards increase beyond this level, say because of an exceptional harvest, or a new discovery of raw materials, population rises accordingly. This increase in population offsets the temporary improvement in incomes. In contrast, when a drought occurs, or the fish harvest drops, population decreases. Population responds to the living standard. While this model explains both the living standard and the level of population, it fails to explain the experience of modern industrialized countries.

Tables 5.4 and 5.5, from Maddison (1991), illustrate population changes over the last five centuries and changes in living standards over the last century for a sample of countries. The cumulative evidence in tables 5.4 and 5.5 rejects the Malthusian model. Not only have living standards risen over the last century, but the populations of these countries have grown as well. Furthermore, Japan and other newly industrialized countries, cf. Vogel (1991), enjoyed rapid increases in their living standards after the US and the Western European countries.

Notice that Japan was much poorer than the other countries in table 5.5. At the onset of the Industrial Revolution, the average Japanese worker was only 20 percent as productive as the average US worker. By the outbreak of World War II, the average Japanese worker was still less than 25 percent as productive as the average US worker. From 1960 to 1973, however, the Japanese worker went from producing only 20 percent of the output of an average US worker to producing almost half as much. By 1989 the average Japanese worker produced almost two thirds the output of the typical US worker. Japan went from a closed and backward society at the beginning of the US Civil War in 1861, to a world naval power during World War I. By World War II, Japan was an industrial and naval power. After World War II, Japan rapidly recovered from its war damages and became an economic superpower.

Table 5.4. *Population (in thousands)*

Year	France	Germany	Japan	UK	US
1500	16,400	12,000	12,000	4,400	0
1600	19,000	16,000	14,000	6,800	0
1700	21,120	15,000	30,000	8,400	251
1760	25,246	18,310	30,000	11,050	1,594
1820	30,698	24,905	31,000	21,240	9,618
1870	38,440	39,231	34,437	31,393	39,905
1900	38,940	56,046	44,103	41,155	76,094
1950	41,836	49,983	82,900	50,363	152,271
1989	56,160	61,990	123,116	57,236	248,777

Table 5.5. *Output per man-hour in 1985 US dollars*

Year	France	Germany	Japan	UK	US
1870	1.15	1.04	0.39	2.15	2.06
1890	1.52	1.52	0.58	2.86	2.82
1913	2.26	2.32	0.86	3.63	4.68
1929	3.30	2.89	1.48	4.58	6.88
1938	4.25	3.57	1.83	4.97	7.81
1950	4.58	3.40	1.69	6.49	11.39
1960	7.17	6.62	2.94	8.15	14.54
1973	14.00	12.83	9.12	13.36	19.92
1987	21.63	18.35	14.04	18.46	23.04

In the neoclassical growth model the rate of return to capital is highest in the poorest countries. Therefore the rate of growth of income should be most rapid in the poorest countries. The experience of the less-developed countries in Africa and Asia reject this prediction. African and many Asian residents have suffered through extremely low rates of income growth, and, for many, living standards have declined! However, population growth in these regions is among the most rapid in the world.

Easterlin (1981), examining the experience of the past two centuries, suggests three important determinants of growth: (1) an increase in the number and the rate of innovations, (2) the diffusion of technology to an increasing set of countries, and (3) the spread of general education. He also notes that the existence of consistent credible property rights is a prerequisite for (1), (2), and (3). The development of government as an institution to protect private property rights is necessary for economic growth. Rosenberg and Birdzell (1986) argue that the invention of private enterprise capitalism explains the development of the industrialized countries. Furthermore the importance of private property rights is borne out by the recent collapse of the centrally planned economies of Eastern Europe and the old Soviet Union.

Under a stable economic system that guarantees private property rights, an inventor or entrepreneur is willing to risk his or her resources, and those of other investors, on the hopes of great returns. The gambles made by these inventors and entrepreneurs provide for continual improvements in the technology. Building a better mousetrap provides the inventor with great returns because the better product provides others with a better living standard. Patent rights are necessary in order to reward the inventor for the improved product. If an invention could be costlessly imitated, then the inventor's hard work would not be compensated. Costly resources spent in the discovery of the new product will never be recovered, and hence no inventor would ever risk his or her effort to produce a new product. Nor will any capital from venture capitalists ever finance inventive and entrepreneurial activity if they cannot receive a return on their investment.

However, diffusion of technological improvements allows living standards to rise in countries previously far behind. Part of the explanation of the Japanese transition over the last 125 years must lie in the diffusion of Western technology. Japan is certainly the most prominent example of technological diffusion, but more recent examples abound. The newly industrialized countries of East Asia (Vogel, 1991), and the Latin American countries engaging in market reforms, as well as the former centrally planned economies provide hope for many more examples of technological diffusion. For the last two groups the most important technology transfer is the reinstitution or institution of private property protection.

Becker provides an explanation for rising living standards and slow population growth for some countries, and stagnant living standards and rapid population growth for other countries. His key insight is the aforementioned changing price of time, particularly for women. This has led to a substitution away from large families toward small families. Unlike his (1960) view, Becker used his (1973) model with Lewis to explain that rising wages for women led to a substitution to high-quality children.

Becker and Robert Barro (1988) allow parents to choose their family size in the neoclassical growth model. Altruistic parents love children and care about their welfare. This model simultaneously determines population growth and the steady state income level. Unlike the Malthusian model, a poverty income level and high fertility does not occur. As in the neoclassical growth model, long-run growth depends on the continuing improvements in technology, left unexplained. If countries have similar preferences and have access to common technology, then all countries will converge to the same living standard and the same rate of population growth.

To explain the divergence in living standards between the industrialized West and the lesser-developed countries, Becker, Kevin Murphy, and Robert Tamura (1990) introduced a rising rate of return to human capital investment. A parent who cannot read or do simple arithmetic finds it costly to educate his or her child, whereas a literate, numerate parent will be more successful at transferring these skills to his or her child. Combined with the time cost of rearing children, this model produces a changing price of child quality relative to family size. High human capital parents have high values of time. Time spent rearing children is expensive in foregone market production. Thus high human capital parents choose small families and high levels of investment per child. Low human capital parents choose large families and low levels of investment per child. This produces two development regimes, a Malthusian regime and a perpetual growth regime.

The crucial point to the perpetual growth of technology and hence income is the long-run constancy of the rate of return on capital investment. Unlike the neoclassical growth model, where return to capital investment falls to zero, here the return on capital investment is always high enough to reward those who postpone consumption. Why does capital investment consistently provide high returns in this model compared to the neoclassical growth model? The answer lies in the special nature of human capital.

Adding better pots and pans in my kitchen raises my cooking productivity a bit, but the returns fall rapidly. However, if I learn new recipes from good cooks, my productivity is enhanced greatly. The cost of raising my cooking productivity is the purchase price of cookbooks and being with good cooks. My time is the most important input into becoming a better cook. This example captures the difference between physical capital, pots and pans, and human capital, cooking knowledge.

The diffusion of technology goes together with the expansion of formal general education around the world. Literate and numerate individuals can learn existing techniques as well as develop new ones that suit their environment best. This learning and discovery process allows persistent expansion of knowledge and improvement in technology. Thus human capital accumulation across generations augments the body of knowledge and improves the technology. Technological improvements, discovered by individuals, are embodied in new physical capital as in the next generation personal computer, and existing physical capital as in better ways to mix existing chemical compounds to produce new pharmaceuticals.

Within a society accumulation of human capital occurs in two ways: expanding the coverage of education (extensive margin), and improving the quality of education (intensive margin). On the extensive margin a greater fraction of the population can receive education and training. In 1940 only 25 percent of the US population over the age of twenty-four had completed at least four years of high school. By 1991 almost 80 percent of the twenty-five and older US population had completed at least four years of high school. In 1940 only one in twenty individuals over the age of twenty-four in the US had completed at least four years of college. By 1991 over 20 percent of individuals at least twenty-five years old in the US had completed at least four years of college. The industrialized countries of Western Europe, Canada, and Japan have experienced similar educational expansion. For the newly industrialized countries, this rapid educational transformation has been compressed into the last two decades.

Human capital accumulation also occurs at the intensive margin, and is often overlooked. In the United States the number of years it takes to become a high school graduate or college graduate has remained constant over the last century. However, over this time period some subjects have been eliminated from the curriculum, geography, foreign languages, etc., while other subjects have been added, computer programming, calculus, sex education, etc. The synthesis of new discoveries in math, science, and other fields has allowed students to receive a different education today than in the past. Thus a college graduate who majored in physics is more knowledgeable about the workings of nature than the greatest physicist in the world in 1800. This intensive margin provides much of the expansion of the frontiers of knowledge and technology compared to the extensive margin. Becker and Kevin M. Murphy (1993) investigate the quantitative magnitude of this effect by calculating the input cost to production of education explicitly accounting for the foregone earnings of students. They find that the contribution of human capital to growth is perhaps double or triple what is currently estimated! This increasing intensive margin contradicts the commonly held view of non-existent productivity growth in teaching.

In another piece (1992), they provide an explanation of how human capital accumulation at the intensive margin is accomplished. They argue that the expansion of the body of knowledge and the improvement in technology occurs through the increasing level of specialization of human capital. Throughout science, math, the social sciences, humanities, engineering, and medicine, new fields have been created and developed. The initial discovery is quickly followed by a synthesis with or sometimes a replacement of the existing body of knowledge. More importantly each discovery unwraps new puzzles to understand. These puzzles require the increasing specialization of human capital. Individuals today can no longer be natural philosophers working in biology, chemistry, and physics. Within each field scientists have become ever more narrowly applied in order to extend the field beyond its current limits.

Public policy

I conclude this chapter with some simple policy implications of Becker's work on human capital, fertility, and growth. Taken for granted is a respect for property rights. Any institution attempting to foster economic growth must respect and protect individual property rights so that individuals have incentives to accumulate human capital and physical capital. The experiences of the centrally planned economies of Eastern Europe and the former Soviet Union and others illustrate the effects of the denial of private property rights. Lacking any ability to claim the fruits of one's efforts, individuals rationally choose to consume more leisure. Why work hard if enjoying leisure provides the same level of material satisfaction? Why attempt to improve production of existing goods or services, or invent new goods and services, if no reward is forthcoming?

The recent passage of the law banning mandatory retirement makes it difficult for individuals and firms to contract to prevent malfeasance by workers. Without continuous monitoring, how does a firm ensure that a worker does not reduce his or her effort on the job? Paying workers less than they produce early in life, and paying them more than they produce later in life serves as an incentive for workers to "behave." By misbehaving a worker forfeits compensation from past work, and this serves as the penalty for bad behavior. However, since workers are paid more than they are producing, an older worker would like to work longer than is efficient. Mandatory retirement allows the use of this "tilted" earnings profile to solve the problem of misbehavior, without introducing the distortion of a career that lasts too long. Therefore eliminating mandatory retirement increases the cost of preventing bad behavior of workers (see Lazear, 1979).

Provision for general education is a primary responsibility of government. Provision for general education does not require government production of education. Becker has long advocated educational vouchers; see Coleman (chapter 4). Competition is the best way to improve the quality of education for all. The implications of Becker's work on fertility and human capital investment for helping the poor escape poverty are simple and intuitive. Although public provision can be limited to financial support, it is crucial that resources are made available to poor parents to finance their children's education. This "subsidy" lowers the cost of high-quality children for the poor.

First, current welfare programs tax savings at a higher rate than the rate that the richest individuals pay. Second, current programs increase welfare payments as the number of children increases in the household. This lowers the cost of quantity of children, while simultaneously raising the cost of quality of children. Finally, delivering income support in kind through Food Stamps, housing subsidies, and Medicaid instead of cash payments raises the price of education or job-training programs. Switching from the current in-kind delivery of income support to a negative income tax system would also allow poor families to send their children to better schools. It is particularly disheartening to place low-income families in subsidized low-income housing projects in high concentrations. The schools in these neighborhoods are not conducive to educational achievement. By providing greater cash assistance, more parents will have the opportunity to live in neighborhoods with higher-quality schools, or to send their children to private schools.

Thus, in addition to educational vouchers, the welfare system can lower the cost of skill acquisition. Providing a negative income tax system and eliminating restrictions on asset accumulation are two methods to raise the rate of return on investments for the poor. Increasing the rate of return to investment will induce poor households to switch to smaller families, and higher quality children. Only then will society begin to solve many of the ills it faces: crime, despair, poor health, low income of a substantial fraction of the population, reduced economic progress, etc.

Taxation of gains from capital appreciation reduces the incentive to invest and retards growth. In the United States, increased valuations of capital assets are taxed at the rate of income, without indexation for inflation. If a business or house appreciates due to inflation this "gain" over the original purchase price is taxed. This lowers the rate of return on capital investments. In the United States most of the jobs created between 1982 and 1990 were created by small business. New businesses are by nature small businesses. This entrepreneurial spirit faces great odds, as risks are high. New businesses arise from the idea that the entrepreneur believes that he or she has a better product or service than currently is available. This combination of human and physical capital effort is the riskiest of investments. High rates of capital taxation implied by the US tax code reduces the incentive for economic growth. One reason that the industrialized European countries have performed as well as they have in the 1980s despite relatively higher income tax rates than the US or Japan is their much lower rate of taxation of capital gains. France, Germany, and the UK are a few of the countries with zero taxation of capital gains. In order to provide the proper incentive for entrepreneurs to accept the risks to form new businesses, government must lower the rate of taxation on capital gains, at the minimum by indexing the gains for inflation so only real capital accumulations are subject to tax, at a rate no greater than the personal income tax rate. Perhaps a zero rate of taxation is best.

The spread of formal education has allowed a greater fraction of US citizens to enjoy improvements in their living standards. Furthermore the expansion of formal education around the world provides the opportunity for an improvement in living standards for an increasing fraction of the world. The establishment of market-based economies in Eastern Europe and the former Soviet Union and market liberalization in South America provide an opportunity to enter into a new era of prosperity. If market reforms and well-defined property rights remain for a decade, the experience of China, where the private sector now accounts for over 50 percent of national output, indicates that people will invest, accumulate, discover, and produce new goods and services at a rate never before seen in these countries. As political differences subside in Africa, and markets develop, so will prosperity return to this continent. A new golden age of prosperity is possible as long as markets are allowed to function, private property exists, and quality education is universally available. Government has the tools; the sooner it begins to use them the sooner the work can commence.

Notes

1 My greatest debt is owed to Gary S. Becker for showing me the unlimited scope of economics. I also thank Robert E. Lucas, Jr., Sherwin Rosen, Barbara McCutcheon, and Kevin M. Murphy. All errors are mine.
2 $\$175,000 = \$16,000\{1 + 1/(1.1) + 1/(1.1)^2 + \ldots + 1/(1.1)^{49}\}$.

References

Barro, Robert and Gary S. Becker. 1989. "Fertility Choice in a Model of Economic Growth," *Econometrica*, 57.

Becker, Gary S. 1960. "An Economic Analysis of Fertility," in *Demographic and Economic Change in Developed Countries*, a conference of the Universities–National Bureau Committee for Economic Research, Princeton, NJ: Princeton University Press, for the National Bureau of Economic Research.

1964. *Human Capital*, Chicago, IL: University of Chicago Press.

1981. *A Treatise on the Family*, Cambridge, MA: Harvard University Press.

Becker, Gary S. and Robert Barro. 1988. "A Reformulation of the Economic Theory of Fertility," *Quarterly Journal of Economics*, 103: 1–25.

Becker, Gary S. and H. Gregg Lewis. 1973. "On the Interaction Between the Quantity and Quality of Children," *Journal of Political Economy*, 81: S279–S288.

Becker, Gary S. and Kevin M. Murphy. 1992. "The Division of Labor, Coordination Costs, and Knowledge," *Quarterly Journal of Economics*, 107: 1137–60.

1993. "Can We Measure the Contribution of Human Capital to Growth?" presented at the Carnegie–Rochester Conference 1993.

Becker, Gary S., Kevin Murphy, and Robert Tamura. 1990. "Human Capital, Economic Growth and Population Growth," *Journal of Political Economy*, 98: S12–S37.

Easterlin, Richard. 1981. "Why Isn't the Whole World Developed?" *Journal of Economic History*, 41: 1–19.

Lazear, Edward P. 1979. "Why is There Mandatory Retirement?" *Journal of Political Economy*, 87: 1261–84.

Maddison, Angus. 1991. *Dynamic Forces in Capitalist Development: A Long-run Comparative View*, New York: Oxford University Press.

Malthus, Thomas. 1970. *An Essay on the Principle of Population and a Summary View of the Principle of Population*, Baltimore: Penguin.

The 1993 Information Please Almanac. 1993. Boston: Houghton Mifflin Co.

Rosenberg, Nathan and L.E. Birdzell Jr. 1986. *How the West Grew Rich*, New York: Basic Books.

Vogel, Ezra. 1991. *The Four Little Dragons: The Spread of Industrialization in East Asia*, Cambridge, MA: Harvard University Press.

6   Marriage market models[1]

Shoshana Grossbard-Shechtman

In 1973, while a first-year graduate student at the University of Chicago, I first became acquainted with Becker's economics of marriage. It was not love at first sight. Some of my fellow students and I thought it was weird to analyze love with economic theories. I still remember how we giggled when we first read a mimeographed version of Becker's theory of marriage prior to its publication. A year later, my attitude started to change. I had become interested in anthropology and had difficulty finding a dissertation topic related to primitive societies. T.W. Schultz – who had been a helpful mentor all along – then offered me access to a perfect data set for an economic analysis of polygamy, a study he was sure Becker would gladly supervise. What started as a hesitating exploration into Becker's controversial theory of marriage soon became the focal point of my career.

Two decades of research later, I realize that Becker's theory of marriage is one of his most important scientific contributions. It has inspired a number of valuable insights and results, some of which are presented in this chapter. In particular, this chapter discusses insights derived from Becker's original theory of marriage regarding the effects of no-fault divorce laws and the effects of marriage market conditions on consumption and labor supply. Two market models of marriage are presented: Becker's original theory and my own version of that theory.

The value of Becker's theory of marriage is far from being universally recognized. Economic models of marriage and divorce have often been labeled as esoteric and outside of mainstream economics. Many people still giggle when they see marriage decisions modeled in terms of utility functions. When modeling labor supply, consumption, and fertility, most economists use two other kinds of models: pooled household models – often labeled neoclassical models – and game-theoretic models of household decision making (also called household bargaining models). This chapter concludes with a comparison between these three alternative theories: Becker's theory of marriage, pooled household models, and game-theoretic models.

Two basic tools

When it was published in 1973 and 1974, Becker's theory of marriage was the first application of economic theory to the analysis of marriage. Like most great ideas, the basic idea in Becker's theory of marriage is simple. It consists of applying two basic tools of economic analysis to the area of marriage: cost–benefit analysis (or rational choice theory) and market analysis. The assumption of rational choice is widely used in economics, both in traditional areas of application such as the theory of the firm and in novel areas of application (including other analyses pioneered by Becker such as the economics of fertility and crime). Accordingly, individuals are viewed as rational agents who marry each other if they are better off married than single.

The economic analysis of marriage also draws on another major tool of economic analysis: market analysis. Whether we like to admit it or not, we are all part of some marriage market to the extent that we all are substitutable to some degree. Markets can operate whenever substitutes exist, whether these markets are visible or not. Sociologists, demographers, and anthropologists have recognized the existence of marriage markets for a long time. Becker derived new insights by applying basic demand and supply analysis of the kind usually applied to studies of firms and consumers.[2]

An application of Becker's theory of marriage which has received much attention is the analysis of the effects of a switch from divorce laws requiring either mutual consent or proof of fault to no-fault divorce laws.

No-fault divorce laws

The adoption of no-fault divorce laws by California in 1970 marks a dramatic change in the legal process of divorce in the United States. By 1987 all states had adopted some form of no-fault divorce law. When California was considering changing its divorce laws, no-fault divorce was hailed by women's groups and others as a civilized step that would put an end to the old fault-based system of divorce. For instance, Lenore Weitzman (1985) – a sociologist who has long been identified with feminist causes – admits to her early enthusiasm for the new divorce laws:

I saw California's law as an exciting experiment in legal reform. I ... shared the reformers' optimism and assumed that only good could come from an end to the old fault-based system of divorce. The sham testimony and vilification that were required to prove fault insulted the dignity of the law, the courts, and all the participants. How much better, I thought, to construct a legal procedure that would eliminate vicious scenes and reduce, rather than increase, the antagonism and hostility between divorcing spouses. How much better to lessen the trauma of divorce for both parents and children. And how much better to end a marriage in a nonadversarial process that would enable the parties to fashion fair and equitable financial arrangements. If I, as a researcher, had a personal or political goal beyond my stated aim of analyzing the effects of the new law, it was to help potential reformers in other states to learn from the California experience.

In 1980, when Weitzman and co-author Ruth Dixon published some of their first results of an empirical investigation of the effects of the change in divorce laws in California, she still sounded like an advocate of no-fault divorce (Dixon and Weitzman, 1980). However, by then she had become disturbed by some of the results of her research. Unexpectedly to her, she found that after the passage of no-fault divorce there were dramatic declines in (1) the percent of wives awarded more than half the value of the house, household furnishings, cash, and stocks, (2) the percent of women receiving alimony, and (3) the standard of living of women after divorce, especially in comparison to the standard of living of men. While other researchers may not agree with the size of the effects of no-fault divorce estimated by Weitzman, there are other studies indicating that no-fault divorce worsened the financial situation of divorced women.[3]

Effect on financial well-being after divorce

These findings come as no surprise to anybody familiar with Becker's theory of marriage. Becker (1981, 1992) has theorized that:

The switch to no-fault divorce laws is expected to have a negative effect on the material well-being of women after divorce.

The new laws gave a spouse a unilateral right to divorce, i.e., no consent was required from the spouse preferring the marriage to last. Under the old legal regime a spouse who wanted to stay married – i.e., a spouse losing from divorce – had a strong bargaining position in comparison with a spouse who wanted a divorce. Consequently, the losing spouse would be "bribed" into cooperating with the divorce procedures by receiving a higher portion of the family assets and privileges than would be the case if divorce could be obtained without the agreement of the losing spouse. Becker's theory implies that spouses who had more to lose from a divorce were more likely to be hurt by a switch from old divorce laws to no-fault divorce laws. The no-need-for-consent aspect of the new laws reduced the bargaining power of the spouse standing to lose from divorce.

There are a number of reasons why women may stand to lose more from a divorce than men, especially if they have devoted much of their marital life to home making and child rearing. As mentioned by Becker

(1981): (1) men typically do not get custody of children and thus are freer to find a new mate, and (2) men may have more opportunities to meet other women while still married. Furthermore, one can add that (3) women who devote time and other personal resources to home making pay an opportunity cost in terms of lost earning capacity at the time of divorce, and (4) as people age, sex ratios of marriage eligibles are increasingly in men's favor (men typically marry younger women much more than vice-versa, and women's life expectancy exceeds that of men). Therefore, women's marriage market conditions deteriorate faster than men's.

Under the old divorce laws based on either consent or fault, women with young children or older women who invested their whole life into a home-making career may not have cooperated with a divorce procedure initiated by their husband, unless they got generously compensated materially. Consequently, prior to the switch to no-fault divorce, many women in those situations would be "housekeepers" after a divorce, i.e., they would keep the house. It also follows that a switch to no-fault divorce laws would be associated with a decrease in real value of alimony and child support. By doing away with the need for consent, no-fault divorce laws reduced the bargaining power of spouses who stood to lose from a divorce, more often the case for women than for men.

Having internalized Becker's theoretical analysis of the consequences of no-fault divorce, I tried to persuade Weitzman – when we were both at Stanford in 1981 – that the detrimental financial consequences of no-fault divorce laws for women were to be expected. By 1985, Weitzman had abandoned her earlier enthusiasm for no-fault divorce.

One can only speculate that if the detrimental financial consequences of no-fault divorce for women had been anticipated – based either on a theoretical analysis such as Becker's or on facts such as those collected by Weitzman – the laws would not have been passed in so many states. People concerned about women's rights and the future of marriage should give serious thought to Becker's (1992) proposal to replace the present divorce laws with laws requiring mutual consent.

Effect on divorce

Another interesting implication of Becker's theoretical analysis of marriage and divorce is his hypothesis that:

No-fault divorce would have no long-run effect on divorce rates.

Changes in divorce laws affect the relative bargaining position of individuals in marriage, but they do not affect the total gain from divorce. The law affects property rights, but it does not affect the decision to divorce.

This hypothesis was also confirmed by facts (Becker, 1981; Weitzman, 1985; Peters, 1986).

Effect on marriage

Furthermore, it is predicted that:

No-fault divorce laws will discourage marriage.

In order to explain this hypothesis, it is useful to think in terms of markets for spousal labor (see Grossbard-Shechtman, 1984, 1993).

The G-version of Becker's theory of marriage

I developed the concept of spousal labor while writing my doctoral dissertation on the economics of polygamy in 1974. I read about the hard work involved in running a household in the Eastern part of Nigeria where my data had been collected. My ethnographic advisor, anthropologist Ronald Cohen, assured me that most women he had interviewed in polygamous households were glad to share the heavy burden of household work with another wife or other wives. Accordingly, I started looking at men as employers of women's spousal labor, and women as the suppliers of such labor. Such a perspective implied that most analytical tools used in traditional labor economics could simply be borrowed when analyzing marriage. This view of women as suppliers of spousal labor applies to our own culture and to men as well, especially if spousal labor is defined in broad terms (to include health care or counseling, for instance).

In this model men and women who can possibly marry each other thus participate in two markets: a market for female spousal labor where women are on the supply side and men on the demand side, and a market for male spousal labor supplied by men and demanded by women. Marriage decisions viewed as decisions regarding demand and supply of spousal labor can be analyzed very similarly to work and employment decisions. Accordingly, decisions women make are influenced by the decisions men make and vice-versa, due to their joint participation in the same markets. In addition, a special interdependence between a particular wife and a particular husband may develop after marriage, similarly to the special interdependence between a worker and a firm. Major differences between this particular application of labor economics and more traditional labor economics are that in the case of marriage (1) there tends to be only one worker and one employer, (2) the worker and the employer employ each other more symmetrically than in labor relations, and (3) costs of separation/divorce tend to be higher than in the case of other labor relations.

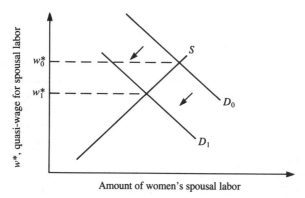

Figure 6.1 Effect of no-fault divorce laws on equilibrium in a market for women's spousal labor

Notes:

D_0: men's demand under pre-1970 divorce laws.

D_1: men's demand with no-fault divorce laws.

For simplicity of presentation, let us focus solely on the spousal labor supplied by women. Given that many women can potentially substitute for each other's spousal labor, and the same can be said for men (in this case in their capacity as employers of spousal labor), there will be markets for spousal labor. Figure 6.1 presents such a market. It has an aggregate upward-sloping supply of spousal labor by women. The demand for this spousal labor by men is downward sloping.

The market equilibrium obtained at the intersection of demand and supply determines both how many people marry and how much time they spend working in marriage. Graphically, both these dimensions of quantity supplied can be seen on the horizontal axis of figure 6.1. As in labor supply theory, a point on the aggregate supply can not specify simultaneously how many people work (in this case, enter marriage) and how much they work (in this case, how much they engage in spousal labor). As in other labor markets, average hours of work tend to be heavily influenced by institutional factors, including customs and cultural expectations.

As is the case with standard labor markets, markets for spousal labor also establish equilibrium wages, shown on the vertical axis of the spousal labor market depicted in figure 6.1. The non-observable compensation for spousal labor is called w^*, as it measures the value of time and w^* is the symbol economists often use for value of time.

When individual men and women employ each other as wife and husband they are initially influenced by the value of their spousal labor as determined in markets for spousal labor (marriage markets). After they marry, their actual value of time may differ from that market value due to the existence of one-to-one ties and divorce costs.

Laws regulating marriage and divorce influence aggregate conditions in markets for spousal labor. Consider the impact of a law which lowers the financial well being of divorced women, such as no-fault divorce laws. Individual decisions regarding spousal labor are made sequentially. The decision to enter marriage, from the perspective of either demand or supply of spousal labor, will be based on expected benefits and costs at various future points in time. The expected benefits from marriage for a woman who intends to engage in substantial spousal labor over her lifetime consist of the present value of her earnings from supplying spousal labor as long as the marriage lasts *plus* the present value of her income as a result of a divorce (weighted by the likelihood of divorce). Men's demand for women's spousal labor also reflects their demand over the life cycle, including the possibility of a future divorce. Given that no-fault divorce laws have lowered the value of divorce settlements women can expect, they can be analyzed as lowering men's willingness to pay for spousal labor (in a particular form). This can be translated as a reduction in men's demand for spousal labor (for instance, from D_0 to D_1 in figure 6.1). Given that women have an upward-sloping supply of spousal labor (see figure 6.1) and that no-fault divorce laws cause a drop in demand, women will be less willing to marry after the passage of no-fault divorce laws than they were prior to the legal change. Also, the present value of the equilibrium compensation for women's spousal labor w^* is expected to decrease as a result of the introduction of no-fault divorce.

Evidence for the hypothesis that no-fault divorce laws have caused lower marriage rates is hard to establish. Marriage rates have definitely declined since 1970, but empirical studies are not available to determine what part of that decline can be attributed to the passage of no-fault divorce laws.

Effect on labor force participation

The same analysis also leads to a further hypothesis:

No-fault divorce laws are expected to encourage the labor force participation of married women.

If married women expect a lower financial settlement in case of divorce, and the present value of quasi-wages for women's spousal labor (w^*) declines, married women (who could possibly divorce in the future) will be more likely to enter the labor force. This follows from a view of spousal labor and regular labor as alternative ways of financial support.[4] Accordingly, Peters (1986) found that in states where no-fault divorce laws had been passed, women were more likely to work than in states which had not passed such laws. In a study comparing states at two points in time, Gray (1993) found that unilateral divorce laws associated with no-fault divorce encouraged labor force participation of married women only in states with community property, such as California. By reducing the expected benefits women could derive from a career in home making, no-fault divorce laws thus encouraged women to engage more in alternative careers in the labor market.

Effect on financial well-being during marriage

Another possible consequence of no-fault divorce laws is that:

No-fault divorce laws are expected to raise the compensation women receive for their spousal labor while married.

No-fault divorce laws have taken away part of the financial benefits women get in the case of divorce. These financial benefits are part of the package of benefits attracting women to marriage under circumstances where they supply more spousal labor than their husbands. It is possible that the passage of no-fault divorce laws results in compensating benefits during marriage so that the overall lifetime compensation from spousal labor to women remains constant. In other forms of employment, if employers are mandated to offer their workers fewer benefits, such as insurance benefits, it is expected that competition for workers will lead employers to compensate their workers by paying them more in cash. Likewise, one expects compensating differentials in marriage. The more such compensating differentials neutralize the effect of no-fault divorce laws on the total expected quasi-wages from spousal labor, the less no-fault divorce laws will have an impact on marriage rates and labor force participation rates of married women.

It is in this light that one may possibly explain Gray's (1993) finding that the introduction of unilateral divorce in community-property states did encourage married women's labor force participation, in contrast to the discouraging effect he found in common-law states. It is possible that in common-law states there have been more compensating differentials, i.e., competition for women's spousal labor has led men to raise the compensation women receive for their spousal labor while married more than has been the case in unity property states. Such higher compensations in marriage would thus discourage some participation of married women in the labor force.[5]

Theories of marriage by Becker and others offer many other useful insights into marriage and divorce, which can not all be covered in this chapter. The next section relates to the contribution of Becker's theory of marriage to our understanding of consumption, fertility, and labor supply. In particular, I discuss how a determinant of marriage market conditions – the relative number of men and women – affects consumption and labor supply.

Applications to consumption and work

It was shown above that the relative financial well being of men and women while married and after divorce can be analyzed with economic theories of marriage. Financial well being is clearly related to consumption and work. The better off an individual is financially, the more he or she is expected to consume and the less he or she is expected to work. No-fault divorce laws are not the only reason we can expect variations in men and women's relative financial well being in marriage or after marriage. Any factor influencing marriage market conditions is likely to have an impact on the consumption and work of men and women.

This section uses Becker's theory of marriage – the original version and the G-version – to analyze sex ratio effects on consumption and work, income effects on consumption, and other marriage market effects on labor supply.

Marriage markets and consumption

Becker's theory of marriage contains many important implications for the study of consumption and fertility. Becker first presented some of these insights in 1973 in the first article he published on the economic analysis of marriage. The same insights also appeared in his *Treatise on the Family* in 1981 in a chapter on polygamy. The limited interest most people have for studying polygamy and the limited degree to which Becker elaborated on these ideas help explain the lack of recognition these ideas have received in the economics profession.

In the section on division of output between mates, Becker (1973) showed how the relative well-being of wives and husbands within marriage depends on factors influencing marriage markets. He mentions possible measurable indicators of such relative well being, such as consumption expenditures benefiting husbands and wives, and leisure time enjoyed by husbands and wives.

In Becker's theory of marriage, individuals compare their output as single to their output as part of a marriage, output including a wide range of activities, goods, and services. Assume women and men can obtain a certain output if they are single (respectively Z_{sf} and Z_{sm}). If they marry, their combined output (Z_{mf}) is expected to exceed the sum of the outputs they can produce if they stay single. This follows from the assumption of rationality, which implies that people do what is better for them. This does not specify how their new joint output is divided amongst them.

Becker's analysis implies that there is a minimum amount each spouse needs to get after marriage: the output they would get while single, so that each individual who marries is at least as well off married as he or she would be if single. In other words, the *opportunity cost* of marriage to an individual is the value of the foregone alternative, namely his or her output while single. Becker showed that under the simplifying assumption that all men are identical and all women are identical, the division of marital output between husband and wife depends on the sex ratio, wage rates, and other factors influencing marriage market conditions.

To follow this argument, consider figure 6.2. The supply of women in the marriage market is their opportunity cost of getting married (Z_{sf}). Each woman in the marriage market adds a point to that supply. If there are N_f women, the supply is horizontal until there are no more women available, at which point it becomes vertical. The demand for women in the marriage market is the maximum amount men are willing to pay in order to marry. Since they too will not agree to receive a share of marital output that is smaller than their output while single, that implies that the maximum amount of joint output husbands are willing to let their wives consume is the difference between marital output and men's output if they remain single ($Z_{mf} - Z_{sm}$). The demand is horizontal until there are no more men available. Assuming that monogamy is imposed and that there are N_m men, the demand becomes vertical when men have entered the marriage market.

This theory of marriage, as well as the G-version presented earlier, can help explain how many different factors influence consumption. It has been shown that divorce laws affect the relative well being of men and women in marriage. Likewise, marriage market conditions will be affected by tax laws and marriage laws. Next, I examine how another determinant of marriage market conditions, the sex ratio, affects consumption in marriage.

Sex ratio effects

The relative share husbands and wives receive out of the marital output depends on their output if single, their combined output if married, and the number of men and women. In terms of figure 6.2, women get a relative output (or income from marriage) which has their output as single as a lower bound (the supply until point N_f) and the maximum portion of marital output men will agree to share with a wife (the demand until point N_m) as an upper bound. If the number of men is less than the number of women ($N_m < N_f$), as depicted in panel (a) of figure 6.2, all men marry and some women remain single. The relatively scarce men are in a good market

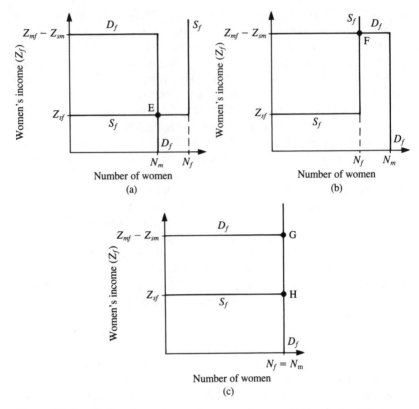

Figure 6.2 Equilibrium in a monogamous marriage market assuming (a) more women than men, (b) more men than women, and (c) equal number of men and women
Source: Becker (1981), figure 3.1.

position and able to reap the entire gain from marriage. Women's share of the marital output will be equal to what they would have if they stayed single, i.e., women are equally well off whether they marry or not. Men get the difference between marital output and women's single output.

The situation is completely different when the number of women is less than the number of men ($N_f < N_m$), as depicted in panel (b). In this case, women are relatively scarce and able to reap the entire gain from marriage. Men have the same income, whether they marry or not, implying that they are equally well off whether they marry or not. Women's income from marriage consists of the combined marital output from which men's single output has been deducted.

A comparison of these two simple cases thus indicates that the gender who is scarce in the marriage market gets more out of marriage. Under these assumptions, if there are more men than women, women gain from marriage but men do not. If there are more women than men, men gain from marriage but women do not. If there are equal amounts of men and women, as depicted in panel (c), the division of output can not be determined by demand and supply.

Using the traditional demographic definition of sex ratio as number of men divided by number of women, it follows from this simple model that:

When the sex ratio is high, women benefit from marriage. When the sex ratio is low, men benefit from marriage.

This suggests that as the sex ratio increases, so will women's share of marital consumption and leisure. The relationship between sex ratio and relative well-being in marriage may not be a smooth mathematical function. Big changes may occur when the balance of the sexes moves from a surplus of men to a surplus of women, or vice-versa.

The insights mentioned above regarding men and women's relative consumption in marriage also follow from the G-version of Becker's theory of marriage presented in the section on no-fault divorce. According to the G-version, marriage functions in part as an institution regulating the supply of spousal labor, where spousal labor is defined as work benefiting a spouse.

Earnings from spousal labor, determined in part in markets for spousal labor, are one possible source of individual income and affect individual consumption by husband and wife. Everything else constant, the more people earn in marriage, the more they can consume what they like (including psychic benefits obtained from working in enjoyable spousal labor). We are now ready to tie relative consumption by husband and wife to sex ratios.

The more men relative to women in a given marriage market – i.e., the higher the sex ratio – the larger the aggregate demand for spousal labor in comparison to the supply, and therefore the higher the market-determined compensation for spousal labor women can obtain if they marry. In terms of figure 6.1, a higher sex ratio (keeping the total population size constant) implies a larger demand by men for women's spousal labor and a smaller supply of spousal labor by women. In turn, this raises the equilibrium quasi-wage for women's spousal labor w^*.

The more women earn from spousal labor, the more it is likely that women consume what they like, and the less it is likely that men consume what they like (mostly because husbands have to pay higher compensations for their wives' spousal labor). We thus get a hypothesis similar to the one derived above from Becker's original theory of marriage:

The higher the sex ratio, the more married women consume in marriage relative to married men.

Male and female income effects

Becker's theory of marriage can also explain why the effect of wages and income depends on whether that income is received by husbands or wives. Consider the consumption effects of income individuals receive regardless of marital status or work status. The effect of income received by women is expected to differ from the effect of income received by men. For instance, if women's income increases regardless of marital status, that implies that their opportunity cost of marriage is higher, and therefore their share of marital output is also likely to be higher. In addition, women's higher income may also translate into a higher marital output, which may also translate into higher consumption levels for women in marriage. If men's income increases, their income is higher regardless of marital status. What that implies for their wives is not so obvious: marital output is likely to increase, which may benefit women's consumption, but the maximum amount of marital output men will agree to let women consume will decrease as men's income increases.

The G-version of Becker's theory of marriage can also explain why the effects of men's unearned income on consumption will differ from the effects of women's unearned income. Given that individual husbands and wives are not conceptualized as merging totally into one unit of production – instead, they are viewed as working for each other – it is obvious that the more income an individual has, the more she (or he) will consume what she likes. Further effects via markets for spousal labor[6] are unlikely to cancel the basic effect of increased individual consumption following from increases in individual income. In sum, it follows from these market theories of marriage that:

Male consumption in marriage is more likely to be affected by male income, whereas female consumption in marriage is more likely to be affected by female income.

A possible application is to study differences in the impact of income on children's well-being, depending on whether the income gets into the mother's or the father's hands. If it is assumed that mothers care more about their children's health and nutrition than fathers do, then the larger the portion of marital output consumed by the wife, the more resources are likely to be spent on children. Under this assumption, it follows from Becker's theory of marriage that if a government transfers funds earmarked for children to mothers (regardless of marital status) this will increase mothers' relative well-being in marriage which will benefit children more than if income is transferred to fathers, the latter causing an increase in fathers' relative well-being in marriage.[7]

Furthermore, one can apply this theory of marriage to the study of fertility. If it is assumed that men and women have different preferences regarding fertility, then the larger the wife's share of marital output, the closer the actual number of children will be to the number of children desired by the wife.

A final application of Becker's theory of marriage, which is the focus of the rest of this chapter, is the effect of marriage markets on labor supply. The main contribution of my own version of Becker's theory of marriage is that it ties the analysis of marriage and divorce with the analysis of labor supply.

Marriage markets and labor supply

According to the G-version of Becker's theory of marriage presented at the beginning of this chapter, people are viewed as producers of home-made goods and services who employ each other's spousal labor and supply spousal labor to each other. Markets for spousal labor, such as the one depicted in figure 6.1, influence the value of time of people engaging in spousal labor.

Economists analyze labor-supply decisions as based on a comparison of the attractiveness of work, measured by the wage, and the attractiveness of staying at home, which is typically denoted by w^* (the value of time).[8] The innovative insight derived from this analysis of marriage markets is that part of the value of time in the home is established in a market for marriage. In contrast, according to traditional labor-supply theory w^* is entirely established in the household and does not vary with marriage market conditions.

According to traditional labor-supply theory, the value of time in the home always depends on the individual's work status. If the individual works, the value of time w^* is equal to the wage, and if she does not work, w^* exceeds the wage. According to this marriage market-based model, for both working and non-working married individuals, value of time is equal to w^* based on a marriage market component. The *quasi-wage for spousal labor* is established in a market for spousal labor. Such quasi-wages may vary for different people, depending on who marries who in a particular society.

The higher the value of time – based in part on marriage market conditions – the less a person is likely to participate in the labor force. The introduction of a component of w^* established in a market for spousal labor (or marriage market) leads to a number of theoretical implications. Most importantly, it leads to the introduction of new variables into the analysis of labor supply, such as sex ratios and group differences in marriage opportunities. It also leads to new interpretations of income and wage effects, and of the backward-bending supply of labor. An insight which follows from the economic analysis of marriage markets which has not received much attention in the past is the idea that the number of men and women in a society affects women's labor supply due to its effect on marriage market conditions.

Sex ratios and female labor-force participation.

As was shown earlier the relative number of men and women – which can be defined as the sex ratio – influences conditions in marriage markets. In terms of the G-version which analyzes marriage as a mutual employment relation, the market-determined value of time w^* varies with demand and supply in the market for spousal labor (see figure 6.1). Comparing people in two different marriage markets with varying sex ratios, the higher the sex ratio – i.e., the larger the relative number of men in a marriage market – the higher the demand for women's spousal labor compared to the supply of spousal labor. Consequently, the marriage market component of the value of time of married women will be higher the higher the sex ratio. This implies lower participation rates of married women in the labor force than if the value of time is lower due to lower sex ratios. At the same time, variations in the number of men and women are also likely to affect labor markets (in the common sense of labor). If sex ratios are high and women are relatively scarce, this may cause increases in women's wages.

Under reasonable assumptions an increase in the relative number of men – which is associated with a higher sex ratio – is predicted to cause an increase in demand for women's spousal labor, which leads to an increase in women's value of time w^*, and therefore a decrease in total female employment. Higher sex ratios may also cause higher wages, which may increase female employment. It can be assumed that sex ratios have more of an impact on women's value of time (due to their impact on marriage market conditions) than on women's wages.[9] It is thus hypothesized that:

Sex ratios are inversely related to women's labor supply in general, and married women's labor supply in particular.

Evidence for this hypothesis can be found in comparisons across different cities in the United States at any given time, or based on changes over time. In a study of cities in the United States in 1930 and 1980, it was found that the higher the sex ratio, the lower the rate of participation of married women in the labor force (see Grossbard-Shechtman 1993).

Sex ratios vary over time due to the tendency of men's age at marriage to exceed women's age at marriage. Consequently, women born during periods of population growth tend to experience bad marriage market conditions when they grow up, whereas men born during periods of population growth tend to experience favorable marriage market conditions. The opposite is true for men and women born during periods of declining fertility, such as the baby-busters now entering marriage and labor markets.

It follows that women born during periods of growing population (baby-booms) are likely to experience low quasi-wages for spousal labor (w^*) and therefore higher rates of labor force participation when married. Everything else constant, one expects higher quasi-wages for women born during periods of declining population (baby-bust) and therefore lower rates of labor force participation. The evidence shows that the most rapid increases in the labor force participation of married women in the United States occurred among women born at the beginning of the baby-boom or slightly earlier, women who must have experienced unfavorable marriage market conditions according to an analysis of demand and supply of spousal labor. Baby-bust cohorts who have recently entered the labor force are experiencing much slower rates of growth in labor force participation (see Grossbard-Shechtman and Granger 1994). This is especially true for married women.

Other factors affecting marriage markets

It also follows from an economic analysis of marriage markets that individual or group differences in marriage opportunities are related to the value of time in the home, and therefore labor supply. Factors influencing an individual's value of time w^* include characteristics of both men and women which are considered as important in marriage markets. It follows that:

The higher a woman's value in the marriage market, the higher her value of time and the lower her labor supply.

Value in the marriage market is not always easy to establish. It probably varies with education, income of family of origin, ethnic origin, and number of previous marriages.

It is generally estimated that African–American women experience worse marriage market conditions in the United States than American women of European descent. This could help explain why the participation rate of married women of African origin has traditionally exceeded that of married women of European origin in this country, even after controlling for all variables usually included in labor-supply estimations.

Furthermore, the pecuniary component of a particular woman's value of time depends not only on her own characteristics, but also on her husband's characteristics. Compensating differentials may exist, whereby husbands who offer relatively low non-pecuniary benefits to their wife make up for such shortcomings by providing their wife with more generous pecuniary benefits than do husbands offering relatively high non-pecuniary benefits. In other words, husbands can make up for an undesirable trait, such as old age or poor health, by sharing a higher proportion of their wealth with their wife. It follows that:

Compensating differentials leading to pecuniary compensations by husbands to wives have a discouraging effect on wives' labor supply.

This could explain why women married to men substantially older than themselves were less likely to participate in the labor force than women married to men who were the same age or slightly older. More hypotheses relating marriage market factors to labor supply include factors associated with a higher probability of divorce and divorce laws. These and other hypotheses are discussed at more length in Grossbard-Shechtman (1993).

A comparison with other theories

The rest of this chapter is devoted to comparing Becker's theory of marriage (which includes his original version and the G-version) with two alternative theories: (1) pooled household models and (2) game-theoretic models.

Becker's theory of marriage versus pooled household models

In these models, the decision maker is conceived of as a household consisting usually of at least two people, usually a husband and a wife. Such models assume either collective decision making or altruistic concerns on the part of a principal decision maker. Widely used in studies of consumption, labor supply, or fertility, pooled household models have often been labeled neoclassical. In fact, these models also owe a large intellectual debt to Becker.

In comparison to pooled household models, models based on Becker's theory of marriage have the following advantages:

1 Becker's theory of marriage provides explanations for various aspects of marriage and divorce. Pooled household models assume a household as given and do not deal with the formation and dissolution of households.
2 In Becker's theory of marriage individual members of a household maintain some degree of independent decision making (more so in the G-version than in the original version). Consequently, according to this theory of marriage income and wealth effects on consumption and work will depend on whether it is the wife's or the husband's income or wealth. In contrast, in pooled household models all resources belonging to the

household members are pooled, and the source of income or wealth does not matter.

3 Factors influencing marriage markets are expected to affect a variety of outcomes (e.g., consumption and labor supply) according to the theory of marriage based on Becker but not according to pooled household models. Such marriage market variables include sex ratios, divorce laws, and tax laws dependent on marital status (see above).

4 Factors influencing the demand and supply of spousal labor are expected to affect a variety of outcomes (e.g., consumption and labor supply) according to the theory of marriage based on Becker but not according to pooled household models. For instance, when substitutes for spousal labor become more expensive (e.g., due to an increase in the wages of live-in maids or a restriction on the employment of illegal aliens working as live-in maids), this is predicted to increase the demand for spousal labor, and therefore likely to affect all the outcomes discussed above.

5 In comparison to pooled household models, marriage models based on Becker's theory of marriage possibly lead to improved methods of estimating outcomes such as divorce and labor supply.

Becker's theory of marriage versus game-theoretic models

To the extent that game theory is an alternative to neoclassical economic analysis, game theories of marriage are an alternative to Becker's neoclassical theory of marriage. Game theory has been applied to the study of marriage at least since Shapley (1962). According to a version of this theory found in McElroy (1990) each household member has a utility function and a threat point, which is the person's maximal level of utility outside the household. Such individual threat points are influenced by prices, incomes, sex ratios, and laws, the same factors which Becker and Grossbard-Shechtman considered when analyzing marriage markets. Outcomes, such as one spouse's consumption or labor supply, vary with all the factors which influence these threat points. Consequently, the individual supplies of labor or demands for goods found in McElroy (1990) are very similar to the supplies of labor and demands for goods found in Grossbard-Shechtman (1984, 1993).

Game-theoretic models do not incorporate marriage market conditions as directly as the marriage market models do. Therefore, it is not straightforward how game-theoretic models of decision making tie into the existing literature on labor supply. In contrast, marriage market models – at least the G-version – tie very easily into traditional models of labor supply.

In sum, many but not all the advantages of Becker's theory of marriage that were mentioned in a comparison between that theory of marriage and pooled household models are shared by game-theory models of marriage. In fact, proponents of game-theory models of marriage have criticized the pooled household models on most of the same grounds that were mentioned above. What has obscured the discussion, however, is that proponents of game-theory models have addressed their criticisms not specifically to neoclassical pooled household models, but to neoclassical models in general. They have overlooked the fact that models based on Becker's neoclassical theory of marriage are substitutes for Nash-bargained models of household behavior. Both kinds of models have considerable advantages over neoclassical pooled models.

Conclusions

This chapter has summarized some of the important insights that can be derived from Becker's theory of marriage. Some of these insights were mentioned by Becker himself, while others can be found in my own model based on Becker's theory of marriage. The insights from Becker's theory of marriage which apply to consumption and labor supply were emphasized, in an attempt to make up for the lack of attention most economists have paid to these implications.

One can only speculate as to the reasons why empirical studies distinguishing between the effects of male and female income on consumption and fertility have preferred to justify such distinctions based on a Nash-bargained household model rather than on Becker's theory of marriage. It certainly is not a function of the chronological order or the complexity of these theories, as Becker's theory of marriage first appeared before game-theoretic models of household behavior became popular. Also, Becker's theory of marriage is simpler to understand than the game-theoretic models, as it links easily to the neoclassical models which dominate other fields of economics.

To the extent that the unfair treatment received by Becker's theory of marriage has resulted from the brevity of Becker's own treatment of the implications of his theory for consumption, fertility, and labor supply, it is hoped that this essay will help correct the situation. Justice was served when Becker received a Nobel prize that was long overdue. Justice will be served even better when due recognition is given to valuable aspects of Becker's contribution which have been ignored by most of the economics profession.

Notes

1 The helpful comments of Gary Becker, Andrea Beller, Jeffrey Gray, Mariano Tommasi, and anonymous referees are gratefully acknowledged.
2 For a more detailed comparison between the economics of marriage and studies of marriage in other disciplines see Grossbard-Shechtman, 1993 (chapter 1). Interested readers wanting to delve more deeply into the economic analysis of marriage are encouraged to start with Becker (1981) and Grossbard-Shechtman (1993).
3 A helpful survey of such studies can be found in Parkman (1992).
4 Peters (1986) derived the same hypothesis.
5 Alternatively, it is possible that no-fault divorce has lowered the present value of women's value of time in marriage (based on the flow of future earnings from marriage) in states with community-property statutes more than in states with common-law statutes.
6 For instance, the larger women's income from sources other than spousal labor, the more women's supply of spousal labor shifts to the left, which is likely to be associated with a reduction in the amount of spousal labor and an increase in the compensation for spousal labor. Depending on other assumptions, this could cause women's income from spousal labor to either decrease or increase.
7 It was found in both the Philippines and in Brazil that income in mothers' hands benefits children more than income in fathers' hands (Senauer, Garcia, and Jacinto, 1988; Thomas, 1990). Furthermore, also consistent with Becker's theory of marriage, in Brazil it was found that mothers preferred to devote resources to improve the nutritional status of their daughters, whereas fathers preferred to devote resources to improve the nutritional status of their sons (Thomas, 1990).
8 This section is based on chapters 3, 5, and 6 in Grossbard-Shechtman (1993).
9 Sex ratios are likely to have little impact on women's wages if male and female workers are easily substituted for each other, and if the demand for female workers is not very elastic.

References

Becker, Gary S. 1973. "A Theory of Marriage: Part I," *Journal of Political Economy*, 81: 813–46.
— 1974. "A Theory of Marriage: Part II," *Journal of Political Economy*, 82: 511–26.
— 1981. *A Treatise on the Family*, Cambridge, MA: Harvard University Press.
— 1992. "Finding Fault with No-Fault Divorce," *Business Week*, December 7.
Dixon, Ruth B. and Lenore J. Weitzman. 1980. "Evaluating the Impact of No-Fault Divorce in California," *Family Relations*, 29: 297–307.
Gray, Jeffrey S. 1993. "Divorce Law Changes, Household Bargaining, and Married Women's Labor Supply," Paper Presented at the meeting of the Population Association of America, Cincinnati, OH, April 1993.
Grossbard-Shechtman, Amyra Shoshana. 1984. "A Theory of Allocation of Time in Markets for Labor and Marriage," *Economic Journal*, 94: 863–82.

1993. *On the Economics of Marriage – A Theory of Marriage, Labor and Divorce*, Boulder, CO: Westview Press.

Grossbard-Shechtman, Shoshana and Clive W. J. Granger. 1994. "The Baby Boom and Time Trends in Women's Labor Force Participation." Paper presented at the meetings of the American Economics Association, January 1994.

McElroy, Marjorie B. 1990. "The Empirical Content of Nash-Bargained Household Behavior," *Journal of Human Resources*, 25: 559–83.

Parkman, Allen. 1992. *No-Fault Divorce*, Boulder, CO: Westview Press.

Peters, Elizabeth H. 1986. "Marriage and Divorce: Informational Constraints and Private Contracting," *American Economic Review*, 76: 437–54.

Senauer, Benjamin, Marito Garcia, and Elizabeth Jacinto. 1988. "Determinants of the Intrahousehold Allocation of Food in the Rural Philippines," *American Journal of Agricultural Economics*, 70: 170–80.

Shapley, Lloyd. 1962. "College Admissions and the Stability of Marriage," *American Mathematical Monthly*, 69.

Thomas, Duncan. 1990. "Intra-Household Resource Allocation: An Inferential Approach," *Journal of Human Resources*, 25: 635–64.

Weitzman, Lenore J. 1985. "The Divorce Law Revolution and the Transformation of Legal Marriage," in Kingsley Davis and Amyra Grossbard-Shechtman (eds.), *Contemporary Marriage*, New York: Russell Sage Foundation.

7 The marriage premium

Kermit Daniel

Married men earn higher wages than single men. Married men are older, better educated, and have more stable employment histories – characteristics associated with higher wages for all workers, married or not. But these differences in characteristics can only partly explain the difference in wages. Economists and others have proposed several explanations for the remaining *marriage premium*. One explanation that has not received the serious attention it deserves is that marriage raises productivity. In this chapter I describe a model of family behavior that explains how it might do so.[1]

The existence of a marriage premium for men is well established. It has been documented in several countries and in the United States as early as the nineteenth century. It remains after accounting for differences in workers' health and the attributes of each worker's job – how dirty, strenuous, challenging, or otherwise unpleasant or pleasant. Estimates of the male marriage premium range from about 10 to 35 percent. Its size differs according to the age and race of the men considered, being larger for older men and for white men. Overall, women do not earn a significant marriage premium.

It is worth noting that some features of marriage tend to lower, not raise, wages. For example, it is usually harder for married men to change jobs when doing so requires moving. Consequently, some married men will receive lower wages than if they were single and could more easily move to a better job. In addition, employers can exploit the relative immobility of married men by paying them a smaller share of the return to their firm-specific human capital. The fact that married men earn more than single men in spite of these factors makes the marriage premium even more striking.

I will argue the reason married men earn more is that marriage makes men more productive. Part of the reason I believe this is so is that other explanations proposed cannot satisfactorily account for the marriage premium.

Alternative explanations for the marriage premium

The fact that all else equal, married men earn higher wages than single men suggests that marriage makes men more productive, but other explanations are possible. Broadly speaking, there are two alternatives. First, although married men earn more than single men, they might not be more productive. Second, even if they are more productive, marriage might not be responsible.

There are two reasons married men might receive higher wages even if they are not more productive. The marriage premium might reflect different choices by married and single men about the form in which to receive compensation, or it might represent discrimination in favor of married men.

Married men might earn more simply because they are more likely to work for employers who pay all their workers more, married or not. Workers receive compensation in many forms. Money is a large part of total compensation, but the quality of the work environment and the nature of the work itself both contribute to total compensation. If these non-monetary features make a job unusually unpleasant, then the employer must pay higher wages than one hiring people to work under more desirable conditions. Robert Reed and Kathleen Harford (1989) have argued that married men should be more willing than single men to trade pleasant work for higher wages. If Reed and Harford are right, the marriage premium merely represents different choices by married and unmarried men about the form in which to receive compensation. In this case the marriage premium should disappear after one accounts for differences in job characteristics.

In fact, while there is some evidence married men tend to work in more unpleasant jobs, accounting for this does not significantly reduce the marriage premium. Furthermore, married men earn more than unmarried men working in the same firm.

Some have suggested the marriage premium simply reflects employer favoritism, but it is not easy to determine whether employers discriminate in favor of married men. It is not enough that employers exhibit a preference for married men. They will do so if married men are better workers. Employers show favoritism only if their preference for married men is not justified.

Employers have at times claimed to discriminate in favor of married men, but it is not obvious that employers discriminated in the true sense of the word. One reason to be skeptical of employers' claims is that talk is cheap, but discrimination is not (see chapter 1). Any effort spent screening out single workers and searching for married workers is wasted if married workers are no better than single workers. Hiring costs are greater than need be, so profits are less than they could be. If high-quality workers are scarce, the cost of discrimination is even greater because some married men hired will not be as productive as the single men whose places they took.

In any event, whether or not employers showed favoritism toward married men in the past, four features of the male marriage premium suggest that discrimination is no longer its only explanation. First, the premium is larger the longer a man has been married. This is true holding constant age, total labor market experience, time on the current job, and other factors affecting wages. Second, its size is influenced by the wife's characteristics and behavior. Third, the premium declines as divorce approaches. Fourth, there is a wage premium among single men living with a woman. Simple discrimination in favor of married men cannot account for these features.

Studies show that married men receive greater compensation and that this premium does not merely reflect discrimination. Together, these facts provide strong indirect evidence that married men are more productive than single men. There is also direct evidence. Numerous studies verify that they are more productive and are less likely to quit or miss work. In addition, married men report expending greater effort on their jobs. Perhaps for this reason they are fired less often, tend to receive higher performance ratings, and are more likely to be promoted.

Married men are more productive, but does being married *cause* them to be more productive? The question may be asked another way: If a given married man had been prohibited from marrying, would he now be less productive? The major difficulty in answering this question is that marital status and productivity may be related even if marital status does not affect productivity. There are at least two reasons marital status and productivity are likely to be related: Some characteristics will enhance both productivity and marriageability, and high earnings increase the probability of becoming and remaining married.

Some characteristics will make any long-term relationship better, whether that relationship is employment or marriage. Many characteristics that enhance a man's productivity within a firm are also likely to enhance his ability at home production. It is easy to think of characteristics that might increase both market and non-market productivity within a marriage, such as dependability, loyalty, intelligence, diligence, creativity, and physical attractiveness.[2] Some of these characteristics will also directly increase his appeal as a husband. To the extent men possess characteristics that increase both productivity and marriageability, married men will be more productive even if marriage does not affect productivity.

Marital status and productivity will also be related because high earnings directly increase the probability of becoming and remaining married. Gary Becker has argued that gains from marriage are probably greater for men with high wages than for those with low wages (because of the greater gains from specialization within marriage), and, all else equal, men with high earnings are probably more attractive spouses. Research supports Becker's argument, suggesting that to some extent high earnings "causes" marriage.

However, researchers have failed to explain all the higher productivity of married men as the result of those who earn more being more likely to marry. For example, a study by David Neumark of young men in the United States accounted for the possibility that high-earning men are more likely to marry and still found a marriage premium of about 15 percent. My own research confirms this result. Using a different technique to account for the possibility that high-earning men are more likely to marry, I found that only about half the marriage premium for young men can be explained by this phenomenon. While it is true that more productive men are more likely to be married, this accounts for only part of their wage premium. Marriage may make men more productive.

A model of the marriage premium

There are several ways marriage might raise productivity. For example, marriage might increase human capital or affect the quality of the job match. A study of how young people look for jobs found that married unemployed youths used more ways to find a job than did those who were single. A study by Kathryn Shaw (1987) found that while married men are less likely to quit a job than are single men, married men with working wives are more likely to quit than those with non-working wives. If this relatively higher quit rate reflects greater opportunities, then married men with working wives will wind up with better, higher-paying, jobs.

A wife might augment productivity by assisting her husband directly in his work, by acting as a "sounding board," by organizing activities, or by performing housework or other chores that increase the other's effectiveness at work. Several authors have described how corporate managers' wives assist their husbands' careers. A study of dual-career marriages by Rosanna Hertz described the advantages (and some disadvantages) accruing to professionals married to other professionals. Cynthia Epstein's study of lawyers provides other examples of the ability of one spouse to augment the other's productivity.

By performing household chores or taking responsibility for child care, a wife could augment her husband's productivity by allowing him more or better sleep. A comprehensive survey of research on medical incidents, auto and truck accidents, and errors in industrial and technical operations concluded that "Inadequate sleep, even as little as one or two hours less than usual sleep, can greatly exaggerate the tendency for error during the time zones of vulnerability [very early morning and mid-afternoon]."

There are many ways a spouse could augment productivity; what they all have in common is that they take time. If one family member wants to augment the productivity of the other, she (or he) must take time away from something else to do so. This simple observation is the foundation of my economic model of the marriage premium. It is not necessary to be very specific about how people use time; it is enough to divide time into three categories: that spent working on a job, that spent augmenting a spouse's productivity, and all remaining time, which I will call non-market time.

In principle, there is nothing to keep men from augmenting the productivity of their wives. The model I describe allows for this possibility, but, as I will explain presently, there are several reasons this is less likely than the reverse. For this reason, and because the evidence shows men earn a marriage premium while most women do not, I will assume for the purpose of describing the model that wives augment the productivity of their husbands. As it turns out, the fact that men are the main recipients of a marriage premium supports the model.

When a man's wife augments his productivity he accomplishes more per minute; his time on the job is more effective. Employers compensate workers according to their productivity, which means they pay for effective time. Productivity augmentation causes a worker's effective time to exceed actual time on the job, so workers benefiting from productivity augmentation are paid more per hour of clock time. This difference in wages per hour is the marriage premium.

Women will differ in their ability to augment their husbands' productivity. One can think of these differences in augmentation ability as arising from differences in *augmentation capital*. Just as a worker's human capital affects the ability to perform a job, augmentation capital affects the ability to augment a spouse's productivity. One woman is better than another at augmenting productivity only if she has more augmentation capital.

There are two fundamentally different ways productivity augmentation can work. A wife might essentially provide her husband with additional capital, or she might provide a flow of services. If she provides a stock of capital, the effect of past augmentation effort persists; if she provides a flow of services, past effort has no direct effect on her husband's current productivity.

All else equal, wives will prefer to provide augmentation as a flow of services rather than as a stock of capital. If a wife augments productivity by giving her husband a stock of capital, then he takes this with him if they divorce. If she augments productivity by providing a flow of services, then her husband loses the benefit of productivity augmentation if they divorce. Providing augmentation through capital enhancement lowers the value of the marriage compared to its value when the same augmentation effect arises from the constant application of the wife's effort. Furthermore, if augmentation takes the form of capital enhancement, the possibility of divorce will lower the wife's optimal investment in augmentation capital, and the marriage premium will be smaller.

Even if it is impossible to choose the form of productivity enhancement, there will be a tendency for it to arise from a constant application of the wife's time. As just explained, the marriage premium is larger, and the net gain from marriage is greater, when productivity enhancement requires a flow of services. As long as the form of augmentation varies across potential marriages, those in which augmentation arises from a flow of the wife's time will be more likely to form and endure.

The marriage premium is likely to arise directly from the time the wife spends augmenting productivity, so it can be understood by thinking about how the quantity of this time is determined. Couples allocate their time to various activities in order to make themselves as well off as possible. This means they will necessarily be equating the value of the last minute spent in each use. A wife who works will spend time augmenting productivity up to the point where the value of another minute spent augmenting is equal to the value of another minute spent working, and will set both equal to the value of another minute of non-market time.

The value of the last minute of each kind of time is called its marginal product. Without knowing much about how productivity augmentation works we can nevertheless be sure that as more time is spent augmenting, its marginal product declines. A wife will do the most obvious and useful things to increase her husband's productivity first. As more time is spent augmenting, she will have less-valuable ways to augment productivity left, and the last minute of augmentation time will have less effect. While the marginal product of augmentation time declines as more time is devoted to this activity, the marginal product is higher the more augmentation capital the wife possesses.

With this in mind, it is possible to explain why men are the main recipients of a marriage premium. There are two related reasons for this. Husbands tend to have higher wages than their wives, and, as a result, women are likely to have more augmentation capital than men. Both of these factors operate to produce a marriage premium for men, even though the logic of the marriage premium is gender neutral: Husbands and wives allocate their time to various activities so as to maximize the couple's well-being.

If a wife spends time augmenting her husband's productivity, she increases his effective time on the job. A husband can similarly increase his wife's effective time. Suppose, as is likely, the husband earns a higher wage than his wife. This implies the couple will choose augmentation times so that the husband's marginal product of augmentation time is larger than his wife's. Assuming his wife has more augmentation capital, this can only be achieved by the husband spending less time augmenting productivity. He must leave more valuable augmentation activities undone, and may spend no time augmenting his wife's productivity. The wife is better at augmenting productivity and spends more time at it, so her husband receives a larger marriage premium than she does. Of course, if the wife earned higher wages and had less augmentation capital the roles would be reversed. Relative wages and augmentation capital determine the marriage premium.

It is easy to verify that husbands tend to have higher wages than their wives, but augmentation capital cannot be observed. There are, however, several reasons to expect wives are better at augmentation than their husbands. All stem from the fact that the higher is one spouse's wage, the greater is the value of the other's augmentation capital. Men tend to have higher wages than women, so women have a greater incentive to develop augmentation capital in anticipation of marriage, and families will tend to invest in more augmentation capital for their daughters than for their sons. For these reasons, even when a woman marries a man with lower earnings, she is likely to have greater augmentation capital and may still provide him with a marriage premium. Thus, the general pattern of men earning more than women will produce a bias toward a male marriage premium. Of course, once married to a higher-earning man, wives have a larger incentive than their husbands to further develop augmentation capital.

The model provides an explanation for the male marriage premium; it simultaneously provides an explanation for the absence of one among women. It also suggests other patterns to the marriage premium. Fortunately, many of the suggested relationships are not predicted by the alternative explanations discussed earlier, so one way to assess whether marriage makes men more productive is to see whether these patterns in fact exist.

The logic of the model suggests the marriage premium should not be restricted to formally married couples. A marriage premium arises when two people coordinate their actions and have the opportunity to augment each other's productivity. Living with another adult indicates the desire and opportunity to engage in joint behavior, so the marriage premium should not be limited to those in a formal marriage or to heterosexual couples, nor should it always arise whenever couples are formally married. A couple living together outside formal marriage reveal a desire and ability to coordinate activities, as evidenced by the fact that spells of cohabitation often end in formal marriage. There should be a "marriage premium" for cohabiters.

Conversely, divorce clearly signals a desire to stop coordinating behavior, a process that surely begins before the date the divorce is formally effected. Couples who live apart prior to divorce have at least begun the process of separating their behavior, and have less incentive, and probably fewer opportunities, to augment each other's productivity. Furthermore, there are reduced opportunities for reciprocity within marriage as divorce approaches, so it seems reasonable to expect that even couples still living together will spend less time augmenting productivity as divorce nears. For both of these reasons, there should be less productivity augmentation among couples near the date of divorce. A decline in time spent augmenting productivity will produce a decline in the marriage premium as divorce nears.

The model has several other implications. The marriage premium should be larger, the larger is the gap between the spouses' earnings. Because married workers spend more effective time on the job per hour of real clock time, they should accumulate specific human capital more quickly and their wages should rise more quickly. Children place demands on their parents' time, so the presence and number of children is inversely related to the time available for productivity augmentation, and should therefore lower the marriage premium. All else equal, wives (or husbands) will spend less time at market work the more productive they are at augmentation. For this reason the marriage premium should be inversely related to the wife's (or husband's) hours of work.

Finally, a major implication of the model is that the important determinants of the existence and size of the marriage premium are the relative productivities of family members in the market and at augmentation. Ignoring differences in augmentation capital for the moment, the marriage premium should be larger, the smaller the spouse's hours of work, and larger, the smaller the relative earnings of the spouse. Compared to black men, white men are less likely to have a working wife, and, when their wives work, they work fewer hours. White men are more likely to earn more than their wives, and the average gap between the husband's and wife's wage is much larger among white men than among black men. Among women, the pattern is reversed. These differences help provide evidence on the model. Overall, black men should receive a smaller marriage premium than white men; black women should receive a larger marriage premium than white women.

If, as seems reasonable, augmentation capital acquired by the four groups reflects current and historic marriage rates, labor force participation rates, and relative wages, then the preceding patterns will be strengthened. White men (or their parents) should invest in less augmentation capital than white women, and the difference should be less or reversed among blacks. White men have less incentive to invest in augmentation capital than black men; black women have less incentive to invest in augmentation capital than white women. Overall, the marriage premium should be smaller for blacks since the lower marriage rate among blacks reduces the expected return to investment in augmentation capital.

Evidence

Having established the basic logic of an economic model of the marriage premium, in the remainder of the chapter I describe the marriage premium found among the men and women surveyed in the National Longitudinal Survey of Youth. The NLSY includes a representative sample of men and women between the ages of fourteen and twenty-one on January 1, 1979. The respondents were first surveyed in 1979 and have been resurveyed each year since. By the end of the data the oldest survey respondents are thirty years old.

This survey has a number of features that make it well suited to a study of the marriage premium. It contains unusually detailed information about survey respondents and their jobs. Because it tracks survey respondents for several years, for many respondents there is wage and other information from both before and after they marry. It also has detailed employment and education histories for almost everyone, as well as their scores on a battery of aptitude tests. By accounting for the many sources of wage differences between people, I can more precisely estimate that part due to being married.

I divided the sample by race and sex, and estimated the marriage premium separately for each of the four groups defined, black men and women, and white men and women. I did so under the assumption that there are unobserved characteristics that simultaneously affect marital status, wages, and the decision to work. These unobserved differences do not account for the male marriage premium. There remains a statistically and economically significant marriage premium for both black and white young men. The marriage premium for white men is about 6 percent; among black men it is about 4.5 percent. As the model suggests, white men earn a larger premium than black men.

Consistent with the model, both black and white men who are cohabiting receive a wage premium and for both groups the marriage premium declines as divorce nears. There is strong evidence that children reduce the marriage premium for white men and weaker evidence of this for black men. As expected, the more hours a man's wife works, the smaller is his marriage premium. This effect is stronger among white men than among black men.

For white women, the net effect of marriage on wages is negative, but this is entirely due to the negative effect of children. Marriage alone has a small positive effect that appears after a few years of marriage. If at least some husbands are augmenting their wives' productivity, then children should reduce the wages of married women, but not of single women, because single women receive no augmentation to be reduced. As predicted, children do not have a statistically significant effect on the wages of single white women. Unlike men, white women do not receive a cohabitation premium and there is no evidence that wages fall as divorce approaches.

Unlike white women, black women earn a significant positive marriage premium of about 3 percent. They do not earn a cohabitation premium. Consistent with the model, children reduce their marriage premium, but have no effect on the wages of single black women.

Also consistent with the model, the marriage premium among white men is larger than that among black men. The relationship between the estimated effect of marriage for white women and black women is also broadly consistent with the model, in the sense that the model suggests there should be a smaller premium among white women than among black women. The difference between races in the relationship between the premium earned by men and that earned by women is also as expected. Given the greater relative earnings of black women compared to black men and the lower relative participation rates of black men compared to white men, the model suggests that difference in the marriage premium between men and women should be less among blacks than among whites. This is exactly the pattern observed.

I also examined the effects of a spouse's education on the marriage premium. I did so under the assumption that education is correlated with augmentation capital. This obviously will be true if education directly creates augmentation capital. It will also be true if there is some underlying ability or characteristic that people have in different amounts that reduces the cost of accumulating both education and augmentation capital.

For white and black men the results are consistent with the interpretation of a wife's education as a proxy for augmentation capital. Educated wives provide a larger marriage premium, holding constant time in marriage, their hours of work, the number and presence of children, and the wage gap. For white and black women, the husband's education has no effect.

As a final test of the model, I directly estimated the effect of relative wages on the marriage premium.[3] As the model suggests, the marriage premium for white men is increasing in the wage gap. The size of the effect for black men is the same as for white men, but it is estimated much less precisely, meaning there is a reasonable probability that the positive estimate arose by chance.

For both black and white women the effect of relative wages is small and not statistically significant. An obvious interpretation of the lack of a significant relationship for white women, combined with the previous estimates of a low or completely absent marriage premium for them, is that white men do not spend much or any time augmenting productivity, and any time they do provide does not vary. Given that black women earn a marriage premium, the absence of a relative-wage effect suggests that black men augment productivity, but the time they spend doing so does not vary with the wage gap. For both blacks and whites, this interpretation is consistent with studies of how people use time. Men do not change the allocation of their time to different activities as much as women do in response to marriage, having children, or changes in their spouse's labor-force participation. These results are also consistent with the labor-supply behavior of men and women. Women vary their time working more than men do in response to wage and wealth changes.

Summary and conclusion

Three of the four groups examined exhibit a positive marriage premium in wages. Among white men, black men, and black women, married workers earn more than unmarried workers. There is a net negative marriage "premium" among white women, but this is entirely due to the negative effect of children on the wages of married women. Among men, there is evidence of a premium attached to cohabitation, and also among men, the premium declines as divorce approaches. Among white men, the marriage premium is inversely related to the wife's hours of work. For white men and black women, the marriage premium is reduced by children. These characteristics of the marriage premium are consistent with the productivity augmentation model and specialization within marriage

The model strongly suggests that the marriage premium should be increasing in the relative wages of the spouses. I presented two types of evidence on this. First, general features of the gender and racial differences are consistent with this model. The model suggests that white men should earn a higher premium than black men, with just the opposite true among women, and the results are generally consistent with this prediction. The model further suggests that the difference in the marriage premium for men and women should be greater among whites than among blacks, and this too is reflected in the estimates.

I also directly estimated the effect of relative wages. Among men, there is direct evidence that the marriage premium is increasing in relative wages. The effect is estimated to be about the same for white and black men, and for white men the effect is statistically significant. The estimates for women are statistically insignificant and numerically small. These results suggest that the augmentation time of wives is more responsive than that of husbands, which is consistent with research on other types of time allocation. For men, there is evidence that the marriage premium increases with the wife's education.

The productivity-augmentation model provides a single simple explanation for the marriage premium and many of its features. There is enough positive evidence to justify serious consideration of the model, and to warrant further research into the exact mechanism by which the marriage premium arises.

Notes

1 This model is described in detail in my Ph.D. dissertation "Does Marriage Make Workers More Productive?" The University of Chicago, 1993.
2 A study of Canadian men found that physical attractiveness was positively related to earnings growth. Interviewers rated physical attractiveness on a scale ranging from "homely" to "strikingly handsome or beautiful." The researchers found that a one-step increase in the attractiveness rating was associated with an increase in annual earnings of $1,266 (Canadian). Of course, because they did not control for marital status, this "attractiveness premium" may just reflect the marriage premium.
3 Because by construction each spouse's wage is correlated with the difference in wages between spouses, this is not as easy as it sounds. I produced the estimates using a statistical technique known as "instrumental variables." Although this approach presents its own difficulties, it has some advantages over the comparisons just described – it is less affected by differences in marriage markets between blacks and whites and it does not rely upon the black/white difference in the husband/wife wage ratio being independent of the processes generating the marriage premium.

References

Bartlett, Robin and Charles Callahan. 1984. "Wage Determination and Marital Status: Another Look," *Industrial Relations*, 23(1): 90–6.
Becker, Gary. 1981. *A Treatise on the Family*, Cambridge, MA: Harvard University Press.
    1985. "Human Capital, Effort, and the Sexual Division of Labor," *Journal of Labor Economics*, 3(1, part 2).
Becker, Gary, Elizabeth Landes, and Robert Michael. 1977. "An Economic Analysis of Marital Instability," *Journal of Political Economy*, 85(6): 1141–87.
Blackburn, McKinley and Sanders Korenman. 1991. "Changes Over Time in Earnings Differentials by Marital Status," The University of South Carolina.
Duncan, Greg and Bertil Holmund. 1983. "Was Adam Smith Right After All? Another Test of the Theory of Compensating Wage Differentials," *Journal of Labor Economics*, 1(4): 366–79.

Epstein, Cynthia. 1971. "Law Partners and Marital Partners," *Human Relations.* 24(6): 549–64.

Goldin, Claudia. 1990. *Understanding the Gender Gap*, Oxford University Press.

Hertz, Rosanna. 1986. *More Equal Than Others: Women and Men in Dual-Career Marriages*, University of California Press.

Holzer, Harry. 1988. "Search Methods Used by Unemployed Youth," *Journal of Labor Economics*, 6(1): 1–20.

Kanter, Rosabeth. 1977. *Men and Women of the Corporation*, New York: Basic Books.

Korenman, Sanders and David Neumark. 1991. "Does Marriage Really Make Men More Productive?" *Journal of Human Resources*, 26(2): 283–307.

Kostiuk, Peter and Dean Follmann. 1989. "Learning Curves, Personal Characteristics, and Job Performance," *Journal of Labor Economics*, (7 April): 129–46.

Mitler, Merrill *et al.* 1988. "Catastrophes, Sleep, and Public Policy: Consensus Report," *Sleep*, 11(1): 100–9.

Neumark, David. 1988. "Employers' Discriminatory Behavior and the Estimation of Wage Discrimination," *Journal of Human Resources*, 23(3): 279–95.

Reed, Robert and Kathleen Harford. 1989. "The Marriage Premium and Compensating Wage Differentials," *Journal of Population Economics*, 2: 237–65.

Rees, Albert and George Schultz. 1970. *Workers and Wages in an Urban Labor Market*, Chicago, MA: University of Chicago Press.

Shaw, Kathryn. 1987. "The Quit Propensity of Married Men," *Journal of Labor Economics*, 5(4): 533–60.

Stoner, James, John Aram, and Irwin Rubin. 1972. "Factors Associated with Effective Performance in Overseas Work Assignments," *Personnel Psychology*, 25(2): 303–18.

Whyte, William. 1956. *The Organization Man*, New York: Simon and Schuster.

IV

Government and politics

8   The process of government

Edgardo Enrique Zablotsky[1]

1 Introduction

Suppose we have a corrupt city government, and we want to improve our understanding of the phenomenon of corruption. A naive explanation would be that corrupt acts are committed because corrupt men are in office. This statement, while very straightforward, does not improve our understanding on the subject. There are too many questions that cannot be answered in such terms. What form does the corruption take? How pervasive is it? Why does it appear in one city and not in another? If we explain corruption in terms of corrupt men, we find ourselves building a set of problems in the background corresponding with the problems in the foreground, but not throwing any light upon the latter.

A more fruitful strategy consists of forgetting moral characteristics and analyzing the acts performed. To do this we must find out what circles of the population those groups represent in each case. We then must work out which other circles of men they injure, and we finally must get some measurement of the extent of the injury and their reaction against injuries of these kinds. When all this is done we will realize that we have learned much more about the phenomena under study than naively attributing municipal corruption to corrupt city officers. This essay will focus on a theory to explain political outcomes (such as corruption): the so-called "interest-groups" approach to public policy.

This approach can be traced back as early as the beginning of this century when *The Process of Government*, a seminal book by Arthur Bentley, was first published. In *The Process of Government* Bentley vigorously attacked instincts, innate feelings and faculties, and even ideas or ideals as causes of the behavior of government officials. He characterizes government as a *process*, in which *interest groups* are the protagonists. Within this framework an *interest group* is defined as a certain number of members of a society engaged in a mass activity, which does not preclude anyone who participates in it from participating in other groups. Every person has not one but many interests, and the more complex their culture becomes, the more interests they have. In these terms a group and its activity are equivalent. There is no group without a specific interest. As the shared interest that defines a group declines, the group itself becomes weaker and may even disappear. Interest groups are the raw material to the comprehension of government behavior, and they are the protagonists of the process of government.

The *process* is defined as the activity of the groups in their relation with one another; no group has any meaning except in its relation to other groups. Groups are in constant activity, jockeying for position, cooperating, competing, forming offensive and defensive alliances, splitting apart, and disappearing, while new groups are being formed. Strong groups dominate, and delineate the existing state of society; a state is in equilibrium, given that it is the end result of the pressure exerted by all the existing interest groups.

The Process of Government was almost ignored by political scientists for two decades but has been rediscovered. By the 1950s, empirical studies of the role of pressure groups in the legislative, judicial, and administrative processes and in molding public opinion had become a major preoccupation of political scientists. However, this work was almost entirely devoid of theory; it usually looked for beneficiaries of a given policy and proceeded to ascribe the existence of the policy to that interest group. It did not explain why some groups were effectively represented in the political process and others were not, or which conditions led a pressure group to be successful in obtaining favorable legislation.

Since the early 1970s some economists (e.g., Stigler, 1971; Posner, 1974; Peltzman, 1976; Becker, 1983, 1985) and members of the Chicago Political Economy School (Tollison, 1989) have followed Bentley's insights, beginning the challenging work of building a general theory able to provide conditions that favor the existence of successful interest groups and explanations of the tactics of the parties to different regulatory policies. Chicago Political Economy is a body of literature that analyzes government from the perspective of price theory and positive economics. Traditionally, the paramount role assigned by economists to government regulation was to correct failures of the private market. Chicago Political Economy hypothesizes that the premier role of modern regulation is to redistribute income. Under this approach the state is a mechanism used by rational economic agents to redistribute wealth. This redistribution is the essence of government behavior.

The following section is devoted to illustrating Becker's contributions to this exciting area of inquiry.

2 The process of government revisited

Becker (1983, 1985) formalizes Bentley's framework, extends the original analysis, and develops many empirical implications. He assumes that individuals belong to particular groups, according to their common interests. These groups expend time and money on political advertising, campaign contributions, taking part in strikes, riots, terrorist acts, political assassinations, and so on, exerting political pressure to gain income transfers from other groups. Competition among interest groups determines the equilibrium structure of taxes and subsidies of the society. This political–economic equilibrium has the property that all groups maximize the well-being of their members by exerting their optimal level of political pressure, given the behavior of all other groups.

An appealing feature of this framework is that groups do not entirely win or lose, since taxed groups invest in political pressure to reduce their taxes until an additional dollar spent lobbying equals the induced reduction on their taxes. Since the government cannot give out more than it raises in revenue, that amount has to equal the total amount available for subsidies, and since the successful groups pay taxes, they are not completely subsidized either. This result differs from the all-or-nothing outcomes implied by majority rule models of political behavior where the majority wins and the minority fully loses.

Becker shows that the political–economic equilibrium depends on variables such as the efficiency of each interest group in producing political pressure, the social costs and benefits of taxes and subsidies, and the size of the groups. Let us examine each of these variables in a little more detail.

If a group increases its *efficiency* in producing political pressure, its optimal level of pressure would be raised for any level of pressure exerted by the other groups. An example of this is the control of free riding, which is an individual's temptation to evade his duties by imposing the burden of producing political pressure on the other members. Each member of a group has an incentive to free ride, and the larger the group, the more significant the problem, since it will be more costly to monitor each member's assignments. If a group has increased success at controlling free riding, then an additional dollar invested by each of its members would produce a larger effect on their well being – a smaller proportion of the marginal dollar would need to be devoted to the control of free riding and a larger to direct political activity.

Since the total amount raised from taxes has to equal the total amount available for subsidies, it is not possible to improve simultaneously the political achievement of all groups. Therefore, the political success of a particular group is not determined by its absolute accomplishment in the control over free riding, but by its relative accomplishment compared to the rest of the groups. If every group becomes more efficient in its control, then the political–economic equilibrium would not be largely modified.

Public policies produce *dead weight costs*, social costs that have no corresponding benefits to any party involved. These costs originate from the distortions induced by the transfers embodied in a given policy (for example, a regulation that increases the income of farmers through restrictions on the use of land would generate inefficient farming practices, or an increased tax on labor income would reduce the labor supply). Larger dead weight costs would reduce the political pressure exerted by subsidized groups because a given revenue from taxes yields a smaller increase in their incomes. In contrast, dead weight costs would increase the pressure exerted by taxpayers because they cause a reduction of their incomes larger than the tax revenue.

Therefore, an increase in the dead weight costs of taxes and subsidies would modify the political–economic equilibrium by reducing the transfers to the subsidized groups. The size of these transfers is limited by the fact that dead weight costs usually increase with the magnitude of the transfers. The findings of many empirical studies seem to be consistent with these predictions.

Under Becker's framework a dichotomy does not exist between the traditional view that governments correct market failures and the modern view that they favor successful interest groups. Actually, as Becker shows, the same analysis of competition among interest groups is also useful to explain governmental policies that correct market failures.

An interesting illustration of these market failures are externalities. An economic situation involves an externality if one agent cares directly about another agent's production or consumption. For example, a consumer could have strong preferences about the amount of pollution produced by others' automobiles. Similarly, a fishery cares about the amount of pollutants dumped into its fishing area, since they will affect its catch. The crucial feature of externalities is that there are goods people care about that are not sold on markets.

Public policies that correct market failures (like externalities) produce more social benefits than social costs. Therefore, they would increase the political pressure exerted by benefited groups because they yield a larger increase in their members' well-being than that gotten from the given revenue from taxes. By the same token, it would decrease the pressure exerted by taxed groups because it would induce a reduction in their members' well-being smaller than the tax revenue. This wedge between benefits and costs provides the groups benefited by this policy with an intrinsic advantage compared to the groups harmed. Therefore, policies that correct market failures are likely to be selected.

Therefore, while the existence of externalities is traditionally an example of why a government *must* intervene, it is, under Becker's framework, a fact that would explain *actual*, observable government behavior.

Quite frequently we hear that the *size of a group* is an important factor in its political success, since small groups are at a disadvantage because they do not have enough votes. There is substantial evidence against this statement; for example, in the agricultural sector. Agriculture is often heavily subsidized in industrial countries (e.g., the United States, European Economic Communities, Japan) where it is a relatively small sector.[2] By contrast, it is frequently heavily taxed in underdeveloped and developing countries, where it is a large sector.[3] Becker's findings are consistent with this type of evidence, since in his framework politically successful groups tend to be smaller than the groups taxed to pay their subsidies.

Becker's work shows an increase in the size of an interest group would produce two effects: i) It would affect its efficiency in producing political pressure; ii) It would reduce the dead weight costs of its taxes or subsidies.

An increase in the size of a group would affect its efficiency in producing political pressure because, on one hand, it would increase the cost of controlling free riding, and, on the other, it would allow the group to take full advantage of economies of scale. That is, in a very small group every member has to perform every task, so a modest increase in its size would allow its members to specialize, which would increase its efficiency in producing political pressure.

Becker argues that when the group is very small the second effect would usually prevail since economies of scale are very beneficial and free riding is not very costly. When the size of the group increases, the effects would reverse because free riding would become a problem and the advantages provided by economies of scale would have been realized. Beyond some point, both effects would become unimportant since further increases in size would induce little additional scale effects or free riding.

Regardless of the effect of the size of a group on its efficiency, a subsidized group would prefer to be financed by a large number of taxpayers because an increase in the size of the taxed group reduces the tax required on each member to obtain a given revenue. This fact would cut down the dead weight costs of taxation, reducing the political pressure exerted by the taxpayers.

In summary, Becker has contributed to eliminating the dichotomy between the traditional view that governments correct market failures and the modern view that they favor successful interest groups. In his framework political pressure tends to be greater from more efficient interest groups, from subsidized groups with small dead weight costs, and from taxed groups with large dead weight costs. These costs not only limit the relative size of the successful groups but also the size of the subsidies that they seek.

The interest-groups theory of government is quite old. Gary Becker has rejuvenated it by extending Bentley's analysis, developing many empirical implications, and motivating further research in the area. The following section discusses one application.

3 Political regime and government policy in Latin America

Most of the empirical work on the interest-groups approach to public policy has been focused on government's microeconomic policy, particularly on regulation. In contrast, this section discusses an application of interest-group theory to a macroeconomic issue – government budgets.

Democracy, while desirable, does not represent an appropriate description of the political regimes that have ruled most countries in the world during a large part of this century.[4] Actually, democracy should be considered an exception rather than the rule!

This fact highlights one major attribute of the interest-groups theory of government – its usefulness to explain public policies not only under democratic regimes but also under totalitarian ones, since it focuses on pressure groups instead of voters, politicians, and political parties. Under Bentley's framework, it is not adequate to talk of despotisms and democracies as absolutely distinct types of governments. Everything depends on the existing interests in each despotism and each democracy, their relations, and their modes of interaction.

However, the political success of particular interest groups is sensitive to the characteristics of the political regime, because they influence the rules under which the groups compete.[5] One usual form of restricting the extent to which popular will is reflected in decision-making institutions is by blocking access to the process of government from one part of the population. South Africa gave a clear illustration of this practice. The elimination of discrimination sharply affects the rules of the political game, and hence, its outcome. This was one critical factor in the white opposition to the complete elimination of political restrictions on blacks.

A change of political regime should bring a new political–economic equilibrium, since it will alter the rules under which the different interest groups compete.[6] This should be reflected in changes in government policies.

Many Latin American countries present regularities consistent with this hypothesis. For example, as Martin Paldam (1987) reports, inflation usually has followed a different path under military and civilian regimes. Paldam finds that inflation usually has grown under civilian regimes (eleven of thirteen cases) and declined under military ones (five of five cases).

A similar regularity is provided by David Greenaway and Chong Hyun Nam (1988), who examine the role of international trade in the process of industrialization and development. They classify forty-one developing countries in terms of their development strategy. Table 8.1 shows their classification of Latin American countries. Only two countries, Chile and Uruguay, present a significant shift in their development strategy between the two periods of analysis; in both of them a change of political regime (a successful military coup d'etat) occurred in 1973.

Table 8.1. *Classification of Latin American countries in terms of their development strategies, 1965–73, 1973–85*

Strategies	1965–73	1973–85
Strong outward oriented	—	—
Moderately outward oriented	Brazil, Colombia, Costa Rica, Guatemala	Brazil, *Chile*, *Uruguay*
Moderately inward oriented	Bolivia, El Salvador, Honduras, Mexico, Nicaragua	Costa Rica, Colombia, El Salvador, Honduras, Guatemala, Mexico, Nicaragua
Strongly inward oriented	Argentina, *Chile*, Dominican Republic, Peru, *Uruguay*	Argentina, Bolivia, Dominican Republic, Peru

Source: David Greenaway and Chong Hyun Nam, 1988.

Similar regularities can be found by case studies, centering our attention on the economic histories of individual countries. Commercial policy in Argentina, for example, seems to have been modified after changes of political regimes during the last thirty years.

To illustrate, I formed an indicator of the degree of "closedness" of the economy, which equals the degree of difference between domestic and international prices.[7] A value greater than zero indicates the existence of an inward-looking policy. The larger the coefficient, the more intense the inward-looking strategy. During the thirty years since World War II the coefficient has grown systematically under civilian regimes and declined under military ones. Table 8.2 summarizes these findings.

Table 8.2. *Coefficient of closedness*

Period	Regimen	Average	Trend
1946/55	Democratic	0.56	—
1956/8	Military	0.27	Decreasing
1959/61	Democratic	0.29	Increasing
1962	Military	0.26	Decreasing
1963/6	Democratic	0.35	Increasing
1967/72	Military	0.31	Decreasing
1973/5	Democratic	0.42	Increasing

Source: Edgardo Zablotsky, September 1992.

These regularities motivate the search for a test of the influence of changes in the rules of the game on the political–economic equilibrium. To study that, I use an index that reflects changes in the outcome of the political game. The indicator,[8] suggested by Katz and Rosenberg (1989), measures the responsiveness of the composition of government expenditure to pressure groups. Assuming that every change in the proportion of the budget spent for a given purpose is due to interest group pressure, the bigger the change in the outcome of the political game, the higher the index should be. Table 8.3 shows that the index tended to increase when there was a change of regime, but remained unchanged when there was just a change of ruler (holding fixed the characteristics of the regime). This is evidence in support of the Bentley approach to public policy.

Table 8.3. *The Bentley approach: some empirical support*

Type of change	Index was increased	Index was not modified
Changes of regimes:		
Military coups d'etat overthrow democratic regimes	5	1
Democratic regimes are restored	5	2
Mass revolutions	1	0
Total	11	3
Changes of rulers:		
Military coups d'etat overthrow military regimes	1	3
Democratic presidential transitions	2	10
Total	3	13

Source: Edgardo Zablotsky, June 1992.

A better understanding of the process of government is an essential requirement to achieve a better understanding of economic life. This is a major motivation for further research in this exciting area of inquiry, motivation that inspired Arthur Bentley's seminal work close to a century ago.

If I may be pardoned a remark from my own experience, I will say that my interest in politics is not primary, but derived from my interest in the economic life; and that I hope from this point of approach ultimately to gain a better understanding of the economic life that I have succeeded in gaining hitherto (Arthur Bentley, 1908, p. 210).

Notes

1 I want to thank Mariano Tommasi and Kathryn Ierulli for very helpful comments.
2 "In the United States, the government pays farmers not to grow grain; in the European Communities, farmers are paid high prices even if they produce excessive amounts. In Japan, rice farmers receive three times the world price for their crop; they grow so much that some of it has to be sold as animal feed at half of the world price ... The main objectives of agricultural policies in industrial countries are to stabilize and increase farmers' incomes and slow the migration of people out of the sector" (World Bank, 1986, p. 110).
3 "Paradoxically, many countries which have been stressing the importance of agricultural development have established a complex set of policies that is strongly biased against agriculture. Thus, some developing countries impose taxes on agricultural exports while lamenting the adverse impact of declining commodity prices on the farm sector. Some pay their producers half the world price for grains ... Many subsidize consumers to help the poor, but end up reducing the incomes of farmers who are much poorer than many of the urban consumers who actually benefit from the subsidies. Most developing countries pronounce self-sufficiency as an important objective, but follow policies that tax farmers, subsidize consumers, and increase dependence upon imported food" (World Bank, 1986, p. 61).
4 "Most governments in the world today are dictatorships of one sort or another ... The average person in our society knows of dictatorships, or autocratic governments, only that they are bad things. I don't deny that they are bad, but they are very, very common" (Gordon Tullock, 1987, pp. 1, 12).
5 "Groups compete within the context of rules that translate expenditures on political pressure into political influence and access to political resources. These rules may be embodied in political constitutions and other political procedures, including perhaps rules about the use of force to seize power" (Gary Becker, 1983, p. 374).
6 For example, a military coup d'etat that overthrows a democratic regime will alter these rules, since the immediate consequence of the overthrow of a

democratic regime will be the establishment of a dictatorship; a situation which will drastically modify the structure of the political organization of society (e.g., the Parliament will be closed, the political parties and the labor unions proscribed, anti-government demonstrations and strikes forbidden, etc.).

7 It measures the deviation of domestic prices from international prices due to protectionist measures such as tariffs and quotas. It is 1 minus the ratio of internal to external terms of trade (see Diaz Alejandro, 1981).

8 The index is defined:

$$\text{Index}_t = \tfrac{1}{2} \sum |S(t)_i - S(t-1)_i| \qquad i = 1 \ldots n$$

where $S(t)_i$, $S(t-1)_i$ are the proportions of the government's budget going to purpose i in years t and $t-1$ respectively, and n is the number of categories in the budget. Thus, its value in year t represents the total sum of the absolute changes in the proportion allocated to the different categories in year t over year $t-1$.

References

Becker, Gary. 1983. "A Theory of Competition Among Pressure Groups for Political Influence," *Quarterly Journal of Economics*, 98(3) (August).

    1985. "Public Policies, Pressure Groups, and Deadweight Costs," *Journal of Public Economics*, 28(3) (December).

Bentley, Arthur. 1908. *The Process of Government*, Chicago: University of Chicago Press.

Diaz Alejandro, Carlos. 1981. "Tipo de Cambio y Términos de Intercambio en la República Argentina 1913–1976," Center for Macroeconomic Studies of Argentina, Working Paper, No. 22, March.

Greenaway, David and Chong Hyun Nam. 1988. "Industrialization and Macroeconomic Performance in Developing Countries Under Alternative Trade Strategies," Kyklos, 41(3).

Katz, Eliakim and Rosenberg, Jacob. 1989. "Rent Seeking for Budgetary Allocation: Preliminary Results for 20 Countries," *Public Choice*, no. 60.

Mitchell, William. 1989. "Chicago Political Economy: A Public Choice Perspective," *Public Choice*, 63(3).

Odegard, Peter. 1967. "Introduction," in Arthur Bentley, *The Process of Government*, Cambridge, MA: The Belknap Press of Harvard University Press,

Paldam, Martin. 1987. "Inflation and Political Instability in Eight Latin American Countries, 1946–83," *Public Choice*, no. 52 (Spring).

Peltzman, Sam. 1976. "Towards a More General Theory of Regulation," *Journal of Law and Economics*, 19(2) (August).

Posner, Richard. 1974. "Theories of Economic Regulation," *Bell Journal of Economics* (Autumn).

Stigler, George. 1971. "The Economics of Regulation," *Bell Journal of Economics* (Spring).

    1988. *Chicago Studies on Political Economy*. Chicago and London: University of Chicago Press.

Tollison, Robert. 1989. "Chicago Political Economy," *Public Choice*, 63(3).

Tullock, Gordon. 1987. *Autocracy*, Dordrecht, The Netherlands: Kluwer Academic Publishers.

World Bank. 1986. *World Development Report 1986*, July, New York: Oxford University Press.

Zablotsky, Edgardo. "A Bentley's Approach to Public Policy. Some Empirical Support," Center for Macroeconomic Studies of Argentina, Working Paper No. 83, June 1992.

La Ley de Sufragio Universal, Secreto y Obligatorio. Su Efecto Sobre la Política Económica Argentina, International Center for Economic Growth (ed.), September 1992.

9 The economic approach to democracy[1]

John G. Matsusaka

Democracy is the worst form of government, except for all
those other forms that have been tried from time to time.

Winston Churchill

1 Introduction

Democracy, as taught in high school civics classes, is a beautiful thing. Citizens keep abreast of the news and when an election comes they listen to what the candidates have to say, discuss the issues among themselves, and come to a decision. On election day, they go to the polls and vote for their representatives. These representatives, commissioned by the electorate to work for the public good, meet in the capitals. They gather and discuss the important issues of the day. After a balanced airing of views and suitable reflection about which policies will advance the national interest, the laws are passed and implemented, and the common good is achieved.

Democracy in practice appears to be an ugly thing. Few citizens keep abreast of the news and even fewer listen to what political candidates have to say. Voter ignorance about the issues is widespread. Political debate is often short on substance and long on symbols. In some circles politics is even considered impolite conversation. On election day, it is remarkable how many citizens do *not* vote: almost 50 percent in presidential elections and up to 70 percent in local elections. The representatives do gather in the capitals to discuss the issues of the day, but public discussions and debates are almost cursory. Most laws are not passed after an impartial evaluation of their social merits. Rather they originate from closed-door deals, and often benefit special interests. Representatives appear to pay as much attention to lobbyists representing well-organized political action groups as they do to common citizens.

The clash of the civics class version of democracy and the version we observe in the United States has led some to bemoan the lack of civic virtue and presage the decline of American civilization. More productively, it has also led to investigation of political behavior by social scientists. One of the most exciting, and perhaps the most fruitful, of these lines of inquiry is the

140

economic approach, which originated with the celebrated book by Anthony Downs, *An Economic Theory of Democracy*, in 1957.

Economics is a theory of human behavior. Its central premise is that *people have objectives that they try to achieve in the least costly way*. Put more starkly, the heart of the economic approach is the assumption that people undertake activities only if the benefits exceed the costs, where both benefits and costs are defined relative to an objective. The economic approach is sometimes misinterpreted to imply that people only care about money. It is important to bear in mind that the relevant benefits and costs may not be monetary. For example, a candidate running for office evaluates his actions in terms of how much they are likely to contribute to his votes, not to his income.

The central premise of the economic approach is sometimes shortened to say simply that people are rational. It pays to be aware that the word "rational" takes on different meanings in other (non-economic) contexts. As used in economics, the rationality assumption is not an assertion that people are all-knowing or never make mistakes. It simply says that people pursue their objectives in a way that appears to them to be the most efficacious.

This chapter discusses a variety of political actions from an economic point of view. In particular, the implications of individual rationality for citizen and representative behavior are explored. It might seem odd at first to introduce the idea of rationality in a context that many believe is plagued by irrationality. But the proof is in the pudding – as the rest of the chapter shows, the economic approach has great power in explaining why we see the political behavior we do. This is its sustaining virtue. The economic approach also leads to an overall evaluation of democracy that shares Churchill's sentiments. It suggests that in spite of the widespread apathy of citizens and the pervasive influence of pressure groups, democracy works fairly well.[2]

2 Voter turnout

The central act in democracy is voting. Yet only 55 percent of eligible Americans chose to cast a vote in the 1992 presidential election. The numbers were even lower for other races. In California, for example, participation in the two US senate races was 52 percent of the eligible population. Turnout for the state's fifty-two congressional races was 51 percent. These numbers look high compared to voter turnout in primary elections. Only 26 percent voted in the presidential primary and 29 percent in the senate primaries.

Why do so many citizens choose not to exercise one of their fundamental rights as citizens? The answer, according to the economic approach, is simple: some people abstain because their cost of voting exceeds the benefit. The cost of voting is mostly a time cost. A person has to make time to register, read up on the candidates, and go to the polls. These costs are admittedly small for most people, but so are the benefits. The benefit to voting is that a person's vote might lead to the election of the candidate of his choice. The benefit in this sense is virtually zero because one vote never decides an election. There is always the chance, of course, that the outcome of an election will hinge on a single vote, but the rational citizen is aware that for all practical purposes his vote will not affect the outcome of the election. Thus, unless he receives a psychic benefit from voting (such as satisfaction that he has done his "duty"), he abstains if there is even a small cost.

There is abundant evidence that citizens employ this kind of benefit–cost calculation when deciding whether or not to vote. For example, one important cost of voting is the time it takes to register. The economic approach implies that participation goes up when registration costs go down. In fact, turnout in Minnesota and Wisconsin (where people can register to vote on the same day as the election) and North Dakota (where registration is not required) is on average 10 to 15 percent higher than in other states. Numerous researchers have found significant positive effects on turnout from a variety of other policies that lower the cost of registering and voting: allowing registration closer to election day, eliminating poll taxes and literacy requirements, keeping longer hours at registration offices, purging election rolls less frequently, and so on.[3] In countries like Australia and Belgium where citizens are required by law to vote – that is, where it is costly *not* to vote – turnout regularly runs in the 85 to 90 percent range.

Another cost that plays a role in whether or not a person votes is the cost of becoming sufficiently informed to decide which way to vote. The cost of information is not a cost of voting per se because there is nothing to prevent a perfectly ignorant person from voting. However, few citizens find it satisfying to vote in elections that they know nothing about. This is why so many people abstain in obscure local races, like those for judges, port commissioners, school boards, and so on.[4]

The importance of information costs in the turnout decision enjoys abundant empirical support. Perhaps the most well-documented voting regularity is that turnout is higher for more educated and older people.[5] Education and age confer stocks of general knowledge, knowledge that makes it easier to process and evaluate political information. In effect, people with more education and older people have lower costs of acquiring information that allows them to come to a voting decision. Conversely, young people have limited stocks of knowledge and correspondingly high costs of processing information, which explains why they have lower participation rates than the rest of the population.

Another empirical regularity is that campaign spending increases voter turnout. This can also be understood from the perspective of information costs. Most campaign spending takes the form of political advertising, which is nothing more than free information for voters. The more of this free information that the candidates provide, the less costly it is for a citizen to make his voting decision, and the more likely he is to vote. Some additional issues relating to the content of political advertising (or lack thereof) are discussed in section 3.

As mentioned above, one reason a citizen abstains is because he believes he cannot affect the outcome. Another reason to abstain is because he expects that the outcome of the election will be to his satisfaction even without his vote. This has implications for participation on ballot propositions. If the issue on a ballot involves a decision that everyone is likely to agree about then the abstention rate will be high. For example, if an election were held on what type of O-rings to use on the space shuttle, abstention would be high. Everyone wants the type of O-rings that will not lead to an explosion. The rational decision for most people, then, is to sit out the election and leave it to those voters with scientific expertise to make the decision. Similar, but more realistic, issues include such things as court jurisdictions and civil service. At the other extreme are issues about which there is fundamental disagreement, for example, issues about tax burdens and moral issues like abortion. For these issues, people are less willing to delegate their decisions (as it were), which leads to higher turnout. I recently documented such behavior for California ballot propositions.[6] Eight hundred and seventy-one measures were identified that had appeared on the ballot from 1912 to 1989. The measures were divided into groups based on how similar people's preferences about the outcomes were likely to be. I found that citizens were 10 percent more likely to vote on issues involving fundamental disagreement than issues where preferences were similar.

3 Voter ignorance

Few will dispute that the average citizen is poorly informed about political matters. Politics is a once-every-four-years diversion for everyone but politicians, academics, and political junkies. Moreover, political campaigns and media coverage do not convey much substantive information about policy issues. They tend to focus on personal or symbolic issues.

There is a good reason the economic citizen remains largely ignorant of political matters even though they can have a large impact on his life. It is the same reason the economic citizen often abstains from voting: the benefit to acquiring information is less than the cost. Critics of voter ignorance often fail to appreciate how costly it is to collect information. To become sufficiently informed to evaluate the nuances of candidate positions on even one issue can take weeks. Some scholars spend years studying a single issue without coming to a definitive conclusion. Against this substantial cost of acquiring information, the economic citizen can see very little benefit. The information he acquires can help him to make a better decision in the voting booth, but because his vote is unlikely to matter in any event, he is not overly concerned with the possibility of making a mistake. In short, facing substantial costs and minuscule benefits, the economic citizen chooses to remain ignorant.

Even so, the economic citizen would like to have at least a little information – he does not want to vote from a position of complete ignorance. Once the economic citizen gives up the idea of becoming informed enough about the issues to evaluate candidates on their policy positions, he looks for other kinds of information to guide his voting decision. Given limited information, an attractive way to pick a candidate is on the basis of personal or symbolic issues. The citizen reasons that if a particular candidate is "just like me" there is a good chance he will implement the sorts of policies the citizen himself would choose (if he was as informed as a representative). As a result, a citizen may choose to pay close attention to the personal characteristics of candidates. The citizen may also look to see how the candidates stand on certain symbolic issues that are not too important in the grand scheme of things, like flag burning and the death penalty, in order to determine which candidate has similar values.

A "just like me" method of choosing a candidate is unlikely to yield as accurate a choice as detailed study of the issues and positions would. But one of the great advantages of representative government is that the average citizen does not need to be a policy expert – that is the representative's job, to specialize in policy formation. Given the cost of information, then, it is easy to understand why political campaigns invariably center on personal and symbolic issues. In contrast to the conventional wisdom, however, the economic approach considers this a reasonable way to hold an election. The electorate is given a relatively inexpensive way to decide which candidate is "just like me."

Voters have another important way to make the right decision without being very informed. They can pay attention to endorsements. Endorsements work on the same principle as other political information. First, a citizen must identify a person or organization who he believes has the same values (is "just like me"). For example, an environmentalist may choose the

Sierra Club. The endorser carefully evaluates the candidates and the issues and boils down all the information to a bottom-line recommendation. The endorsing person or group in effect is acting as an information economizer. In fact, most voters pay close attention to the advice of others who are more informed, especially to political parties. If a citizen manages to find a person or group who represents his interests, he can cast the right vote *even if he has no information about the candidates or the issues*. That is, even though he has no information he can cast his vote exactly as if he had full information. Thus, the fact that the average citizen is fairly uninformed in no way implies that his voting decision is unintelligent.

This may seem rather theoretical. Fortunately, there is hard evidence that popular votes reflect efficient information processing by the electorate. Or put more crudely, there is statistical evidence that voters are sophisticated enough to cast the right vote in spite of their ignorance. The evidence appears in a remarkable study by Sam Peltzman.[7] The study focused on the relation between macroeconomic factors like aggregate income and inflation and votes for president, governor, and senator from 1950 to 1988. The main question was how well voters use aggregate data to "settle up" with elected officials. Does the electorate punish representatives who deliver poor economic performance?

Peltzman found broad evidence consistent with voter rationality. One finding was that increases in output and decreases in inflation at any point in a president's, governor's, or senator's term in office was rewarded when he (or his party's subsequent nominee) stood for reelection. Thus, voters do not have short memories as some have suggested. They do not focus solely on events in the few months immediately preceding the election. The second finding was that voters rewarded increases in permanent income and did not reward increases in transitory income. Thus, the electorate is not fooled by pump-priming before an election. Third, modern macroeconomic wisdom holds that unexpected inflation is more costly than expected inflation (individuals can adjust their contracts to take into account expected inflation). Vote totals were found to reflect this as well – increases in unexpected inflation cost the incumbent votes but increases in expected inflation did not. The president is likely to have more control over aggregate income than over the income of any particular state. This is because there are idiosyncratic factors involved in a particular state's income, like discovery of oil. The rational voter should not reward or punish the president for the idiosyncratic fluctuations in state income, but only for fluctuations that are linked to aggregate income. Peltzman found evidence for this as well. Taken together, the results are consistent with efficient use of information by voters, or in Peltzman's words, "the broad picture that emerges here is of self-interested voters who correctly process relevant information. Indeed, one would be hard put to find nonpolitical markets that process information better than the voting market."

4 Representatives

How do elected representatives decide which bills to support and which to oppose? According to the economic approach, they decide on the basis of the benefits and the costs. At first this might seem perplexing: why should there be a benefit or a cost to a representative, other than the satisfaction of doing the right thing or the guilt of doing the wrong thing?

The primary concern of a successful representative is getting elected. Whatever his ideology and whatever policies he hopes to implement, nothing can be achieved if he loses his office. Thus, the central objective of a representative is to maximize the votes he receives in the next election. To be sure, some representatives will forego vote maximization in order to cast votes in favor of causes that are of personal interest to them, but such actions will be infrequent or the representatives will enjoy only a short stay in office. For this reason, at any point in time a typical legislature acts in such a way as to increase the votes of its members.

The main consequence of vote maximization is that it leads a representative to try to implement policies that please his constituents. The more a senator can deliver to his home state, the more likely he will be reelected. Thus, representatives seldom give their ideologies free rein, nor are they particularly concerned with vague notions of the "national interest" (except insofar as ideological and national concerns coincide with the interests of their constituents). Instead, their attention is focused on how proposed legislation benefits their constituents. The economic approach, then, tends to agree with former House Speaker Tip O'Neill's assertion that "all politics is local."[8]

The economic approach suggests that public debate by legislators serves primarily to remind a representative's constituents that he is fighting for their interests. Issues are seldom settled on the basis of these debates nor do they provide much useful information for a legislator's decision. Further, rhetoric to the contrary, policies are not often chosen based on their merits to the country as a whole (supposing this is a well-defined idea). Rather, they are decided on the basis of the local benefits they deliver to each legislator's constituents.

An interesting study by Peter Pashigian highlights the primacy of local interests.[9] In the study, Pashigian investigated congressional votes on amendments to the Clean Air Act. The Clean Air Act, passed in 1970, set minimum national air quality standards that were uniform across the country. In order to meet the national standard, states with dirty air had to impose tough emission controls on industrial producers and utilities. These states, located primarily in the northeast and Great Lakes regions, were concerned that pollution regulation might cause industry to relocate to states with clean air. Pashigian's study focused on amendments to the act that required regions with cleaner air than the national standard to prevent significant deterioration of existing air quality (called PSD standards). In effect, regions that started out with clean air were to be held to a tougher standard than regions with dirty air. A predictable consequence of the PSD standards was to prevent industry from moving from the polluted states to clean air states in the south and west.

We might expect that votes on an issue like this were determined by environmental ideology and concerns over the national interest, but Pashigian found that local interests were dominant. Over 70 percent of congressmen from the northeast supported tough PSD standards, and the standards commanded substantial support from rust belt congressmen as well. Tougher standards were opposed by more than 70 percent of the congressmen from all regions of the south, and over 60 percent of those from the mountain west. These voting patterns fit nicely into the economic framework. Clearly, each congressman was paying close attention to the effects of the amendments on his constituents.

In light of the discussion above concerning voter ignorance, it is natural to ask whether vote maximization is really likely to lead representatives to pursue constituent interests. A representative will do the right thing for his constituents as long as he thinks they will notice and reward him with reelection. If constituents have as little information as it seems and as theory predicts, how is the good senator going to be identified and reelected and the bad senator replaced?

In answer to this question, it is noted above that although voters are ignorant about issues, they may still be able to cast the right vote if they have access to endorsements. From a representative's point of view, then, it is not essential that each voter be kept informed of his actions on behalf of the voter, but only that some person or group the voter trusts observes the action. Thus, a representative with many environmentalists in his district makes sure to confer with representatives of the Sierra Club before and after an important environmental vote. This points out again the central role played by organized interest groups in the political system. Equally important, it shows that the ignorance of individual voters does not in principle prevent them from rewarding a representative who looks out for their interests.

The desire for reelection pushes representatives to pursue the interests of their constituents. But it would be an exaggeration to say that the process leads to perfect representation. Because of voter ignorance, a representative has at least a little leeway to act in opposition to voter interests.[10] In a recent study of state fiscal behavior from 1960 to 1990, I compared the state and local governmental finances of states that allow citizens to initiate and pass laws by popular vote ("direct legislation" states) and states that allow laws to be passed only by an elected legislature ("pure representative" states).[11] I found that direct legislation states have lower levels of government expenditure than pure representative states. This implies that representatives systematically spend more than the electorate would like. My estimates of the excess were on the order of 4 percent for combined state and local expenditure and 12 percent for expenditure by state governments alone. In another study over the same time period, Sam Peltzman showed that governors who presided over spending and tax increases were punished at the polls.[12] Thus, the voters are aware of and settle up with these undesirable actions when their representatives pursue them. However, the settling up does not appear to be strong enough to entirely deter the objectionable activity.

The economic approach does not condone or condemn vote-maximizing behavior – the main objective is to understand the consequences of such behavior. Still, it is worth noting that there is something to be said for vote maximization. The desire to be reelected leads representatives to pay close attention to the desires of constituents. This is, after all, the way democracy is supposed to work.

5 Policies

The economic approach helps us to understand the political actions (or inactions) of citizens in a democracy and sheds light on the behavior of elected representatives. The actual policies of a democratic government result from the interaction of citizens and representatives. We have seen above that these policies tend to reflect constituent interests. This section evaluates *which* constituents' interests are the most influential in determining policy outcomes.

A central implication of the economic approach is that policies at some level always reflect the interaction of political pressure groups.[13] In a democracy, pressure groups function as the key intermediaries between citizens and their representatives. First, they monitor legislators and convey this information to the voters. Second, they keep legislators informed about the wishes of their constituents. The term "pressure group" here and below is taken to include not only registered lobbying organizations and political action groups, but also grass roots movements, community organizations, church groups, and the like.

The groups that exert the most pressure on a particular issue will have the issue resolved in their favor. Pressure in a democracy ultimately derives from the ability to deliver votes at the next election because votes are what ultimately matters to representatives. A group can deliver votes in two ways. The most effective way is to endorse a candidate and motivate group members to go to the polls and vote for the candidate. The other way is to contribute money to a candidate's election campaign. Candidates do not value contributions in themselves, but rather for their ability to generate votes. The more money a candidate has available to spend, the more he is able to get his message out to his supporters.

It should be noted that although pressure groups are often disparaged, sometimes considered a sickness in the body politic, from an economic point of view they are the lifeblood of democracy. Pressure is how constituents ensure that their representatives pay attention to their interests. Absent pressure by political groups, the rational ignorance of the electorate would free representatives to pursue objectives unrelated to the interests of their constituents.

Pressure tends to push policy in the direction of the greatest good for the greatest number. Other things equal, large groups are able to exert more pressure (deliver more votes) than small groups. Causes that people care the most about are able to attract the most funds to contribute to campaigns. Both effects push representatives to implement policies that are the most important to the greatest number of people. This is not inconsistent with democratic ideals.

Nevertheless, casual observation reveals there are many policies that benefit small groups at the expense of the majority. This is made possible by the rational ignorance and abstention of the average citizen. His passivity gives a political edge to small groups that are well organized and can keep their members informed and motivated.

Large groups are also disadvantaged by what is called the free-rider problem. When a member of a group exerts effort to achieve a policy favorable to his group, he is providing a benefit not only to himself but also to everyone else in his group. For small groups, members know each other, monitor each other, and encourage each to pull his weight. For large groups, however, individuals have an incentive to "free ride" on the efforts of others rather than exert effort of their own. Another way to see this important point is to note that in a small group, each member is aware that the ultimate success of the group may depend on his contribution. In a large group, any one individual's action is unlikely to be decisive for the group's success.

The free-rider problem implies that small groups have an advantage over large groups in organizing their members. This does not guarantee that they are able to exert more pressure, however, because they are numerically smaller. Small size may in the end prevent a group from delivering substantial pressure. The logic of collective action so described does give an explanation of how tiny groups can sometimes gain benefits at the expense of the rest of the population.

A notable example is sugar growers. Because of government import protection, the price of sugar in the United States is several times what it is in the rest of the world. The high price hurts American consumers while providing a benefit to sugar growers. The sugar interests are able to exert more pressure than consumer interests because sugar growers are a small, well-organized group and the stakes are individually high to them, while consumers are a large group, prone to free-riding problems, and the cost to individual consumers of the sugar protection program is small. Thus, sugar growers, although they comprise only a tiny fraction of the population, are able to impose huge aggregate costs on the rest of the population in order to capture private benefits. Prices for most agricultural products, for example, dairy products, honey, peanuts, and oranges, are supported by the US government, costing consumers billions each year. The benefits from agricultural subsidies accrue to a tiny minority – farmers make up less than 3 percent of the population. This is testimony to the organizational advantages of small groups.

The economic approach can explain why so often government regulation appears to benefit the regulated industry. Industry groups are small and organized and stand to gain a lot individually while consumer groups are large and poorly organized. This observation gave rise to the "capture" theory of regulation, that was developed to explain why so many regulatory boards appear to be acting in the interests of the regulated industry. A notable example of this phenomenon was the Civil Aeronautics Board (CAB), established in 1933 to regulate the airline industry. For most of its history the CAB was devoted to promoting the interests of the airline industry. Entry was essentially prohibited – the CAB did not allow a new trunk airline to enter the industry after 1936 – and competition was restricted. As a result consumers paid high prices and airlines enjoyed huge profits.

There are many other examples of regulations that were promoted as being in the public interest but that turned out to benefit primarily industry groups. One of the earliest and most influential studies of this phenomenon was published by George Stigler and Claire Friedland in 1962.[14] The study concerned the regulation of electric utilities. Electric utilities were essentially unregulated until public service commissions were established in New York and Wisconsin in 1907. An ostensible purpose of regulation was to guarantee low electricity prices to consumers. Studying the period from 1912 to 1937, during which almost all electric utilities came to be regulated,

Stigler and Friedland found that prices did not change after regulation. More surprisingly, and in contrast to the idea of consumer protection, the utilities with the lowest prices were the first to be regulated. A third finding was that stockholders of regulated companies did better than stockholders of unregulated companies. The market value of sixteen regulated firms rose on average by 312 percent over 1907–20, while the market value of unregulated utilities rose only 250 percent over the same period. A final discovery was that regulated utilities tended to provide cheap electricity to industrial and commercial users, and relatively high prices to domestic consumers. This led Stigler to conclude some years later that the prime beneficiaries of electric utility regulation were industrial users.

Turning to more modern examples, one of today's most influential pressure groups is senior citizens. The influence of this group has turned the social security program from a social insurance retirement program to a full-scale transfer of wealth from non-retired people to retirees. On average, a retiree is repaid the value of his lifetime contributions after only three years. Because most live well beyond this point, senior citizens now end up collecting several times what they originally contributed.

Another influential group is public school teachers. Public school teachers are government employees so all aspects of their work are regulated and susceptible to political pressure. Real wages of teachers rose 3.3 percent faster than the wages of the rest of the labor force from 1960 to 1983. The teacher lobby also managed to push down the average class size from 25.8 students to 19.0 students over the period 1960–80, despite research evidence that such reductions in class size do not improve student learning.[15]

6 Conclusions

The economic approach suggests some interesting conclusions about the nature of politics. Consider a policy that would make every single person in the country better off. Clearly there would be some pressure in favor of this policy, no pressure against it, and it would be implemented in short order. It follows that if there are any programs of this sort, they are already in effect. The flip side is that there are no unenacted policies that would make every single person better off. Thus, any new policy is detrimental to some group in society. Economists have a term for social outcomes with this property: Pareto optimal. We can summarize the preceding discussion by saying that democratic outcomes are Pareto optimal.

There is more to this than meets the eye. First, it implies that *all politics is distributional*. Any issue that takes center stage invariably involves the tradeoff of one group's interests for another's. That there are winners and losers from any new policy will not be disputed by many. Still, it is remarkable how often interest groups try to portray policy debates as battles between the national interest and special interests. Or, noting that everyone has special interests, perhaps it should be said that special interests *are* the national interest.

Second, the view that government outcomes are Pareto optimal helps to clarify the role of government. Consider a situation where the Pentagon pays a Navy contractor hundreds of dollars for a hammer. Critics would say that the Pentagon is not behaving optimally. The critics are correct if the objective of the Pentagon is to build a ship in the least costly way. However, unlike private businesses, the government's objective is not to minimize costs. If it were then there would be no welfare payments, housing subsidies, or agriculture subsidies.

According to the economic approach, a $300 payment for a hammer to a defense contractor should be seen as a subsidy to the contractor, just like sugar price supports are a subsidy to sugar growers and welfare checks are a subsidy to the poor. Judged by a cost-minimization objective, all these programs are suboptimal. However, each of these programs is likely to be the most efficient way to deliver favors to the groups exerting pressure, and this is the sense in which they are optimal. We might disagree with subsidies to these groups, but that does not mean the payments are inefficient means to effect them.

In the end, the economic approach suggests that democracy in practice is not as hopeless as it might appear when compared to the high school civics class ideal. True, it implies that citizens and representatives pay as much attention to their own narrow interests as they do to the interests of others in society. Through and through, their decisions are guided by a tradeoff between benefits and costs. Thus, the civics class ideal of saintly citizens and representatives who consistently forsake their own interests in order to pursue the common good cannot be found. However, the policy outcomes that result from rational behavior may not be that far from the civics class ideal. A key insight of the economic approach is that by pursuing their self-interest, citizens and representatives adopt policies that tend to be in their collective interest. These policies are somewhat optimal in that they do not omit programs that would make everyone better off. Moreover, they tend to trade off group interests on the basis of group size and intensity of preference. This is more or less what democracy is supposed to achieve.

Notes

1 I thank Lee Fischman, Thomas Gilligan, and Mariano Tommasi for helpful comments.

2 The economic approach holds that individual rationality is a general characteristic of human behavior – it is not restricted to particular persons, places, or times. However, for concreteness, the discussion in the chapter focuses on the United States.

3 Two notable studies are John E. Filer, Lawrence W. Kenny, and Rebecca B. Morton. 1991. "Voting Laws, Educational Policies, and Minority Turnout," *Journal of Law and Economics*, 34 (October): 371–93; and Raymond E. Wolfinger, David P. Glass, and Peverill Squire. 1990. "Predictors of Electoral Turnout: An International Comparison," *Policy Studies Review*, 9 (Spring): 551–74.

4 This reasoning is developed in detail in John G. Matsusaka, "Explaining Voter Turnout Patterns: An Information Theory," *Public Choice*, forthcoming.

5 Raymond E. Wolfinger and Steven J. Rosenstone, *Who Votes?*, New Haven: Yale University Press, 1980.

6 John G. Matsusaka. 1992. "Economics of Direct Legislation," *Quarterly Journal of Economics*, 107 (May): 541–71.

7 Sam Peltzman. 1990. "How Efficient is the Voting Market?" *Journal of Law and Economics*, 33 (April): 27–63.

8 Thomas P. O'Neill, Jr. with William Novak. 1987. *Man of the House: The Life and Political Memoirs of Speaker Tip O'Neill*, New York: Random House.

9 B. Peter Pashigian. 1985. "Environmental Regulation: Whose Self-Interests Are Being Protected?" *Economic Inquiry*, 23 (October): 551–84. There are many other studies that have documented the link between representative behavior and constituent interests, notably, Sam Peltzman. 1984. "Constituent Interest and Congressional Voting," *Journal of Law and Economics*, 27 (April): 181–210; and Thomas W. Gilligan, William J. Marshall, and Barry R. Weingast. 1989. "Regulation and the Theory of Legislative Choice," *Journal of Law and Economics*, 32, (April): 35–61.

10 Joseph P. Kalt and Mark A. Zupan. 1984. "Capture and Ideology in the Economic Theory of Politics," *American Economic Review*, 74 (June): 279–300; and Joseph P. Kalt and Mark A. Zupan. 1990. "The Apparent Ideological Behavior of Legislators: Testing for Principal–Agent Slack in Political Institutions," *Journal of Law and Economics*, 33 (April): 103–31.

11 John G. Matsusaka. 1994. "Fiscal Effects of the Voter Initiative: Evidence From the Last 30 Years," USC School of Business Administration Working Paper No. 93–17, March.

12 Sam Peltzman. 1992. "Voters as Fiscal Conservatives," *Quarterly Journal of Economics*, 107 (May): 327–61. As an interesting aside, George Bush's defeat in the 1992 presidential election is consistent with these results because federal spending under the Bush administration grew faster than under any previous administration since Franklin Roosevelt's.

13 Gary S. Becker. 1983. "A Theory of Competition Among Pressure Groups for Political Influence," *Quarterly Journal of Economics*, 98: 371–400; and Gary S. Becker. 1985. "Public Policies, Pressure Groups, and Dead Weight Costs," *Journal of Public Economics*, 28: 329–47.

14 George J. Stigler and Claire Friedland. 1962. "What Can Regulators Regulate? The Case of Electricity," *Journal of Law and Economics*, 5: 1–16. Reprinted in George J. Stigler, *The Citizen and the State*, Chicago, IL: University of Chicago Press.
15 Eric A. Hanushek. 1986. "The Economics of Schooling," *Journal of Economic Literature*, 24 (September): 1141–77.

V

Health, religion, and mass behavior

10 The economic approach to addictive behavior

Michael Grossman

1 Introduction

Much of Gary Becker's recent work has focused on the economic approach to addictive behaviors, particularly harmfully addictive behaviors (Becker and Murphy, 1988; Becker, Grossman, and Murphy, 1991; Becker, 1992; Becker, Grossman, and Murphy, 1994; Chaloupka, Grossman, Becker, and Murphy, 1993). Examples of these behaviors are cigarette smoking; gambling; consumption of such illegal drugs as heroin, marijuana, and cocaine; and excessive alcohol use. As in almost every other study discussed in this book, Becker's research on addiction extends the boundaries of economics to an area usually reserved for another discipline – in this case, psychology.

Experimental studies of harmful addiction by psychologists have usually found reinforcement, tolerance, and withdrawal (Donegan, Rodin, O'Brien, and Solomon, 1983; Peele, 1985). Reinforcement means that greater current consumption of a good raises its future consumption. Tolerance means that given levels of consumption are less satisfying when past consumption has been greater. Withdrawal refers to the negative physical reaction and other losses in satisfaction as consumption is terminated. Becker incorporates these insights into an economic framework in which consumers are rational or farsighted in the sense that they anticipate the expected future consequences of their current actions to challenge the conventional wisdom that the consumption of harmfully addictive substances is not responsive to price.

In the next section of this chapter, I indicate how addiction is defined in economic terms and I identify some key concepts used in this approach. Then, I briefly review theoretical and empirical economic contributions in this area that either assume that consumers are myopic or that they have stable but inconsistent short-run and long-run preferences. I follow this review with an outline of theories of rational addiction with a focus on

Becker and Murphy's (1988) contribution and extensions developed by Becker, Grossman, and Murphy (1991). Then, I describe empirical applications of rational addiction to the demand for cigarettes, gambling at horse-racing tracks, excessive alcohol consumption, and leisure time. Included is an analysis of the implications of these empirical studies for policies to legalize such substances as marijuana and cocaine. I conclude with a discussion of research dealing with the supply side of the market for addictive goods.

2 Definitions and basic concepts

In economic analyses of addictive behavior, the consumption of a certain good is termed to be an addiction or a habit if an increase in current consumption of the good leads to an increase in future consumption. Of course, this means that current consumption is positively related to past consumption. A harmful addiction is one in which current consumption has detrimental effects in the future, such as reductions in health and therefore in utility caused by cigarette smoking and excessive alcohol use. Similarly, a beneficial addiction is one in which current consumption has favorable effects in the future, such as increases in future utility from attending and acquiring additional information about operas today. Other examples of beneficial addictions are attending church, jogging, or playing tennis on a regular basis. Note that I follow most of the literature in using the terms addiction and habit as synonyms.

Consumers are myopic if they ignore the effects of current consumption on future utility when they determine the optimal or utility-maximizing quantity of an addictive good in the present period. On the other hand, they are rational or farsighted if they take account of future effects of current consumption when they determine the optimal quantity of an addictive good in the present period.

Both myopic and rational models of addiction stress that choices today depend on choices made in the past. This stands in contrast to the standard treatment of consumption choices over time, which assumes that consumers maximize a lifetime utility function that is the discounted sum of utility in each period, where utility each period depends only on current period consumption. From there, a demand function for current consumption is obtained that depends only on the current period price and on the marginal utility of wealth. For our purposes it is important to note that this formulation rules out addiction because an increase in consumption in period t affects utility in period t alone.

To allow for the possibility that at least some goods are addictive, the utility function at time t is allowed to depend on consumption of a non-addictive good in that period, consumption of an addictive good, and the stock of the addictive good. An increase in the stock lowers utility if the addiction is harmful, while an increase in the stock raises utility if the addiction is beneficial. Regardless of the nature of the addiction, an increase in the stock must raise the marginal utility of the addictive good in order for an increase in past consumption of that good to increase current consumption.

Note that harmfully addictive goods exhibit the psychological properties of tolerance, reinforcement, and withdrawal mentioned in section 1. In particular, an increase in the stock *lowers* utility (tolerance) but *raises* the marginal utility of current consumption of the addictive good (reinforcement). Withdrawal also is present because a reduction in current consumption lowers current utility. Reinforcement and withdrawal, but not tolerance, also are present in the case of beneficial addiction.

3 Myopic models of addiction

Interest in addictive behavior by economists dates to Alfred Marshall. Writing in 1920, he noted: "Whether a commodity conforms to the law of diminishing or increasing returns, the increase in consumption arising from a fall in price is gradual; and, further, habits which have once grown up around the use of a commodity while its price is low are not quickly abandoned when its price rises again" (Marshall, 1920, p. 807). In this quote Marshall anticipates the differences between long-run and short-run price responses that play an important role in rational models of addiction. Most economists who have studied this behavior since Marshall have assumed myopia or imperfectly rational behavior. I classify two types of models under the general rubric of myopia. In one class of models, consumers ignore the effects of current consumption on future utility when they determine the optimal quantity of an addictive good in the present period. In this class of models, past consumption affects current consumption through an accumulated stock of habits. Economists who use this type of model frequently view it as one in which tastes are endogenous since the stock measure in the current period utility function depends on past decisions (for example, Houthakker and Taylor, 1970; Pollak, 1970). In the second class of models, consumers have stable but inconsistent short-run and long-run preferences (for example, Schelling, 1978; Thaler and Shefrin, 1981). At any one point in time the individual is both a "far-sighted planner and a myopic doer" (Thaler and Shefrin, 1981, p. 392), with the planner and the doer in conflict.

Empirical applications of myopic addiction focus on the first class of models and are based on the pioneering work by Houthakker and Taylor

(1970). They argue that the stock of a commodity should have a positive impact on its current consumption in the presence of habit formation if the commodity is non-durable. If it is durable, a negative stock effect is possible due to inventory adjustment. Houthakker and Taylor fit dynamic time-series demand functions for the US and several countries in Western Europe. They find a considerable amount of evidence in support of habit formation.

More recent examples of myopic demand functions are contained in studies by Grabowski (1976), Johnson and Oksanen (1977), and Baltagi and Levin (1986). The first two studies report positive and significant impacts of past consumption of alcohol on current consumption of alcohol. The third study contains the same finding for cigarette consumption.

4 Rational models of addiction

In rational models of addiction, consumers take account of future effects of current consumption when they determine the optimal quantity of an addictive good in the present period. Becker and Murphy (1988) use the notion that the utility function is not additively separable over time as the point of departure for a specific model of rational addiction that among other things contains the first explicit derivation of the long- and short-run demand function for addictive goods in the case of farsighted consumers. Contrary to conventional wisdom, Becker and Murphy stress that the demand for addictive goods is likely to be quite responsive to price in the long run. They also stress that the quantity demanded of an addictive good is negatively related not only to the current price of the good but also to its past and future price. That is, cross-price effects are negative, or the quantities of an addictive good consumed in different periods are complements.

Becker, Grossman, and Murphy (1994) show that under some conditions (when the utility function is quadratic and the rate of depreciation on the addictive stock is one), the demand function for consumption of an addictive good in period t (C_t) has the form

$$C_t = \alpha C_{t-1} + \beta \alpha C_{t+1} + \alpha_1 P_t + \alpha_2 e_t + \alpha_3 e_{t+1}. \tag{1}$$

Here P_t is the price of C_t, $\beta < 1$ is the time discount factor, e_t and e_{t+1} reflect the impact of unmeasured exogenous life-cycle variables on utility, and the intercept is suppressed. Since α is positive and α_1 is negative, current consumption is positively related to past and future consumption (C_{t-1} and C_{t+1}, respectively) and negatively related to current price. In particular, α measures the effect of an increase in past consumption on the marginal utility of current consumption. By symmetry, it also measures the effect of an increase in future consumption on the marginal impact of current consumption on the next period's utility. The larger the value of α the greater is the degree of reinforcement or addiction.

Equation (1) highlights the source of negative cross-price effects (intertemporal complementarity) in the rational addiction model. Negative cross-price effects arise because increases in past or future consumption (caused by reductions in past or future prices) cause current consumption to rise. Put differently, the reinforcement property of an addictive good, which is emphasized by psychologists, suggests that an increase in past consumption raises the marginal benefit of current consumption. By symmetry, an increase in future consumption also raises the marginal benefit of current consumption.

Equation (1) also implies that the short-run price elasticity, which holds past consumption constant, must be smaller than the long-run price elasticity, which allows past consumption to vary. Since this property does not hold for a non-addictive good, the price elasticity of demand is expected to be larger for the former than for the latter. (The price elasticity of demand is defined as the percentage change in consumption caused by a 1 percent change in price.) Put differently, since past consumption reinforces current consumption, the price response grows over time in the case of an addictive good. For example, a price hike in 1993 would reduce consumption in 1993 which in turn would cause consumption in 1994 and in all future years to fall. Indeed, the long-run price response is greater the greater is the degree of addiction or reinforcement. But the ratio of the short-run price effect or elasticity to the long-run price elasticity falls as the degree of addiction rises. This perhaps is the basis for the conventional wisdom that addictive goods are not responsive to price, although the actual short-run price elasticity may be greater for addictive goods.

Equation (1) is the basis of the empirical implementation of the model in most of the studies described in section 5. The statistical significance of the coefficient of future consumption provides a direct test of a rational model of addiction against an alternative model in which consumers are myopic. In the latter model they fail to consider the impact of current consumption on future utility and future consumption. That is, the myopic version of equation (1) is entirely backward looking. In it current consumption depends only on current price, lagged consumption, the marginal utility of wealth (which is one of the determinants of the current price coefficient), and current events. Current consumption is independent of both future consumption, C_{t+1}, and future events, e_{t+1}. Because of these distinctions, myopic models and rational models have different implications about responses to future changes. In particular, rational addicts increase their current consumption when future prices are expected to fall, but myopic addicts do not.

Extensions of the above framework imply differential price responses by age, income, and education in the case of addictive goods. The total cost of addictive goods to consumers equals the sum of the good's price and the money value of the future adverse effects, such as the negative effects on earnings and health of smoking, heavy drinking, or heavy dependence on crack. Future costs tend to be less important to poorer, less educated, and younger consumers because they generally place a smaller monetary value on health and other harmful future effects than richer, more educated, and older consumers who have higher wage rates. Moreover, the poor, youths, and the less educated are likely to have lower time discount factors (higher rates of time preference for the present) than the rich, adults, and the more educated. It follows that the poor, youths, and the less educated are more sensitive to changes in money prices of addictive goods, whereas the middle- or upper-income class, adults, and the more educated respond more to changes in the perceived or actual harmful consequences that take place in the future.

Interactions between peer pressure and addiction also predict greater price sensitivity by youths. Bandwagon or peer effects are much more important in the case of youth smoking or alcohol consumption than in the case of adult smoking or alcohol consumption. That is, youths are much more likely to smoke or drink if their peers also engage in this behavior. Initially, a fall in the price of an addictive good subject to peer pressure causes each consumer to increase his demand for the good for two reasons. There is a direct price effect and an indirect price effect operating through peer consumption. Over time, the increase in current consumption stimulates future consumption due to the reinforcement property of an addictive good. In turn, reinforcement makes the peer effect larger.

The final notable component of the rational addiction model is its treatment of unstable steady states. A steady state is one in which annual consumption of an addictive good is exactly equal to depreciation of the addictive stock, so that the stock remains constant over time. An unstable steady state is one in which a price change or the occurrence of a stressful life event such as unemployment or divorce causes persons to start or stop consuming the addictive good or to change their consumption by a very large amount. Strong complementarity between current and past consumption leads to unstable steady states. The existence of these states is one of the key features of the rational addiction model since it helps explain the binge behavior and "cold turkey" quit behavior observed among addicts. Furthermore, these unstable steady states imply that there will be a bimodal distribution of consumption. That is, they imply that few people will consume small amounts of highly addictive goods, with the majority either not consuming or consuming large quantities. Cigarette consumption is a good example of such bimodality.

5 Empirical applications

Becker, Grossman, and Murphy (1994) fit models of rational addiction to cigarettes to a US time series of state cross sections for the period 1955–85. The study capitalizes on substantial variations in the price of cigarettes among states at a moment in time due primarily to large differences in state excise tax rates on cigarettes. Cigarette consumption is measured by the per capita number of packs of cigarettes sold in each state over time.

The estimated coefficient of current price in equation (1) is negative and statistically significant, while the estimated coefficients of past and future consumption are positive and significant. These results imply both that cigarette smoking is addictive and that consumers are rational rather than myopic. The sizable long-run price elasticity of demand of approximately -0.75 is almost twice as large as the short-run price elasticity of -0.40. That is, a 10 percent increase in price in 1993 and in all future years will cause annual consumption to fall by 4 percent in 1993 and by 7.5 percent after a number of years have elapsed. Smoking in different years appear to be complements: cigarette consumption in any year is lower when both future prices and past prices are higher. To be specific, a 10 percent reduction in the current price increases cigarette consumption by approximately 1.5 percent next period and by approximately 0.7 percent in the previous period.

Additional evidence in support of the rational addiction model in aggregate data on cigarette consumption is contained in a study by Keeler, Hu, Barnett, and Manning (1993). They use monthly data on per capita cigarette consumption in California for the years from 1980 through 1990 and capitalize on the dramatic increase in the tax on cigarettes in that state from 10 cents to 35 cents per pack on January 1, 1989. They find that an increase in past or future consumption raises current consumption, a short-run price elasticity of -0.36, and a long-run price elasticity of -0.58. Clearly, these estimates imply that the cumulative effect of the California excise tax hike will exceed its short-run effect.

Even though the preceding estimates indicate that the equilibrium aggregate amount of smoking is stable, unstable steady states may greatly affect the overall response of cigarette smoking to changes in cigarette prices. This conclusion is supported by the evidence that almost all the effect of higher prices on teenage smoking and more than half the effect on adult smokers are due to a decline in the number of smokers (Lewit, Coate, and Grossman, 1981; Lewit and Coate, 1982). The possible role of unstable steady states is inferred from the fact that the large decline in the number of smokers is not due entirely to heterogeneity in the amount smoked, whereby people who smoke only a few cigarettes per day stop smoking when cigarette prices increase. Data from the second National Health and Nutrition Examination Survey reveal that 60 percent of persons who had stopped smoking for less than one year smoked at least one pack of cigarettes per day during the last year in which they smoked. The same survey indicates that 68 percent of persons who had stopped smoking for one or more years smoked at least one pack a day during their period of maximum consumption. Even a modest increase in cigarette prices could induce smokers who happen to be near unstable steady states to cease. The existence of unstable steady states means that some people who smoke a lot will be the "marginal" smokers with respect to changes in cigarette prices and other variables.

Chaloupka (1991) provides further evidence in support of the rational model of cigarette addiction in a microdata set: the second National Health and Nutrition Examination Survey. Using measures of cigarette consumption in three adjacent periods, he fits demand functions similar to those described above. He finds a short-run price elasticity (-0.20) that is less than one-half of the long-run price elasticity of -0.45. His significant future consumption coefficient is further evidence against myopic addiction.

Chaloupka (1991) also finds that smoking by the less educated is considerably more responsive to changes in cigarette prices than is smoking by the more educated; a similar result has been obtained by Townsend (1987) with British data. Lewit, Coate, and Grossman (1981) and Lewit and Coate (1982) report that youths respond more to cigarette prices than adults. By contrast, the information that began to emerge in the early 1960s about the harmful long-run effects of smoking has had a much greater effect on smoking by the rich and more educated than by the poor and less educated (Farrell and Fuchs 1982 for the US; Townsend 1987 for Britain).

Mobilia (1990) applies the rational addiction framework to the demand for gambling at horse-racing tracks. Her data consist of a US time series of horse track cross sections for the period from 1950 through 1986 (tracks over time are the units of observation). She measures consumption by the real amount bet per attendant and price by the takeout rate (the fraction of the total amount bet that is retained by the track). Takeout rates are legislated by states and vary considerably among them. Mobilia's findings are similar to those in the rational addictive studies of cigarettes. The long-run price elasticity of demand for gambling at horse tracks equals -0.7 and is more than twice as large as the short-run elasticity of − 0.3. Moreover, an increase in the current takeout rate lowers the real amount bet per attendant in past and future years.

Mobilia also considers attendance per capita as a dependent variable. She finds no support in favor of the rational addiction model with this outcome. Her results are plausible because the amount bet per attendant is a much better measure of addiction to gambling than attendance per capita. That is, a considerable number of people attend horse racing tracks for entertainment and place very modest bets. These persons are not addicted to gambling. Moreover, Mobilia cites data that indicate that 20 percent of betters account for 80 percent of all bets.

Hotz, Kydland, and Sedlacek (1988) and Bover (1991) apply variants of rational addiction models to the demand for leisure time or the supply of hours of work over the life cycle. Both studies use panel data on males in the University of Michigan's Panel Study of Income Dynamics. Both report evidence of rational addiction in the sense that current hours of work are positively related to past and future hours of work. These studies suggest that reductions in real wage rates due to increases in income tax rates can have substantial negative effects on hours of work in the long run even if their short-run effects are modest.

Excessive alcohol consumption is perhaps the most common example of a legally addictive good next to cigarette smoking. Attempts to apply rational addiction models to the demand for alcohol consumption are, however, difficult and challenging. The reason is that alcohol consumption is not nearly as addictive as cigarette smoking since many persons consume relatively small quantities of alcohol but not cigarettes. Put differently, the distribution of alcohol consumption is more continuous than the bimodal distribution that is likely to characterize consumption of an addictive good.

In work in progress, Chaloupka, Grossman, Becker, and Murphy (1993) apply the rational addiction model to alcohol outcome measures in a time series of state cross sections for the years 1962 through 1984. These measures are per capita consumption of distilled spirits, total per capita ethanol consumption (an aggregation of the ethanol in beer, wine, and spirits), and the age-adjusted death rate from cirrhosis of the liver of persons aged thirty and over. The price of alcohol is based on the prices of the three leading brands of spirits in the period from 1958 through 1984. As in the case of the cigarette studies, this research capitalizes on substantial cross-sectional variations in alcoholic beverage prices among states of the US due primarily to the very different rates at which states tax these beverages.

When per capita consumption of distilled spirits or total per capita consumption of ethanol is used as the dependent variable, they do not find much evidence in support of the rational addiction model. This is not surprising since alcohol consumption is not nearly as addictive as cigarette smoking, as pointed out above. That is, the results indicate that the aggregate data are dominated by the behavior of light and moderate drinkers.

More promising results are obtained when the age-adjusted cirrhosis mortality rate is used to develop a measure of excessive alcohol consumption. Deaths from cirrhosis of the liver reflect chronic, long-term drinking. While not all these deaths result from excessive drinking, about 75 percent are alcohol related.

Chaloupka, Grossman, Becker, and Murphy assume that the cirrhosis mortality rate in the current year is a function of excessive alcohol consumption in each previous year with exponentially declining weights. They find that this proxy for current excessive alcohol consumption is positively related to past and future excessive alcohol consumption. These results suggest that the behavior at issue is addictive and that consumers are farsighted rather than myopic. The long-run price elasticity of demand of −1.00 is substantial and 20 percent larger in absolute value than the short-run price elasticity of −0.79. The estimates indicate either that heavy drinkers greatly reduce their consumption when alcohol becomes more expensive or that the number of heavy drinkers is sensitive to the price of alcohol.

To summarize, the evidence from smoking, gambling, leisure time, and heavy drinking rather strongly supports the rational addiction model. In particular, long-run price elasticities are sizable and bigger than short-run price elasticities, and higher future as well as past prices reduce current consumption. In addition, lower-income persons respond more to changes in prices of addictive goods than do higher-income persons, whereas the latter respond more to future harmful effects. Finally, younger persons respond more to price changes than older persons.

This evidence has implications for the probable effects of the frequently debated policy to legalize such substances as marijuana, heroin, and cocaine. Legalization surely will reduce the prices of these harmfully addictive drugs. By the law of the downward-sloping demand function, their consumption will rise. But by how much? It seems reasonable to suppose that what holds for other addictive behaviors tends to hold also for drug use although direct evidence is not yet available, and many experts on drugs would be skeptical. Lacking the evidence, I will simply indicate what to expect from various price changes if drug addicts do behave rationally for the most part.

To fix ideas, consider a large permanent reduction in the price of drugs (perhaps due to partial or complete legalization) combined with much greater efforts to educate the population about the harm from drug use. The addiction model predicts that much lower prices could significantly expand use even in the short run, and it would surely stimulate much greater addiction in the long run. Note, however, that the elasticity of response to large price changes would be less than that to modest changes if the elasticity is smaller at lower prices.

The effects of a fall in drug prices would be countered by the education program. But since drug use among the poor would be more sensitive to the price fall than to greater information about harmful longer-run effects, drug addiction among the poor is likely to become more important relative to addiction among the middle classes and rich. For similar reasons, addiction among the young may rise more than among other segments of the population.

A misleading impression about the reaction to permanent price changes may have been created by the effects of temporary police crackdowns on drugs, or temporary federal "wars" on drugs. Since temporary policies raise current but not future prices (they would even lower future prices if drug inventories are built up during a crackdown period), there is no complementary fall in current use from a fall in future use. Consequently, even if drug addicts are rational, a temporary war that greatly raised street prices of drugs may well have only a small effect on drug use, whereas a permanent war could have much bigger effects, even in the short run.

Clearly, I have not provided enough evidence to justify whether or not the use of heroin, cocaine, and other drugs should be legalized. A cost–benefit analysis of many effects is needed to decide between a regime in which drugs are legal and one in which they are not. What the analysis shows is that the permanent reduction in price caused by legalization is likely to have a substantial positive effect on use, particularly among the poor and the young.

6 Monopoly and addiction

Research on the supply side of the market for addictive goods is much more limited than research on the demand side and focuses on the cigarette industry. Previous analyses of this industry have concluded that cigarette companies have significant monopoly power. Discussions of pricing by cigarette companies have not, however, paid attention to the habitual aspects of cigarette smoking, even though that greatly affects optimal monopoly pricing and other company policies.

Becker, Grossman, and Murphy (1994) illustrate the relation between pricing and addiction in a simple monopoly pricing model. In each period a monopolist sets a price where marginal revenue is below marginal cost, as long as consumption is addictive, and future prices tend to exceed future marginal costs due to the monopoly power. The reason is that future profits are higher when current consumption is larger, and current price is lower, because greater current consumption raises future consumption. As it were, a monopolist may lower price to get more consumers "hooked" on the addictive good.

This analysis that incorporates addiction into pricing policy may be helpful in understanding the rise in cigarette prices in recent years. Much of the drop in demand for cigarettes since 1981 is due to greater information about health hazards, restrictions imposed on smoking in public places, and the banning of cigarette advertising on radio and television. Several studies have commented about the apparent paradox that cigarette companies have been posting big profits while smoking is declining, and have documented the faster rise in cigarette prices than in apparent costs (Harris, 1987; Dunkin, Oneal, and Kelly 1988). Indeed, according to Adler and Freedman (1990, p. 1), "One of the great magic tricks of market economics ... [is] how to force prices up and increase profits in an industry in which demand falls by tens of billions of cigarettes each year."

Incorporation of the addictive aspects of smoking into the analysis resolves this paradox if cigarette companies have some monopoly power. An increase in current prices would raise cigarette companies' profits in the short run if they were pricing below the current profit-maximizing point (in order to raise future demand through the addictive effect of greater current smoking). Addictive behavior can also explain why current prices rise: the decline in future demand for smoking reduces the gains from maintaining a lower price to stimulate future consumption. Indeed, Showalter (1991) develops and estimates more elaborate models of the behavior of rational monopolistic producers of cigarettes who sell to rational consumers. This study reports that a drop in future consumption causes a positive and statistically significant increase in current price.

Incorporation of the addictive aspects of smoking also leads to a test of whether the cigarette industry is oligopolistic or competitive. If smokers are addicted and if the industry is oligopolistic, an expected rise in future taxes and hence in future prices induce a rise in current prices even though current demand falls when future prices are expected to increase. This cannot happen in simple models of competitive behavior.

A higher federal excise tax on cigarettes was widely expected to go into effect at the beginning of 1983. Cigarette prices increased sharply not only in 1983 but also prior to the tax increase during 1982. The price increase in 1982 has been taken as evidence that "the tax increase served as a focal point [or coordinating device] for an oligopolistic price increase" (Harris, 1987, p. 101). That is possible, but a price increase in 1982 may have occurred even if oligopolistic cigarette producers had no such coordinating problems because the higher future cigarette tax reduced future demand, and hence the gain from lowering the current price.

7 Conclusion

The most fundamental law in economics is that of the downward-sloping demand function. The theory of rational addiction stresses that the consumption of these goods is not an exception to this rule. More importantly, it implies that consumption is likely to be quite sensitive to price, particularly in the long run. The theory also implies negative relationships between future price and current consumption and between future consumption and current price. On the demand side, a reduction in future consumption due to an increase in future price will cause current consumption to fall. On the supply side, monopolistic or oligopolistic producers of addictive goods will raise current prices in response to an anticipated decline in future consumption. Studies completed since 1990 contain a considerable amount of empirical support for the implications of the rational addiction model. Indeed, the political debate surrounding the 1991 increases in the federal excise tax rates on cigarettes, beer, wine, and distilled spirits did call attention to long-run reductions in smoking and heavy drinking that are likely to accompany these policies. As data measuring the full cost of consuming illegal drugs (money price, probability of conviction, and penalty) become available and the debate concerning the legalization of drugs continues, insights from the theory of rational addiction should become even more prominent in guiding empirical research and the formulation of public policy.

Note

Research for this paper was supported by grant 5 R01 AA08359 from the National Institute on Alcohol Abuse and Alcoholism to the National Bureau of Economic Research and by grant 1 R01 DA07533 from the National Institute on Drug Abuse to the National Bureau of Economic Research. I am grateful to Gary S. Becker and Mariano Tommasi for helpful comments on an earlier draft. This paper has not undergone the review accorded official NBER publications; in particular, it has not been submitted for approval by the Board of Directors.

References

Adler, Stephen J. and Alix M. Freedman. 1990. "Tobacco Suit Exposes Ways Cigarette Firms Keep the Profits Fat," *Wall Street Journal*, March 5.
Baltagi, Badi H. and Dan Levin. 1986. "Estimating Dynamic Demand for

Cigarettes Using Panel Data: The Effects of Bootlegging, Taxation and Advertising Reconsidered," *Review of Economics and Statistics*, 68(1) (February): 148–55.

Becker, Gary S. 1992. "Habits, Addictions, and Traditions," *Kyklos*, 45: 327–46.

Becker, Gary S., Michael Grossman, and Kevin M. Murphy. 1994. "An Empirical Analysis of Cigarette Addiction," American Economic Review, 84(3) (June): 396–418.

  1991. "Rational Addiction and the Effect of Price on Consumption," *American Economic Review*, 81(2) (May): 237–41.

Becker, Gary S. and Kevin M. Murphy. 1988. "A Theory of Rational Addiction," *Journal of Political Economy*, 96(4) (August): 675–700.

Bover, Olympia. 1991. "Relaxing Intertemporal Separability: A Rational Habits Model of Labor Supply Estimated from Panel Data," *Journal of Labor Economics*, 9(1) (January): 85–100.

Chaloupka, Frank J. 1991. "Rational Addictive Behavior and Cigarette Smoking," *Journal of Political Economy*, 99(4) (August): 722–42.

Chaloupka, Frank J, Michael Grossman, Gary S. Becker, and Kevin M. Murphy. 1993. "Alcohol Addiction: An Econometric Analysis," presented at the annual meeting of the American Economic Association, Anaheim, California, January.

Douglas, Stratford and Govind Hariharan. 1992. "The Hazard of Starting Smoking: Empirical Results from a Rational Model," Presented at the annual meeting of the Southern Economic Association, Washington, DC, November.

Dunkin, Amy, Michael Oneal, and Kevin Kelly. 1988. "Beyond Marlboro Country," *Business Week*, August 8, pp. 54–8.

Farrell, Phillip and Victor R. Fuchs. 1982. "Schooling and Health: The Cigarette Connection," *Journal of Health Economics*, 1(3) (December): 217–30.

Grabowski, Henry G. 1976. "The Effects of Advertising on the Interindustry Distribution of Demand," *Explorations in Economic Research*, 3(1) (Winter): 21–75.

Harris, Jeffrey E. 1987. "The 1983 Increase in the Federal Cigarette Excise Tax," in Lawrence H. Summers (ed.), *Tax Policy and the Economy*, vol. I, Cambridge, MA: MIT Press.

Hotz, V. Joseph, Finn E. Kydland, and Guilherme L. Sedlacek. 1988. "Intertemporal Preferences and Labor Supply," *Econometrica*, 56(2) (March): 335–60.

Houthakker, H. S. and Lester Taylor. 1970. *Consumer Demand in the United States: Analyses and Projections*, Second and Enlarged Edition, Cambridge, MA: Harvard University Press.

Johnson, James A. and Ernest H. Oksanen. 1977. "Estimation of Demand for Alcoholic Beverages in Canada from Pooled Time Series and Cross Sections," *Review of Economics and Statistics*, 59(1) (February): 113–18.

Keeler, Theodore, E. Teh-Wei Hu, Paul G. Barnett, and Willard G. Manning. 1993. "Taxation, Regulation, and Addiction: A Demand Function for Cigarettes Based on Time-Series Evidence," *Journal of Health Economics*, 12(1) (April): 1–18.

Lewit, Eugene M. and Douglas Coate, 1982. "The Potential for Using Excise Taxes to Reduce Smoking," *Journal of Health Economics*, 1(2) (August): 121–45.

Lewit, Eugene M., Douglas Coate, and Michael Grossman. 1981. "The Effects of Government Regulation on Teenage Smoking." *Journal of Law and Economics*, 24(3) (December): 545–69.

Marshall, Alfred. 1920. *Principles of Economics*, Eighth Edition, London: The Macmillan Company.

Mobilia, Pamela. 1990. "An Economic Analysis of Addictive Behavior: The Case of Gambling," Ph.D. dissertation, City University of New York Graduate School.

Peele, Stanton. 1985. *The Meaning of Addiction: Compulsive Experience and its Interpretation*, Lexington, MA: Lexington Books.

Pollak, Robert A. 1970. "Habit Formation and Dynamic Demand Functions," *Journal of Political Economy*, 78(4, Pt. 1) (July/August): 745–63.

Schelling, Thomas C. 1978. "Egonomics, or the Art of Self-Management," *American Economic Review*, 68(2) (May): 291–94.

Showalter, Mark H. 1991. "Monopoly Behavior with Intertemporal Demands," Ph.D. dissertation, Massachusetts Institute of Technology.

Thaler, Richard H. and H. M. Shefrin. 1981. "An Economic Theory of Self-Control," *Journal of Political Economy*, 89(2) (April): 392–406.

Townsend, Joy L. 1987. "Cigarette Tax, Economic Welfare and Social Class Patterns of Smoking," *Applied Economics*, 19: 355–65.

11 Household production, human capital, and the economics of religion[1]

Laurence R. Iannaccone

Economic language has found its way into discussions of religion. We hear talk these days of "religious markets" and "religious entrepreneurs." Religious "consumers" are said to "shop" for churches much as they shop for cars: weighing costs and benefits, and seeking the highest return on their spiritual investment. Religious "producers," the erstwhile clergy, struggle to provide a "commodity" at least as attractive as their competitors'. Religion is advertised and marketed, produced and consumed, demanded and supplied.

One is tempted to dismiss such statements as a passing fad, misguided and possibly pernicious symptoms of a materialistic age with little or no appreciation of religion's true nature. This response is in my opinion mistaken. The logic of economics and even its language are powerful tools for the social-scientific study of religion. Economic theory offers a new paradigm for religious research, one that may eventually replace or encompass many of the approaches now competing for scholars' attention. The economic approach is both conceptually clean and empirically fruitful. It accounts for much of what is already known about religious participation, generates new predictions that suggest new avenues for empirical research, and forges links between the study of religion and a growing body of economic research on other "non-market" institutions and activities.

Modeling religious behavior

Economic theories of religious behavior assume that people approach religion in the same way that they approach other objects of choice. They evaluate its costs and benefits and act so as to maximize their utility. Hence they *choose* what religion (if any) they will accept and how extensively they will participate in it. These choices need not be permanent – people can and do change their religious identities or levels of religious participation over time. As in any other market, the consumers' freedom to choose constrains

172

the producers of religion. Ultimately, it determines the content of religious commodities and the structure of the institutions that provide them. These effects are felt most strongly where religion is relatively unregulated and, as a consequence, competition among religious firms is pronounced.

Economic theory raises questions that we might otherwise ignore, questions such as: How do people produce religious "commodities" and how do these commodities differ from standard, secular commodities? Why are religious commodities usually produced and consumed collectively; why are they not more often packaged and sold for money? What are the costs, both direct and indirect, of different religions and different religious practices? How do personal attributes, social settings, and technology affect these costs? Do "cheap" religions, which promise much and demand little, enjoy more success than costly religions? What are the consequences of religious market structure; does it matter if a given market is monopolistic or competitive, regulated or free? These are the kind of questions that I have sought to answer in my research. This essay focuses on a few such questions – questions about church attendance, contributions, and religious affiliation. It illustrates the value of the economic approach through a simple model of religious behavior.[2] The model explains observed patterns in denominational mobility, religious intermarriage, conversion ages, the relationship between church attendance and contributions, and the influence of upbringing and interfaith marriage on levels of religious participation. The model rests upon the concepts of household production and human capital.

Household production and human capital

Religious commodities are not physical goods, like cars or computers, that are readily manufactured, packaged, and sold in stores. Nor are they services, like hair cuts or banking, that we have others do for us. Rather, they fall into a third category that economists call "household commodities."

The study of household commodities, sometimes called "the new home economics," was pioneered by Gary Becker in the 1960s (Becker, 1964, 1965). Since then it has greatly expanded the boundaries of economics, enabling economists to analyze behaviors traditionally deemed beyond their reach: fertility, education, marriage and divorce, health, discrimination, and even crime (Becker, 1976). Its central feature is that families are viewed as quasi-firms engaged in the production of "household commodities." These commodities may be as concrete as meals and laundry or as abstract as relaxation and love. Unlike the products of a commercial firm, household commodities are consumed by family members rather than being sold. But like the products of a firm, household commodities can only be produced with scarce resources; they require inputs of purchased goods, household labor, and human skill. For example, a traditional, home-cooked meal is produced when a family member combines purchased inputs (such as meat, milk, and flour) with machine services (of sink, stove, refrigerator) and his or her own skilled labor to produce a valued output, which is promptly consumed by family members. As this example suggests, a fair amount of household production is just a scaled-down version of market production. But the real strength of the household production approach lies in its applicability to abstract commodities such as recreational enjoyment, relaxation, health, and child rearing. So, for example, even though we can not quantify the relaxation and enjoyment that come from recreational activities, we may usefully speak of households "producing" this commodity by combining purchased inputs (such as ski equipment, automobile services, or VCRs, TVs, and stereos) with their own skilled labor and time.

Productive skills enter analyses of both commercial and household production because people's skills critically affect the quality and quantity of what they produce. Such skills are just as important in child rearing and home maintenance as in construction and banking. Economists often refer to productivity-enhancing skills as "human capital." They do so because human skill and physical capital both are needed to turn raw labor and physical inputs into valued commodities, and because people typically accumulate their skills through a process of investment (via education and practice) that parallels the investment that firms make in physical equipment. The importance of human capital is underscored by studies which find that economic progress in developing countries is more often constrained by workforce inadequacies, such as low levels of health, education, and training, than by limited access to modern equipment and technology.

Human capital derives from various sources: native ability, general education that contributes to one's productivity across the board, and so-called "specific" education or training that enhances the ability to perform specific tasks. Cooking skills provide a concrete example of each source: native ability may endow one with a fine palate or ability to memorize complex recipes; general education helps one to plan nutritious meals, buy wisely, and benefit from cook books; and specific training teaches one specific recipes, cooking techniques, and so forth. General education and specific skills likewise affect one's ability to produce abstract commodities such as recreation and child rearing. In the home as in the workplace, most general training is acquired through schooling, and most specific training is acquired "on the job" through experience, experimentation, and the imitation of others.

Religious production and religious capital

Religious practice can also be viewed as a productive process. Purchased goods, household time, and human capital affect a family's capacity to "produce" religious satisfaction just as they affect its capacity to produce meals, health, offspring, and recreational enjoyment. To be sure, religious products are complex and largely unobservable (though possibly no more so than recreational enjoyment). Nevertheless, the *inputs* to religious production are measurable and indeed are already routinely measured by researchers. These inputs include purchased goods, such as Sunday attire and transportation, sacrificial offerings, and money contributions which finance a church's operation and facilitate its charitable works. They also include family members' time and labor, such as time spent attending and traveling to and from church services, devotional time spent praying, meditating, and reading scriptures, and time and effort required for religious charity or other conduct motivated by religious concerns. Human capital, particularly human capital pertaining specifically to one's religion, comprises a third class of inputs. It is the input class most central to my analysis.

Although we are all familiar with the concept of a skilled clergy, we sometimes dismiss rank and file church members as passive consumers of religion. The household production approach reminds us that church members do not merely rely upon the skills of experts, but also employ their own skills and experience to produce religious satisfaction. The skills and experience specific to one's religion include religious knowledge, familiarity with church ritual and doctrine, and friendships with fellow worshipers. It is easy to see that these skills and experiences, which I will call *religious* human capital, are an important determinant of one's ability to produce and appreciate religious commodities. For example, the quality of fellowship experienced within a congregation depends strongly on what has been invested in relationships, and over time this fellowship can become a major source of satisfaction and a major motive for continued church participation. Likewise, it is difficult if not impossible to appreciate religious services without first becoming familiar with the doctrines, rituals, and traditions that underpin them. It is also true that religious capital is an important *product* of religious activity. Many religious activities are explicitly "marketed" as a type of personal investment: religious services are designed not only to inspire or entertain the participants but also to instruct them; religious acts of charity and love are supposed not only to better the lot of others but also to better the actor as well; and in one way or another virtually every religion promises improved prospects in this life or the next.

These examples illustrate a fundamental interaction between religious capital and religious participation. Religious capital is both a prerequisite for and consequence of most religious activity. Religious capital – familiarity with a religion's doctrines, rituals, traditions, and members – enhances the satisfaction one receives from participation in that religion and so increases the likelihood and probable level of one's religious participation. Conversely, religious participation is the single most important means of augmenting one's stock of religious human capital. Religious activities yield a stock of specialized skills that enhances the satisfaction received from subsequent religious activities. In this last respect, religion is like many other household activities that involve learning by doing. It is, to use a term introduced by Stigler and Becker (1977), a form of "consumption capital."

Putting the model to work

In religion as in economics the concepts of household production and human capital prove their value by generating testable predictions. Some of these predictions provide theoretical explanations for facts that are already well known but not well understood. Others suggest new lines of empirical research. The discussion below concerns predictions about denominational mobility, religious intermarriage, conversion, and religious participation. My purpose is to illustrate the value of an approach rather than to prove any particular hypothesis. Hence, the treatment of each subject is brief, limited to a statement of the model's predictions and a summary of the empirical evidence relating to them.

Denominational mobility

Religious training, unlike general education and occupational training, is received directly from parents and the religious institutions they support. Hence, children are more likely to remain within their parents' denominations than to remain within their parents' occupations. Most children's religious human capital is acquired in a context determined and favored by their parents. As children mature and decide for themselves what beliefs they will accept and what church they will attend, they naturally gravitate to those of their parents. And even those who do switch religions will tend to switch to religions that are similar to the one in which they were raised. Hence the likelihood of conversion between particular religious groups should be greater the more similar the groups, and that overall rates of conversion to and from a particular group should be lower the more nearly unique the group.

Empirical evidence These predictions are confirmed by James Kluegel's (1980) statistical analysis of denominational mobility. Drawing on merged data from five years of the National Opinion Research Center's General Social Surveys, Kluegel cross-classified about six thousand white adult respondents by their current denomination and "background" denomination (in which they were raised). Members of all denominations showed a strong tendency to maintain their background affiliation and this tendency was stronger in groups that have fewer close substitutes. The two most distinctive major religious groups in America, Jews and Catholics, had retention rates of 87 percent and 85 percent respectively. The less distinctive Protestant denominations had lower retention rates, ranging from 78 percent for Lutherans to 55 percent for Disciples of Christ. Those raised with no religious affiliation, and hence little or no religious capital, remained unaffiliated only 38 percent of the time. Moreover, those who had changed religious affiliation manifested a clear affinity for denominations that were similar to their background denomination. Similar patterns appeared in Samuel Mueller's (1971) study of intergenerational religious mobility.

Conversion ages

The human capital model predicts that religious switching, like job changing, will tend to occur early in the life cycle as people search for the best match between their skills and the context in which they produce religious commodities. Over time the gains from further switching diminish as the potential improvement in matches diminishes and the remaining years in which to capitalize on that improvement decrease, whereas the costs of switching increase as one accumulates more capital specific to a particular context. Conversions among older people should be very rare.

Empirical evidence These predictions are strongly confirmed by empirical studies (see Iannaccone 1990 for details). Three studies conducted about the turn of the century found that people made their first personal religious commitments at a mean age of sixteen or seventeen. In 1928, a large survey found that religious "awakenings" usually began at age twelve, but clear-cut conversion experiences usually occurred around age sixteen. In 1954, the most common age of "converts" at Billy Graham crusades was fifteen. Not surprisingly, the typical religious commitment in all these studies was a personal affirmation of the religion in which the subject had been raised. Decisions to join a different church usually come later. For

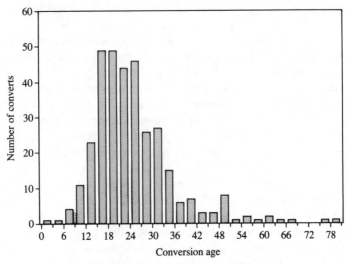

Figure 11.1 Age distribution of conversions

example, my own analysis of data from the 1988 General Social Surveys finds that people are most likely to switch religions in their late teens and early twenties (figure 11.1). Dean Hoge (1981) obtained a similar result in his study of 210 Catholic converts. The basic conclusion is clear: the decisions that lead to new religious commitments cluster in the early part of the life cycle. Eleventh-hour conversions of aging sinners preparing at last to meet their Maker are mostly mythical.

Religious intermarriage

A household can produce religious commodities more efficiently when both husband and wife share the same religion. Shared-faith households benefit from "economies of scale." A single car drives everyone to church; there is no question as to how time and money contributions will be allocated over different religions; and parents need not debate the religion in which their children will be raised. (The magnitude of these costs is underscored by Becker *et al.* [1977] who found significantly higher rates of divorce for intermarried couples even when other traits were held constant.) Hence, the same forces that lead people to remain with the religion of their parents also lead them to choose mates from within their religion. Moreover, even those who do intermarry will have a strong incentive to later adopt the religion of their spouse (or vice versa). The efficiency gains from such marital realignments will tend to be greater when the less religious spouse converts to the faith of the more religious spouse.

Empirical evidence Empirical studies find patterns in religious intermarriage very similar to those of intergenerational religious mobility. (This is to be expected, since most intergenerational mobility is due to one spouse adopting the religious affiliation of the other.) The tendency to marry within one's denomination is always very strong; *intra*marriage rates are higher in denominations with fewer close substitutes; and the *inter*marriage that does occur tends to be between people from relatively similar religions. These patterns have been verified in both Canadian and US data.

Intermarriage and participation

Empirical studies consistently find rates of church attendance to be much higher among marriage partners sharing the same religion. The reason for this finding, however, has been unclear, prompting one pair of researchers to remark that "a convincing explanation, if found in future research, would probably have far-reaching implications for understanding motivations for church participation today" (Hoge and Roozen, 1979, p. 47).

The household production model provides a simple explanation for the higher rates of church attendance within shared-faith marriages. Partners of the same religion can produce religious commodities more efficiently. Their religious activities tend to be complementary, lowering the overall costs and raising the overall benefits of religious participation. In mixed-faith marriages, complementarity is replaced by competitive (or at best neutral) use of family resources. Since this argument applies to any religious activity that permits a sharing of partners' resources, we would also expect more contributions and perhaps even more prayer and Bible reading in shared-faith marriages. On the other hand, a shared faith should have only indirect effects on personal belief.

Empirical evidence I have tested and confirmed these predictions with regression analyses of data from a wide range of surveys – two national surveys of American Catholics (conducted in 1963 and 1974), a 1963 survey of church members in the San Francisco Bay Area, and the 1972–1991 General Social Surveys. In each case, I found that married respondents reported much higher rates of church attendance, contributions, and prayer if married to a spouse of the same religion. Indeed, the differences were of the order of 30 to 40 percent.[3] These differences remained strong and statistically significant even after "controlling" for background variables, such as age, income, education, and denomination (see Iannaccone, 1990 for details).

There is, however, an alternative explanation for these results that has more to do with sampling bias than productive efficiency. People who are more serious about their religion, and so more likely to participate in it, may well be more likely to marry in their faith. If much of this sorting goes on, members of shared-faith marriages will average higher rates of religious participation than their mixed-faith counterparts *even if marriage itself has no impact on an individual person's participation.* Although the household production model predicts some sorting (since people desiring high levels of religious participation gain more than others from a shared-faith marriage), the model also predicts higher rates of participation in shared-faith marriages *even if no sorting occurs.* Stated differently, the model predicts that members of shared-faith marriages will not only participate more than members of interfaith marriages, but also more than they themselves would have done had they remained single. We can therefore measure the relative importance of pure sorting versus pure efficiency effects by comparing religious participation rates among single, mixed-faith, and shared-faith respondents. Under pure sorting, average participation rates for single people should equal those of married people as a whole, with mixed-faith marriages averaging less and shared-faith marriages averaging more. Under pure efficiency, average participation rates for single people should be less that those of married people as a whole, with mixed-faith marriages averaging about the same and shared-faith marriages averaging more.

As it turns out, the household production model passes this test. Statistical results indicate that production efficiency has an impact that is independent of and stronger than the impact of sorting alone. For every measure of religious *participation* – attendance, contributions, and prayer – mixed-faith married respondents participate only slightly (and never significantly) less than single respondents, whereas shared-faith married respondents participate substantially (and significantly) more than single respondents. On the other hand, in regressions measuring belief (in the Bible and in an afterlife) marriage effects are insignificant. Both these sets of results are consistent with the "efficiency" model but contradict the pure "sorting" model.

Religious upbringing

Since religious capital accumulates largely as a by-product of religious participation, and since religious capital provides an incentive for further religious participation, the household production model predicts that people's adult rates of religious participation correlate strongly with their childhood religious participation and training.

Empirical evidence It comes as no surprise that a strong religious upbringing constitutes a "leading indicator" of adult religious participation. Nevertheless, it is worth noting that careful statistical analyses support this prediction as well. In the 1974 Catholic American survey, both childhood religious instruction and parents' frequency of mass attendance (while the respondent was growing up) have positive effects on the respondents' current contributions and mass attendance. The effect of childhood religious instruction is also positive in a 1963 church member study (which did not include information on parental church attendance). And the effect of parental church attendance is again positive in the 1972–1991 General Social Surveys (which do not include information on childhood religious instruction).

Time versus money

The concept of "input substitution" underpins many of the most distinctive and important predictions of household production theory. Virtually all production processes, whether household or commercial, require both purchased inputs and labor inputs. But the *ratio* of these inputs can often be varied. Home cooked meals and restaurant meals can be equally good (or bad), but the former require much greater inputs of household time relative to purchased goods. In like manner, lawns can be watered by hand or by automated sprinklers, trips can be taken by bus or by plane, and children can be cared for by parents or preschools. In each of these cases, the efficient method of production will depend on the monetary value of the household's time. The higher the value of time, the more likely it is that the household will substitute time-saving, "money-intensive" forms of production for money-saving, "time-intensive" forms. Hence, it comes as no surprise that people with high wage rates are more likely to dine out, install sprinklers, travel by air, and enroll their children in preschools.

Applied to religion the concept of input substitution yields a uniquely economic prediction: people with high monetary values of time will conserve on their time by engaging in money-intensive religious practices. In particular, their money contributions will be high relative to their rates of attendance and vice versa. People with low monetary values of time will adopt more time-intensive practices and so do the opposite. These predictions provide a strong test of the proposed model since they have no precedent within traditional models of religious participation.

Empirical evidence The three surveys discussed above support the prediction that religious participation is more "money intensive" among people with high values of time. Regression analyses show that income is one of the strongest predictors of the ratio of attendance to contributions. Richer people contribute more dollars per service they attend and, conversely, attend less per dollar they contribute. Hence, higher income leads to participation that is more money intensive and less time intensive. This finding must be kept in proper perspective, however. People's participation in religious activities becomes less time intensive (and hence more money intensive) whenever their time inputs decrease *relative* to their money inputs. But this relative decrease need not be accompanied by a decrease in the *absolute* amount of time devoted to religious activity. So, for example, the attendance statistics show that income has a positive, albeit small, effect on absolute levels of attendance. In other words, the attendance/contribution ratio decreases simply because contributions have increased much more rapidly than attendance. This leads one to ask whether the concept of substitution between time and money really has relevance. Might not the regression results simply reflect people allocating to religion a fixed fraction of their time (e.g., one morning per week) and a fixed fraction of their income (e.g., 5 percent per year)?

Figures 11.2 and 11.3 help to distinguish between these two competing interpretations by providing a different view of the data. Figure 11.2 plots respondents' average rates of contributions and church attendance as a function of their ages. Notice that attendance and contributions are in no sense static over the life cycle – people do not merely allocate a fixed fraction of their time to religion, nor do they merely allocate a fixed fraction of their income. Attendance displays a strong upward trend which begins to level out, and only after age seventy.[4] Contributions increase steadily and far more rapidly than income between ages twenty-five and forty-five, remain fairly stable from forty-five to sixty-five, and decline thereafter. Despite these differing patterns, the average *ratio* of attendance to contributions (plotted in figure 11.3) reveals a life-cycle pattern that is both regular and consistent with the household production model: compared to people in their prime earning, middle years, the young and the old attend much more relative to each dollar they contribute.[5] Conversely, the age groups with the highest monetary values of time contribute the greatest number of dollars per hour of church attendance.

In short, the data across both age groups and income strata support the prediction that people substitute money for time in the production of religious commodities. How might this substitution occur? My own, admittedly unsystematic, observations suggest that richer congregations opt for a variety of time-saving, money-intensive, practices: shorter

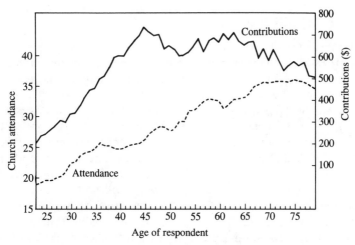

Figure 11.2 Yearly attendance and contributions

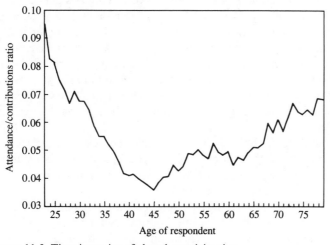

Figure 11.3 Time intensity of church participation

services, more reliance on professional staff (such as clergy, custodians, choir directors, and paid soloists), larger and more costly facilities (permitting less use of members' homes for special meetings), less reliance on volunteered labor, and more reliance on purchased goods and services (such as catered meals in place of pot-lucks). A careful, comparative study is needed to determine whether these observations really reflect an overall pattern.

Is religion "addictive"?

We saw in figure 11.2 that rates of religious participation, particularly church attendance, increase with the age of the respondent. Numerous other surveys taken in the past fifty years confirm this finding and leave little doubt that the observed pattern is indeed linked to age.[6] Household production models offer two very different explanations for this pattern. The first, due to Azzi and Ehrenberg (1975), rests on the assumption that most people attend church and contribute in order to accumulate afterlife rewards. If in fact most religious activities constitute a form of afterlife investment, then rational people will tend to defer their religious investing until they are relatively old and, conversely, will devote most of their youthful energies to secular pursuits. An alternative explanation, which I introduced in my doctoral thesis, is that religion is habit forming. If, as I have argued throughout this essay, religious satisfaction depends critically upon the stock of religious human capital that people accumulate, and if this stock of human capital is the product of prior religious participation, then religious involvement will tend to be self-reinforcing. As people age, they will tend to become more religious because, in a very real sense, they become more adept at being religious. Compared to the afterlife explanation, habit formation has several attractive features: it does not invoke unique assumptions about the nature of religious commodities; it rests on the same basic concept that we have used to explain other aspects of religious behavior; and it fits the data somewhat better[7] (see Iannaccone, 1984 for details).

I have described the habit formation model because it illustrates the unexpected synergies that often arise in the study of "non-market" behavior. When I first began studying religious behavior for my thesis, it became immediately apparent that upbringing and past religious involvement exerted a major influence on a person's current religious practices. As a student of Gary Becker, it was only natural that I try to model this tendency as the consequence of rational choice and the accumulation of human capital. The resulting model (Iannaccone, 1984, 1986) formalized Stigler and Becker's (1977) treatment of addiction. Subsequently, Becker and Murphy (1988) greatly extended this line of research in their "Theory of Rational Addiction." The economics of religion thus benefited from and contributed to a very different line of research.

Conclusion

The economic concepts of household production and human capital generate a powerful model of religious participation. Although the model sidesteps questions about what religion "really" is,[8] it nevertheless illuminates a great many issues: denominational mobility, religious inter-marriage, the timing of conversions, the influence of religious upbringing, the ratio of attendance to contributions, and the impact of mixed-faith marriage.

In each case, the model's predictions receive strong empirical support. Conversions are concentrated in the early stages of the life cycle, as people search for the best match between their religious skills and the context in which they produce religious commodities. Religious mobility, like career mobility, diminishes as people age. The patterns of mobility also fit the model's predictions. People switch denominations in ways that preserve the value of their religious human capital. Rates of intergenerational mobility tend to be low, particularly for people raised in distinctive religious traditions, and the switching that does occur tends to be among similar denominations. Religious intermarriage displays similar patterns. People seek out partners whose religious human capital complements their own, and the productive efficiency inherent in shared-faith marriages leads to higher levels of church attendance and contributions. Religious upbring-ing, probably the most important source of religious human capital, is a major determinant of religious belief and behavior. Money and time substitute for each other in the production of religious commodities. People with high monetary values of time display higher ratios of contributions to attendance, suggesting that they engage in more "money-intensive" forms of religious activity. There is even some evidence that religious activity tends to rise with age because it is habit forming.

None of these findings is by itself very surprising. It is, however, surprising to see so many different findings emerge as predictions of a single model. The economic concepts of household production and human capital deserve researchers' attention precisely because they explain so much of what we already have observed. They further deserve attention because they raise new empirical questions, such as those concerning the substitu-tion of money for time. Indeed, the human capital approach to religious participation illustrates the threefold contribution of economic theory to social scientific research: integrating numerous predictions within a single conceptual framework; providing theoretical explanations for observed empirical regularities; and generating new hypotheses to guide future empirical research.

Notes

1 Part of this essay is adapted from "Religious Practice: A Human Capital Approach" (Iannaccone, 1990).
2 See Iannaccone (1992) for a more sophisticated model that takes account of the club-like, congregational setting in which most religious activities occur.

3 In the 1974 Catholic survey, shared-faith couples contributed 71 dollars per year more than mixed-faith couples (relative to an overall average of 193 dollars), and Catholics married to other Catholics attended mass 11.8 times per year more than Catholics married to non-Catholics (relative to an overall average of 39). In the GSS survey, which surveyed people of all faiths, the corresponding differences are 86 dollars per year and 9.2 services per year (relative to means of 376 dollars and 23.6 services, respectively).

4 For the purpose of my analysis it does not matter whether the observed increase is due to age, period, or cohort effects. Nevertheless, studies suggest that most of the observed trend is in fact related to age (Hout and Greeley, 1987).

5 Note, in particular, that the attendance/contributions ratio is nearly the same for people in their thirties and sixties, despite the fact that the latter attend twice as frequently as the former.

6 If the pattern were not so pervasive we might instead suspect that it was due to "secularization" – a progressive decline in religiosity that induces each new generation to be less religious than its immediate predecessor.

7 The afterlife model predicts ever-accelerating rates of religious participation, whereas the habit formation model predicts eventual convergence toward a steady state. As is seen in figure 11.2, observed patterns in attendance and contributions are more consistent with the latter prediction.

8 Such sidestepping is quite common and arguably beneficial in economic discourse, since it facilitates the construction and application of abstract theories. For example, agricultural economists rarely worry about the essential characteristics of apples or why people enjoy eating them. Yet, by studying the external forces that govern the supply of and demand for apples – weather, price, income, familiarity with the product, and so forth – they generate valuable insights and information.

References

Azzi, Corry and Ronald Ehrenberg. 1975. "Household Allocation of Time and Church Attendance," *Journal of Political Economy*, 84 (3): 27–56.

Becker, Gary S. 1964. *Human Capital*. New York: National Bureau of Economic Research.

Becker, Gary S. 1965. "A Theory of the Allocation of Time," *Economic Journal*, 75 (299): 493–517.

Becker, Gary S. 1976. *The Economic Approach to Human Behavior*, Chicago: University of Chicago Press.

Becker, Gary S., Elizabeth M. Landes, and Robert T. Michael. 1977. "An Economic Analysis of Marital Instability," *Journal of Political Economy*, 85 (6): 1141–87.

Becker, Gary S. and Kevin M. Murphy. 1988. *A Theory of Rational Addiction*, 96(4) (August): 675–700.

Hoge, Dean R. 1981. *Converts, Dropouts and Returnees*, New York: The Pilgrim Press.

Hoge, Dean R. and David A. Roozen (eds.). 1979. *Understanding Church Growth and Decline: 1950–1978*, New York: The Pilgrim Press.

Hout, Michael and Andrew Greeley. 1987. "The Center Doesn't Hold," *American Sociological Review*, 52(3): 325–45.

Iannaccone, Laurence R. 1984. "Consumption Capital and Habit Formation with an Application to Religious Participation," Ph.D. dissertation, University of Chicago.

1986. "Addiction and Satiation," *Economics Letters*, 21: 95–9.

1990. "Religious Practice: A Human Capital Approach," *Journal for the Scientific Study of Religion*, 29: 297–314.

1992. "Sacrifice and Stigma: Reducing Free-Riding in Cults, Communes, and Other Collectives," *Journal of Political Economy*, 100: 271–91.

Kluegel, James R. 1980. "Denominational Mobility: Current Patterns and Recent Trends," *Journal for the Scientific Study of Religion*, 19(1): 16–25.

Mueller, Samuel A. 1971. "Dimensions of Interdenominational Mobility in the United States," *Journal for the Scientific Study of Religion*, 10(2): 76–84.

Stigler, George J., and Gary S. Becker. 1977. "De Gustibus Non Est Disputandum," *American Economic Review*, 67: 76–90.

12 The blind leading the blind
Social influence, fads, and informational cascades

David Hirshleifer

1 Introduction

Why do teenagers at one school take drugs while at another they "just say no"? Why do Americans act American, Germans act German, and Indians act Indian? Why did English and American youths enthusiastically enlist to fight in World War I, whereas pacifist sentiments were more popular before World War II and in the 1960s? These are all examples of one of the most striking regularities of human society: *localized conformity*.

Localization in either time or place seems to cast doubt upon the idea that people make rational and intelligent choices. If illegal drug use is a bad idea, why do people participate in waves of abuse of different kinds of drugs at different times? If the sale of marijuana is illegal in America, why is it sold legally in Amsterdam drug cafes? If the Chinese know that cold drinks harm the digestion, are Americans blundering when they guzzle Coke?

Part of the explanation is that people in different places don't observe each other's behavior. Germans do many things differently from me, but I don't know specifically what most of these things are. A high school student who sees his friends taking drugs may not realize that members of other cliques do not take drugs. Or, even ignoring this, he may wrongly attribute these divergences to differences in the costs and benefits from taking drugs.

Rapid changes over time pose an even greater challenge. Why was cohabitation of unmarried couples in the US viewed as scandalous in the 1950s, flaunted in the 1960s, and hardly noticed in the 1980s? College students who flirted with the counterculture in the sixties were succeeded by pre-MBA go-getters in the eighties. The recent collapse of communism in the Eastern Bloc was rapid and unexpected. Religious movements, revivals, and reformations, started by a few zealots, sometimes sweep across populations with astonishing rapidity. Social attitudes toward and popularity of alcohol, cigarettes, and illegal drugs have also fluctuated rapidly.

The main theme of this chapter is that *learning by observing others* can

Figure 12.1

explain the conformity, idiosyncrasy, and fragility of social behavior. When people can observe one another's behavior, they very often end up making the same choices; thus, localized conformity. If the early movers erred, followers are likely to imitate the mistake; hence idiosyncrasy. If later on a few people start behaving differently for whatever reason, then a sudden phase change can occur in which the old convention is swept away by the new; hence fragility. Such imitation can explain either transient fads or permanent choices among alternative products, sexual and marital options, scientific theories, and religious beliefs.

My first crucial point is that imitation can be sophisticated, being based upon rational weighing of pros and cons. Even if the blind are leading the blind, as in Breughel's painting (figure 12.1) the followers need not be fools – each individual realizes that he is somewhat ill-informed and that his predecessors are also.

How "social influences" such as imitation can lead to instability was analyzed by Gary Becker in "A Note on Restaurant Pricing and Other Examples of Social Influences on Price," which carries a heavy punch for a paper of eight pages.[1] The puzzle that interested Becker follows:

A popular seafood restaurant in Palo Alto, California, does not take reservations, and every day it has long queues for tables during prime hours. Almost directly across the street is another seafood restaurant with comparable food, slightly higher prices, and similar service and other amenities. Yet this restaurant has many empty seats most of the time.

Why doesn't the popular restaurant raise prices, which would reduce the queue for seats but expand profits?

The explanation Becker provides is that people would rather dine at the "in" restaurant where others are dining as well. The problem with raising prices is that if this drives away a few customers, the lines get shorter, making the restaurant less fashionable. This lower "in-ness" itself deters a few more customers. If the price is raised just a little too high, this process can feed upon itself (so to speak) until the restaurant's clientele suddenly vanishes.[2]

If the restaurant manager knows *precisely* how much customers value the "in-ness" of the establishment, he can boost the price to the maximum level that avoids unraveling. At that price there are long lines. But if the manager does not know demand perfectly, he may set the price just a bit too high, and the restaurant fails. A seller's attempt to boost revenue by raising prices pushes buyers near the edge of the precipice.[3] Hence, Becker's analysis explains at the same time why popular restaurants (or movies) don't just raise the price more, and why, surprisingly often, fashionable restaurants that are packed one year vanish the next.

As with restaurant seats, initial public offerings (sales of stock by new companies) are sometimes rationed – bidders do not receive as many shares as they would like to buy. Why don't the sellers just raise the price? Welch (1992) focuses on the fact that buyers arrive in sequence, so that later buyers gain information from earlier buyers. Translated into the restaurant context, Welch assumes that each person knows something about the quality of the two restaurants. Thus, the choices of the diners who arrive ahead of you *provide information* about which restaurant is better. If the queue is long at one restaurant, then other people think the food is good, so perhaps you should follow – even if your own limited information possibly suggested otherwise![4]

Because of this self-reinforcing tendency, the seller has a strong incentive to induce early movers to buy. New restaurants sometimes employ people to hang out and eat long meals to make their establishments look popular. Musicians and stage companies have hired claques to provide enthusiastic applause (or, in the case of competitors, to heckle), and professional mourners were engaged at ancient Roman funerals. Another way to get the ball rolling is to charge a low price aimed especially at early purchasers. Thus the familiar phenomenon of new products offered at drastically reduced introductory prices.

Bikhchandani, Hirshleifer, and Welch (1992) have analyzed more generally how limited information can explain conformity and fads. As first defined by Welch, an *informational cascade* occurs when the information implicit in predecessors' actions (or resulting payoffs) is so conclusive that a rational follower will *unconditionally* imitate them, without regard to information from other sources. We show that cascades often spontaneously develop on the basis of very little information. People converge upon one action quite rapidly, and their decisions are *idiosyncratic*.[5]

In our model, a sequence of individuals make successive choices (e.g., between two restaurants) based on both private information (information received by a single individual) and on the observed decisions of earlier movers. If there are many individuals, then we show that with virtual certainty a point in the chain of decisions will be reached where an individual ignores his private information and bases his decision solely upon what he sees his predecessors do. (He's not ignoring his information *foolishly*; it's just that the accumulated evidence from many previous individuals dominates even when his private information points in the opposite direction.) Once this point is reached for some individual n, his decision becomes uninformative to later choosers. Everyone knows that individual n was just following the bandwagon, so people do not take his action as reflecting any *additional* evidence for or against. In consequence, individual $n + 1$ is in the same position as individual n, so she also joins the cascade. This reasoning extends to all later individuals. (Of course, this conclusion does not *always* follow: later movers may have different costs and benefits from adopting, or different accuracy of their private information signals.)

Consider the submission of a manuscript for publication. If a journal's referee is aware that a paper had previously been rejected elsewhere, he should rationally tilt toward rejection. After all, the previous rejection indicates that some other expert reviewer disliked the paper, very likely (though not necessarily) for good reason. If it becomes widely known that several journals have rejected a paper, even a good submission may become unpublishable.

The publication or failure of a few papers can make or break a young professor's career: "Up or out, publish or perish!" But the problem of cascades is hardly limited to academics. Consider the stigma placed upon gaps in a personal resume. "Well," the interviewer thinks, "You haven't held a job for over 16 months. Clearly other employers have rejected you – I *wonder* why!" He reasonably infers that other employers have probably detected something negative about the applicant. Thus, even an otherwise-strong applicant may be virtually frozen out.

Cascades are often involved in the formation of a crowd or a queue. In communist Eastern Europe, it is said, long shopping lines would precipitate whenever a few people happened to stand together.

On the other hand, since cascades are based upon very little information, they can be easily reversed. If an imitator realizes that the rationale for his choice is weak, then it only takes a very small piece of news to change his mind. So the restaurant that is "in" this week may be "out" next week for no clearly visible reason. Much the same may hold for clothing styles and political election campaigns.[6]

The crucial point is that the system bounces around randomly until it reaches a point of *precarious* stability. As decisions are made, evidence (as reflected in people's decisions) gradually accumulates in favor of one action or another. An action is fixed upon when the weight of the evidence grows to be just enough to overcome *one person*'s opposing information. At that point, if the next individual is similar, he is also *just barely* willing to ignore his own information signal, i.e., he is in a cascade. This reasoning extends indefinitely, so all further individuals do the same thing. Thus, a very small preponderance of evidence causes a landslide majority to take one action over the other. In this situation, a very small shock to the system – such as new public information – can affect the behavior of many people. Owing to informational cascades, society often lands precariously close to the borderline, like a car teetering at the edge of a cliff.

This is unlikely to last forever, of course. Aside from external shock, in some cases new information is almost sure to arrive to tip things one way or the other. Consider a newly opened trendy restaurant that is packed with first-time customers. If all they care about is the food, then after a few meals they will learn about the quality quite accurately. So an initially mistaken cascade will be corrected quickly. Of course, if the cascade is for a non-repeated activity (such as seeing a given movie or buying shares of a given initial public offering) or an infrequent activity (such as buying a car), this corrective force is less powerful.

In contrast with the cascades model, most theories of conformity (Becker's model being an exception) imply rigid behavior in the face of changing circumstances. For example, the different though related theories of Akerlof, Kuran, and Coleman are founded on the threat of *sanctions upon deviants*.[7] Sanctions can lock social policy in place, even when it becomes evident to most people that a change would be desirable. A small shock can affect the behavior of many people only in very rare circumstances in which society happens to be at a razor's edge balance between alternatives.[8]

A second class of theories is based on *payoff interactions*, in which one person's action directly increases the benefit to someone else of doing the same thing (see Schelling, 1978; Arthur, 1989). For example, conventions such as driving on the right- (or left-)hand side of the road are self-enforcing.[9]

A third theory, *conformity preference*, holds that people directly prefer to do the same things that others are doing. As everyone hits upon the same actions, that action is stabilized, but it may not be the best one (see Jones, 1984; Becker, 1991).

The fourth and fifth theories can be mentioned together: *parallel reasoning* and *direct communication*. In parallel reasoning, everyone independently is wise enough to figure out the best choice. In direct communication, those who figure out the best choice simply explain the benefits of alternatives to others. This also implies convergence toward the correct outcome if communication is credible and costless. Neither theory explains why mass behavior is error-prone.

Among the questions to be covered here are (1) how likely are cascades, (2) how likely it is that the wrong cascade occurs (can a good job candidate be so badly stigmatized by failure as to become unemployable?), (3) what makes fashions change (why did the business major replace the "counter-culture" in college life), (4) how effective are public information releases (e.g., a campaign to publicize the health effects of smoking), and (5) to what extent subsequent individuals free ride on information purchased by earlier individuals (would an employer who knows that a job applicant has a large gap in his resume even bother inviting the applicant to an interview?).

2 The basic model

Consider a setting where each individual observes only the *actions* of predecessors, not their information signals. (Since actions speak louder than words, the information conveyed by actions may be more credible than verbal reports in any case.) Assume a sequence of individuals deciding between one of two actions: say smoking or not smoking. Each individual observes the decisions of all those ahead of him. People are lined up in sequence, and everyone knows his position in the queue. Everyone has the same costs and benefits from adopting the behavior. If smoking has no adverse health consequences, let its net value be $+\$1$, but if smoking is harmful, let its value be $-\$1$. These possibilities are initially equally likely to begin with in each person's private calculations. Each person then privately observes his own information signal: H (high, or favorable to smoking) versus L (low, or unfavorable). An example of an L signal could be reading about an adverse scientific study. An example of an H signal could be seeing an advertisement in which smoking seems pleasurable.

Suppose all individuals observe similar *types* of signals. Specifically, suppose that adoption is the right thing to do, and that each person has a three-fourths chance of observing H, and a one-fourth chance of observing L. But given the true value of adopting, the signals are independent, so Arnie may see H, and Betsy may see L.

Each person forms a probability belief about whether smoking or not

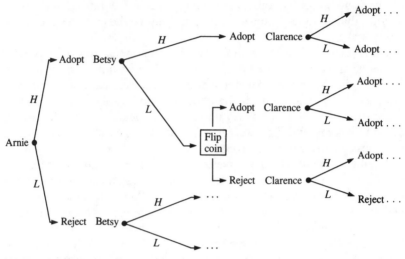

Figure 12.2

smoking is superior based on his information signal and on what he sees his predecessors do. He then makes his own decision. (If exactly indifferent, he flips a fair coin.) In figure 12.2, Arnie, the first person, adopts if his signal is H and rejects if it is L. So Betsy can deduce that if Arnie adopted, his signal was H; if he rejected, his signal was L. If Arnie adopted, Betsy should also adopt if her signal was H; in this case the H's outnumber the L's by 2 to 0. However, if Betsy's signal is L, her L signal is offset by Arnie's H signal, so the expected value of smoking is exactly 0. So Betsy tosses a coin to decide. By similar reasoning, if Arnie had rejected, Betsy rejects if her signal is also L, and tosses a coin if her signal is H.

When we get to Clarence, cascades can start. There are three possible situations: (1) both predecessors have adopted, (2) both have rejected, or (3) one has adopted and the other rejected. If both Arnie and Betsy have adopted, then Clarence will adopt too. He knows that Arnie observed H, and that quite likely Betsy did too (although she may have seen L and flipped a coin). A probabilistic calculation shows that Clarence will adopt *even if he sees an L signal*. This situation, in which Clarence adopts regardless of his signal, may be termed an UP cascade.[10] Similarly, in the second case, if both Arnie and Betsy rejected, then Clarence will reject too, even if he sees an H signal. This is a DOWN cascade.

In the third case, Arnie adopted and Betsy rejected (or vice versa), Clarence knows that Arnie observed H and Betsy observed L (or vice versa). These signals cancel out, so Clarence will follow his own signal, just as if he were the first person in the queue.

Returning to the cascade case where both predecessors adopted, since Clarence adopts regardless of his signal, his action *provides no information to his successors* about the desirability of smoking. Deedee, who has seen adverse medical reports, would reject smoking if only she knew that Clarence had an L signal. Instead, she continues the cascade. This reasoning extends to Edgar, Fifi, Gerard, Harriet, Ivan, Joy, and so on. Since opposing information remains hidden, even a mistaken cascade lasts forever. An early preponderance toward either adoption or rejection, which may have occurred by mere coincidence or for trivial reasons, can feed upon itself until the air is choking with smoke (or becomes particle-free).

The overall outcome here is idiosyncratic and history dependent. Actions may be poorly attuned to costs and benefits even if the information possessed by individuals would, if combined, suffice to make very accurate decisions. To understand this last point, suppose that a restaurant rating bureau were to interview Arnie, Betsy, Clarence, and so on. Walter's Restaurant Guide could then identify with extremely high accuracy which restaurant was better, and could inform later patrons. Jointly, the diners have enough information to decide correctly, but in fact they may end up flocking to the wrong place.

As evidence of the sort of imitative behavior that can lead to cascades, consider the adoption of hybrid corn from 1928–41. Ryan and Gross (1943) interviewed Iowa farmers and found that the most frequent reason given for adoption of hybrid corn was that neighbors adopted. (The importance of neighbors' adoption is a common finding in studies of adoption of innovation.)[11]

Laboratory experiments have been performed in which people are paid by the experimenter for making correct decisions based upon partial information (see Anderson, 1994; Anderson and Holt, 1994). Just as in the cascades model, their decisions are made in sequence and later individuals get to observe the choices of early individuals. These experimental tests have confirmed that people do fall into cascades. Furthermore, people imitated in these experiments primarily when it was sensible to do so based upon the circumstances, rather than irrationally following predecessors out of a taste for the status quo or for conformity.

The fallibility of cascades causes them to be fragile. If some people have more precise signals than others (as will be discussed in section 2.1), or if public news is revealed at a later date (as in section 3.1), or if the relative desirability of adopting versus rejecting changes (as in section 5), then cascades can easily be broken.

An important proposition in our setting is that *cascades will always arise eventually*. To see why, suppose that someone fairly late in the sequence, Zorro, is *not* in a cascade. This means that he and everyone before him must be making decisions that make use of their personal signals. So the actions of each and every predecessor conveys some information to Zorro. If Zorro is far enough down the line, then by combining the information of all his predecessors, with virtual certainty he can infer almost perfectly the true value of adoption. But then, Zorro's own signal contributes virtually nothing to his overall assessment, so he should ignore his signal and follow the action taken by most of his predecessors. In short, he is in a cascade. One may be tempted to think from this line of reasoning that people will ultimately converge on the *correct* action. This is far from the case. A cascade will take a long time to form only if early information is conflicting. As soon as a fairly mild preponderance of evidence favors one or the other action, a cascade starts, preventing decisions from becoming very well informed.

Typically cascades begin surprisingly soon. Calculations show that even when information signals are very noisy (so that H is only slightly more likely to arrive when the adoption is good than when it is bad), the probability of a cascade forming after ten individuals is greater than 99 percent!

The probabilities of an UP cascade, no cascade, or a DOWN cascade after two individuals *given that in fact adopting is superior* are easily calculated in the model. The probability of a correct cascade increases with the accuracy of the signal, but, even for very informative signals, the probability of the wrong cascade can be remarkably high.[12]

Owing to cascades, final outcomes depend heavily on chance early choices. It is tempting to search for deep logical causes of massive social trends, but these may not exist. Early origins may be trivial.[13] Such history dependence is not unique to the cascades theory; it can arise from some of the other theories of conformity mentioned in the introduction as well.

An important extension of the cascades model allows for differing costs and benefits to different individuals (see Lohmann, 1992a). In such a scenario, an adoption cascade that is correct for early adopters may be undesirable for followers who have a lower value of adoption. Followers can be fooled because they don't know for sure whether predecessors have greater or less gain from adoption.

A more radical deviation from the basic model would allow people to observe previous *information signals*, not just previous actions. This makes the outcome less uniform, idiosyncratic, and fragile. Even if someone smokes although his private signal suggested he should not do so (a cascade), that signal joins the common pool of knowledge. A long enough series of adverse information signals eventually cause later movers to choose not smoking.

2.1 Fashion leaders

Cascades will often be wrong. This blind-leading-the-blind phenomenon is bad enough when someone follows a series of similar predecessors. But when people are different, it may take only a single person to start the ball rolling. As an absurd extreme, one person's decision to eat oat bran (for example) can cause millions of others to follow.

Suppose different people have different information precisions (accuracy).[14] Suppose Arnie is a doctor, while Betsy is a computer programmer. Everyone thinks that Arnie has at least slightly better information about whether or not to eat oat bran. Assume that there is an equal prior probability, before signals are observed, as to which is superior. Then if Arnie observes his signal and decides first, a cascade starts *immediately*. Betsy should eat oat bran if and only if Arnie does, because she knows he is better informed. So Betsy's action is uninformative to the next person. So if Clarence, like Betsy, has a lower precision signal, he will follow Arnie just as Betsy did, and so on indefinitely.

Thus, everyone will blindly follow Arnie's action, even if Arnie is better informed than the others only by the slimmest of margins. Betsy's willingness to imitate Arnie is reasonable as far as it goes. But Arnie's information is not necessarily better than the *combined* information of ten people like Betsy, or a thousand.

While I have taken the order of moves as given, often the highest-precision person will decide first, because people who are poorly informed have stronger reason to wait and see what others do. Thus cascades should form extremely rapidly (after one person). But unless the first person's information is very much superior to that of followers, this may be disastrous.

In contrast, suppose the person who goes first has slightly *lower* information precision than those who follow. Then Arnie's action does *not* start a cascade, because Betsy should follow her own information rather than Arnie's. This is too bad for Betsy; she'd rather that Arnie was better informed, so she could exploit his information by imitating him. But Clarence, on the other hand, is *glad* that Arnie is slightly less well informed. Clarence gets to see the actions of both Arnie and Betsy and now *both of these actions are informative*. In fact, everyone from Clarence onward benefits substantially from having Arnie being slightly less well informed instead of slightly better informed than the others.

So small early differences in precision can make a huge difference later. A slightly higher information precision of an early individual can lead to an immediate cascade that is even less informative (and so potentially even more fragile) than when people have equally accurate signals. If a higher-precision individual shows up later, he can shatter a cascade, because he is more inclined to use his own information than those that preceded him. Cascade reversal tends to improve matters, because more information can be aggregated than if only a single cascade occurred.

Thus, from a social point of view it will often be desirable to order decision makers inversely with their precisions. As one example, in US Navy court-martials, the judges vote in *inverse* order of seniority. More generally, in judicial systems with courts of appeal, the judges sitting in lower-ranking courts making initial judgments are less prestigious and experienced (less precise?) than those in higher courts.[15]

There is a lot of evidence that low-precision decision makers imitate high-precision ones. In setting up territories, animals new to a habitat tend to locate close to previous settlers more than do animals that are familiar with the habitat (Stamps, 1988). Psychological experiments have shown that a human subject's previous failure in a task raises the probability that in further trials he will imitate a role model. Young children instinctively imitate their parents and teachers. Teenagers discover that in many areas their parents' information precision is no longer greater than their own, a rational reason for them to rebel. The tendency to imitate high-prestige individuals may be based on a belief that high-prestige individuals are well-informed decision makers.[16]

3 Fragility of cascades: further considerations

The uniformity stemming from the factors described in the introduction usually becomes more robust as the number of adopters increases. Cascades, on the other hand, remain brittle, so that the arrival of a little information, or the mere possibility of a value change (even if the change does not actually occur) can shatter an informational cascade.

3.1 The public release of information

Cascades can be sensitive to public information releases, for example, on the hazards of smoking or the effects of medical procedures (e.g., tonsillectomy), drugs (e.g., aspirin), and diet (e.g., oat bran). This subsection examines three questions: (1) Does the release of a single item of information, e.g., a report on aspirin and heart disease, make all people who have not yet decided better off? (2) How easily can such information reverse a cascade? (3) Does the release of multiple items of information over time eventually make people better off? For example, if medical science gradually generates information about the adverse consequences of tonsillectomy without special medical indications, will all doctors eventually reject this practice?

The answer to the first question is that the release of public information prior to the start of a cascade can make some people worse off (in an *ex ante* sense). For example, a newspaper restaurant review, although providing some valid information, can still make some diners worse off. Public information release has two effects on an individual: (1) It directly provides information, and (2) It changes the decisions of predecessors, and thus the information conveyed by their decisions. It may be that the restaurant review provides very noisy information, so that it is only slightly useful to Betsy; but it does affect Arnie's decision. In particular, it can work out that Arnie's choice becomes less informative to Betsy. This indirect disadvantage to Betsy can outweigh her direct benefit from the review.

Thus, it is not obvious that public health authorities should act quickly to disseminate noisy information. Sketchy disclosures of advantages of oat bran and fish oil, by triggering fads, can be harmful.[17] Of course, clearcut information such as the evidence that cigarettes cause illness are likely to benefit all consumers.

So much for disclosures made *before* a cascade. In contrast, once a cascade starts, and if people are identical, then everyone welcomes public information. To see this, suppose there is no disclosure. If everyone is identical, once a cascade starts people's decisions don't convey any further information. So a public disclosure at this point directly conveys information without reducing the information conveyed by people's decisions.

Such a public disclosure may therefore be beneficial. Of course, if the cascade is very resilient, the disclosure might not make any difference. If Ivan is attached to the belief that Le Burger is better, based on his observation that many earlier people selected Le Burger, then perhaps a restaurant review won't sway him. But, as we have seen, cascades are delicate. How much public information does it take to shatter an established cascade? A public signal can do the trick even if it is less informative than the private signal of just one person. The restaurant reviewer doesn't need to be a genius of connoisseurship. As long as his information is about as good as yours or mine, he can change the behavior of thousands of people.

Recall the illustrative model where a cascade of adoption ensues as soon as there is a majority of two for adopt over reject. Suppose that adoptions and rejections are evenly split until Edgar and Fifi both decide to adopt. At this point, everyone recognizes two possibilities: (1) both of them received favorable (H) signals, or (2) Edgar observed an H signal and Fifi observed L, leading her aggregate evidence to be HL, so that she flipped a coin. Consider a restaurant review that is as informative as a typical diner's information signal. Gerard can reason that even if Edgar and Fifi *both* observed *H*, a negative restaurant review cancels out one *H*. So if Gerard observes *L*, he is on the fence, and may well switch to reject. Since there is a significant probability that in fact Fifi observed *L*, Gerard should in fact reject. This reasoning remains valid even if the restaurant review is slightly less accurate than an ordinary diner's signal. The public signal is still enough to break the cascade.

Since even a minor public information release can shatter a cascade, one may wonder whether the arrival of many useful public disclosures will eventually guide people into the correct cascade. This is in fact the case, because eventually the weight of evidence would tip the balance. Although the proposition strictly holds only "eventually," numerical calculation suggests that a moderate amount of public information release can go a long way toward bringing people around to the right decision.

3.2 Summary

Each person with a bit of information is a valuable resource to those who decide later. An individual benefits from his ability to observe predecessors, which provides him with useful information. However, his ability to observe predecessors can harm his successors, because if he is in a cascade his action is uninformative. Cascades therefore can lead to bad decisions in which most of the potential gain from observing others is lost. For example, if the first 100 people were prevented from observing each other's decisions, each would decide based on his own signal. This could greatly benefit the next 10,000 people if they get to observe the decisions of the first 100.

Even with cascades, some of the benefit of information diversity will generally be recovered because cascades are so easily broken. The blunders of an early few can be rapidly reversed if someone with more precise information appears later in the sequence. The public release of information can also break incorrect cascades, and eventually can persuade people to do the right thing.

4 Some examples

Cascades occur when individuals with private information make decisions sequentially. Cascades can still occur even when non-informational factors (sanctions against deviants, payoff interdependence, desire to conform) are present. Having recognized that factors other than information are important, I will focus on cascades and try to avoid repeated qualifications in the examples that follow. Several criteria are relevant for evaluating the applicability of the cascades model to actual behavior. The first group of criteria pertains to model assumptions: (i) Do individuals observe the actions of others?; (ii) Do individuals learn from direct discussion with others?; and (iii) Are informational effects more important than other effects?

Point (ii) carries little weight, since actions speak louder than words. With regard to point (iii), sometimes one individual's action reduces another's gain from that action, in which case the payoff interaction *opposes* uniformity. If Wellcome observes that Merck is working on an Alzheimer's drug, then Wellcome has a good reason *not* to do so: it would have a competitor. If Wellcome still imitates, this suggests that information is involved. Even when payoff interactions support uniformity, cascades may still play a role in determining which alternative is fixed upon.

The second group of criteria pertain to implications of the theory: (i) Is behavior localized and idiosyncratic (often mistaken)?; (ii) Is behavior fragile?; and (iii) Do some individuals follow the crowd and ignore their own private information?

4.1 Politics

The political scientist Bartels (1988) has discussed "cue-taking" in presidential nomination campaigns, in which one person's assessment of a candidate is influenced by the choices of others: "the operative logic is, roughly, that '25,000 solid New Hampshirites (probably) can't be too far wrong'." Political scientists who have studied how candidates build political momentum have developed survey measures (called "thermometer ratings") in which respondents score numerically how much they like the candidate. Several studies have found that after controlling for relevant factors, a candidate is rated more favorably when respondents are aware of more favorable poll results. Bartels points out (consistent with the cascades theory) that "There need not be any actual process of persuasion ... the fact of the endorsement itself motivates me to change my substantive opinion of him [the candidate]."

An alternative hypothesis is that voters strategically throw support behind candidates who have a better shot at winning. A vote for a sure loser is "wasted," after all. Strategic voting does explain why early successes of a candidate may lead people to vote for him. However, it does not explain why the candidate's thermometer ratings should increase. In the cascades model, the numerical evaluation of the candidate should go up after he wins early victories. In a study of the 1984 Hart–Mondale contest for the Democratic nomination, Bartels found that there was an "internalized effect" on individuals' thermometer ratings, particularly in the early stages of the campaign.

In the 1976 US presidential campaign, an obscure Democratic candidate named Jimmy Carter focused on the Iowa caucus to obtain an early success. In the 1988 presidential contest, Democratic candidate Richard Gephardt campaigned for one year in the first two states (Iowa and New Hampshire), with less success. A common criticism of the primary system is that voters in early primaries carry more weight than voters in late primaries. As a result, many Southern states have coordinated their primaries on the same date ("Super-Tuesday"). In Spain, publicizing opinion polls within twenty-four hours of an election is legally prohibited. Similarly, it has been argued that the early reporting of election results is undesirable because later voters may be influenced (either in their choice of candidate, or in their decisions of whether to vote).

Voting is only one of many kinds of political action. Susanne Lohmann has examined a model of political revolution in which public protests, demonstrations, and riots occur repeatedly over time, and turnout fluctuates until a cascade forms. Since different people have different gains from a regime change, and since people choose when to protest, protests convey information bit by bit over time. She shows that "In some cases, a small number of political actions may have a large impact on public opinion; in other cases, a huge turnout may be followed by the sudden collapse of the protest movement." If more people turn out than expected, even if the numbers are very small, this communicates to others that opposition to the regime is greater than expected, which can stimulate still others to turn out. Conversely, if a huge turnout is expected, then even a large turnout may be a negative surprise, in which case the protest can peter out. Eventually, either a cascade of revolt against or acceptance of the current regime occurs. Lohmann (1992a,b) argues that informational cascades provide the most satisfactory explanation for the process by which communism fell in then East Germany, based on patterns of turnout over five cycles of protest in Leipzig.

4.2 Zoology

Zoologists have found that animals frequently copy the behavior of other animals in territory choice, mating, and foraging. Imitation has obvious adaptive benefit, since it is better to learn by watching than by hard experience. Innovations known to have spread by imitation include sweet potato washing by Japanese macaques (Kawai, 1965), and milk bottle opening by British tits (Hinde and Fisher, 1952).

Various studies have found that animals cluster in their territory choice more than can be accounted for by the fact that high-quality sites may be located close together. Zoologists have found that territories are clumped idiosyncratically, in the sense that they are not necessarily located at the best available sites (Stamps (1988) discusses the relevant studies). According to the cascades theory, the location of clusters will be fairly arbitrarily determined by the choices of a few early settlers. Indeed, some biologists have argued that clustering occurs because of males using the presence of other males as an indicator of high resource quality in nearby territories.

Numerous studies have shown that females copy other females in choosing a male to mate with. Pomiankowski (1990) discusses how "in both fallow deer and sage grouse, the rate at which females enter male territories correlates with the number of females already present." When experimenters placed a stuffed female grouse on the territory of an unattractive male, the number of females entering the territory increased. A recent study by Gibson, Bradbury, and Vehrencamp (1992) found that sage grouse females became markedly more unanimous in their mate choices when they arrived at the male mating display area together, so that they could observe each others' choices. The unanimity of mate choice is not explained by the characteristics of males or their sites observable to human researchers. This arbitrariness is consistent with informational cascades. Copying in these species occurs despite some significant waiting costs.

Lee Alan Dugatkin and his co-author provide some remarkable evidence on the mate choices of the Trinidadian guppy *Poecilia reticulata*. Dugatkin shows that "females copy the choice of mates made by other females by viewing such interactions, remembering the identity of the chosen male, and subsequently choosing that male in future sexual endeavors."[18] In a study of guppies, Dugatkin and Godin (1993) find that "younger females copy the mate choice of older females, but older females do not appear to be influenced by the mate choice of younger individuals." This is consistent with the "fashion leader" model at the end of section 2, since older females presumably have more precise information than younger females. Greater experience in choosing mates presumably allows older females to interpret environmental cues more accurately. Most remarkable of all, in a 1992 paper Dugatkin and Godin have established that

... copying can even override a female's original preference of mates ... That is, a female's preference for a particular male ... can be reversed if she has the opportunity to see a (model) female choose the male she herself did not choose previously.

This experiment identifies a key aspect of an informational cascade, that an individual's private information can be overridden by the observation of others' actions. It would be interesting to verify whether a female's mate choice is more likely to be reversed if she observes *multiple* females choosing differently than when she observes only a single other female.

4.3 Medical practice and scientific theory

The cascades theory predicts fads, idiosyncrasy, and imitation in medical treatments. (The practice of bleeding to remove bad blood, popular until the nineteenth century is a familiar example.) Most doctors are not at the cutting edge of research; their inevitable reliance upon what colleagues have done or are doing leads to numerous surgical fads and treatment-caused illnesses ("iatroepidemics") (Robin, 1984; Taylor, 1979). It appears that many dubious practices were initially adopted based on very weak information. An example is the popularization in the 1970s of elective hysterectomy, the surgical removal, without any special medical indications, of the uterus of women past child-bearing age.[19] In the *New England Journal of Medicine*, John Burnum discusses "bandwagon diseases" diagnosed by physicians who behave "like lemmings, episodically and with a blind infectious enthusiasm pushing certain diseases and treatments primarily because everyone else is doing the same." In the fashion leader version of the cascades model, even one adoption can start a cascade. So our advice to patients seeking a second opinion is to withhold the first doctor's diagnosis.

Even science (not to mention academia in general) is subject to fads and fashions. The sheer complexity and volume of material a scientist must deal with makes it impossible to examine critically the evidence bearing on all major theories. At best scientists can investigate thoroughly only narrow subfields. But knowledge is interrelated, so a scientist is forced to accept useful ideas and theories because *others have done so.*

Furthermore, there is a strong "fashion leader" phenomenon in academics, including the sciences. In the fashion leader model, the decision by the first (well-informed) individual was enough to persuade everyone after to imitate. In academics and science as well, nascent theories of course enjoy much greater success when the initiator is famous and from a top university than when he is unknown and from a minor school. This can explain the "Matthew effect" described by Robert K. Merton, a well-known sociologist of science.[20] When a minor league researcher proposes a good idea, it is often dismissed by editors and reviewers as wrong or uninteresting, whereupon it slips into oblivion. The idea is not linked to any name in people's minds, because almost no one has even noticed its existence. In contrast, when a distinguished scientist proposes the same idea, it gains credibility by virtue of the endorser, and becomes linked to the distinguished name in people's minds.

The cascades theory implies that the rise of academics to eminence is itself idiosyncratic. It is very costly, even for a pro, to assess accurately the achievements of another researcher. So to a large extent we view someone as eminent because we observe that others have done so.[21] For example, if you are hired at a top school, prestige rubs on to you (and vice versa). Just as the eminence of academics may be the result of cascades of esteem, a job applicant who receives early job offers may become a "star." In the annual rookie market for professors, later schools give close attention to the interviews or offers granted by earlier schools. Similarly, to be granted tenure or receive a chaired professorship at a university it is helpful to receive tenured or chaired offers elsewhere. Eminence is of course far from meaningless. But academic stature can be surprisingly noisy. Since eminent academics become academic fashion leaders, these errors in turn can cause substantive errors in the acceptance or rejection of new ideas.

4.4 Finance

Foresi and Mei (1991, 1992) provide evidence consistent with firms imitating each other in choosing levels of investment. They report in both US and Japanese data sets that a firm's investment level can be explained partly by the investment levels and profitability of its *competitors*.[22]

A very important kind of discrete investment is the purchase of another firm. A firm that receives a takeover bid is said to be put "into play," and very frequently receives sudden competing offers. Yet from the bidder's viewpoint, competing for an in-play target is more expensive than buying another target that is not sought after by a competitor. This suggests that potential bidders learn from the first bid that the target is an attractive candidate for takeover. More broadly, takeover markets have been subject to booms and crashes, such as the wave of conglomerate mergers in the 1960s, in which firms diversified across different industries, and the subsequent refocusing of firms through restructuring and bustup takeovers in the 1980s.

Providers of capital to firms also may imitate in their investment decisions. When a distressed firm asks creditors to renegotiate the terms of its debt, the refusal of one creditor may affect the decisions of others. Similarly, if some bank depositors withdraw their funds from a troubled bank, others may follow, leading to a bank run. In both these examples, there is a payoff interaction as well as an informational interaction between different people. If I get my money out first, this leaves less for you. However, at the very start of the bank run, when only a few people have withdrawn, the information conveyed by their actions may be the dominating influence upon others. An analysis of informational cascades at the start of bank runs is provided by Corb (1993). Chen (1993) examines contagious cascades of runs between banks.

It is natural to wonder whether cascades apply to stock market investments. After all, market price fluctuations have been described with such

phrases as "manias," "panics," "fads," "animal spirits," "investor senti-
ment," and "bubbles." The basic cascades model is too simple to capture
these phenomena, because the cost of "adopting" the action of buying a
stock is not constant. As the price rises, it becomes more expensive to buy
the stock. Lee (1992) has shown that market booms and crashes can occur
in a modified cascades model. Currently there is little evidence as to the
validity of this explanation.

4.5 Peer influence and stigma

In *The Mask of Command*, John Keegan describes Alexander the Great as
"the supreme hero. Nowhere do the dimensions of his heroic effort show
more clearly than in his personal conduct on the battlefield." For example,
"at Multan, he attempted to take the city virtually single-handed. It was
thus that he suffered his nearly fatal wound." After confusion led to a delay
in bringing up the siege ladders, Alexander

seized one himself, set it against the wall, held his shield over his head and started up
... Reaching the battlements, he pushed some of the Indians off it with his shield,
killed others with his sword and waited for his followers to join him in the foothold
he had won. They were so anxious to reach him ... that they overcrowded the
ladder, which broke, decanting those at the top on to those at the bottom and so
stopping anyone getting to Alexander's help. He, "conspicuous both by splendor of
this arms and by his miraculous courage," was now under attack by bowmen at
close range. He could not remain where he was. He would not jump down to safety.
He therefore jumped into the city and began to lay about him with his sword as if
Gulliver among the Lilliputians.

As Keegan's book makes clear, Alexander's courage was "exemplary":
his example encouraged others to fight harder.[23] More generally, in battle,
waves of optimism or pessimism often make the difference between victory
and defeat. If others desert, those remaining may not only lose the aid of
their comrades (payoff interaction), but may infer that their comrades
viewed victory unlikely (du Picq, 1921). The ancient emphasis on heroic
leadership has an informational interpretation. As in the fashion leader
model, officers will normally know better than their troops about the
prospects for victory. Thus, courage by officers should have a disproportionate effect on the morale of the troops. Rank distinctions aside, it
would be very interesting to study whether the actions of a very few early
deserters or early fighters can have a disproportionate effect on the morale
and behavior of the others.

It may be objected that information is not the only explanation for a
motivating effect of heroism. Does not brave behavior by officers shame the
troops into bravery? Possibly, but on the other hand, many troops would

rather be shamefully alive than honorably dead. Given the intense emotions and challenges to self-command associated with battle, it is easy to see how some commentators could misinterpret a rational information effect as "shaming."

Conformity to peers in general is often assumed automatically to be due to coercion rather than informational effects. Contrast the cliched, judgmental phrase "peer pressure," with the neutral "peer influence." Conformity may often occur voluntarily when people are faced with similar decisions, especially those with little information or experience, and obtain information from the decisions of others. In a famous set of experiments, the social psychologist Salomon Asch found that people asked to compare the lengths of lines tended to follow the comparisons made by other members of their group. While this is usually viewed as due to a pressure to conform, it is also possible that people genuinely change their beliefs after observing others' choices.

Genuine coercion can arise from the threat of stigma, a shared negative treatment of someone who violates the norm of the group. But those who stigmatize may have informational reasons for doing so. Social psychologists have found evidence suggesting that stigma is specific to the group, and that people learn to stigmatize by observing the actions of others such as parents (see Ainlay, Becker, and Coleman, 1986). Just as gaps in one's resume are damaging, a frequent job-switcher may be treated with suspicion. The traditional (and now weakened) stigma carried by divorced persons provides another example.

5 Fads

Customs and standards sometimes shift abruptly without obvious reason. In the basic cascades model, people very quickly start to do the same thing, which is quite often a mistake. The initial cascade forms based on very little information. Because of this, if the model is changed by adding small shocks to the system, a persistent behavior among early individuals can become unpopular among later individuals.[24] This section considers one kind of shock to the system that leads to seemingly whimsical shifts in behavior. Suppose that there is a small probability that the underlying value of adopting versus rejecting can change after the hundredth person (say). Then the cascade can very easily switch. So much is obvious – if it used to be better to adopt, and now it is better to reject, then it is possible people will notice this fact, and act accordingly.

What is interesting is that the cascade can switch not just because the right action has changed, but because people *think it may* have changed. This means that even if adopting (for example) was the right thing to do and the original cascade correctly involved adopting, for example, individual 101 may happen to observe an L signal and wrongly switch to rejecting because he thinks that rejection has now become more preferable. In effect, the possibility of the value change shakes up a precarious balance. As a result, the likelihood of an action change (from a cascade of rejection to one of acceptance, or *vice versa*) can be far greater than the probability that the correct choice has changed. Bikhchandani, Welch, and I provide a numerical example in which, after the hundredth person, there is a 5 percent chance of a switch in best action (from adopt to reject, or *vice versa*). This leads to a probability of over 9.35 percent that the cascade is at some point reversed, which is 87 percent higher. The effect of cascades is to create temporary uniformity (during the time after the initial cascade starts in the first 100 individuals), but the situation becomes highly volatile at the time of the shock (just before individual 101). Since people were not very sure that the cascade was correct in the first place, they shift at the slightest provocation.

I have focused on one kind of shock – value changes – that causes fads. Other types of noise or shocks can have the same effect. For example, if I can't observe or remember perfectly what previous people did, or if I think their costs and benefits differ from mine, I may be inclined to switch. Again, this can lead to abrupt shifts in the behavior of many people.

6 The decision to acquire information

Information is costly to acquire; it's cheaper to rely on the cheap information conveyed by the decisions of others. Suppose that each person decides whether or not to investigate (which is costly), and then decides whether to adopt or reject. Then whenever anyone declines to acquire information, everyone who follows will do likewise. To see this, suppose that Deedee does not buy information. Then Edgar's decision about whether to invest in information is based on precisely the same public information that Deedee had. Since Deedee didn't buy information, neither should Edgar. Repeating this reasoning shows that no one later in the queue buys information.

Since a cascade is virtually sure to form by the time a late individual is reached (see section 2), any information he might purchase would have no value. So individuals who are late in the queue virtually never acquire information. An early individual, for whom a private signal may prove decisive, is of course more likely to acquire information. In confirmation, Rogers and Shoemaker (1971) conclude from twelve empirical studies on diffusion of innovations that "early adopters seek more information about innovations than later adopters."

Interestingly, even when people can observe the *signals* of their predecessors (not just their actions), cascades can form and bring about idiosyncratic behavior and fragility. As soon as early investigating individuals generate information with a fairly mild preponderance of evidence in favor of one action or another, a point is reached where later individuals will imitate regardless of their own signals. At this point, they have no reason to investigate, so the general pool of public knowledge stops growing. As with the basic model, society therefore ends up fixed upon an action based on weak evidence; and, of course, it only takes a small shock to dislodge such an ill-informed cascade.

7 Conclusion

People often seem to end up doing the same thing without any obvious sanctions against deviants. The theory of informational cascades helps explain why conformity occurs, how it is maintained, and how it is broken. Furthermore, cascades explain why the conformist outcome is often wrong. The reason is that cascades start readily based on very small amounts of information. Once the past history of adoptions or rejections becomes just informative enough to outweigh a person's private information signal, he follows his predecessors. At this point his action is uninformative to later decision makers, so later followers join the bandwagon. But while this cascade of identical or conformist behavior can become quite *long*, it is not *strong*. A small shock, such as a public information disclosure, a value change, or even the possibility of such a change, can lead to an abrupt shift.

The cascades theory should be contrasted with some other theories of instability. Many models of behavior imply that the actions of large groups can be fragile under *special circumstances*. In these alternative models, there is instability only if the system coincidentally is balanced near a knife edge. In contrast, when there are informational cascades the system *systematically* moves to a precarious position – everyone is doing the same thing but just barely prefers to do so.

In most actual conformist situations, one or more forces may be operative: information transfers, sanctions against deviants, payoff interactions, and direct desire to conform. None of these are inconsistent with informational cascades. In a big group, the behavior of the first few individuals probably doesn't impose sanctions on others, nor directly affect others' payoffs very much, nor does it create much immediate pressure to conform. However, according to cascades theory, the actions of the first few individuals will still be extremely influential.

The basic cascades model implies occasional, irregular bouts of sudden change because people reestimate the costs and benefits of different alternatives. In some theories of fads or fashion, change occurs regularly because how much some people value different alternatives directly depends on what others are doing. For example, some people may have a direct preference for change. Or, some people may have a direct preference for deviating from the actions of others. For example, whether a short skirt is acceptable this season depends on who else decides to wear a short skirt.

In a setting where most people want to conform, many outcomes may be possible. Will pink be the fashionable color next year or black? It may be that neither color is much superior to the other, but people do care about wearing the popular color. If so, people who need to buy clothes early will try to forecast what others will be doing. Even in such cases, the choices of early individuals can start cascades, because the followers may infer from the early choice of black (say) that early people have reason to suspect that black will be "in." Thus, even though this setting is rather distant from the basic cascades model, cascades can still help to explain choices. The key ingredient of the cascades approach is that individuals make decisions more or less in sequence, with later decision makers observing something about the choices of earlier decision makers. This sequentiality is probably present in the introduction of clothing fashions and in the start of political revolutions, as well as in other applications mentioned earlier. Thus, cascades can help explain the *process* by which society switches from one steady state to another.

I will mention two possible extensions of the model. The first is to include liaison individuals, i.e., people who link two or more cliques. For example, a cascade in France may go in the opposite direction from a cascade in England. If someone can observe both cascades, and if his decision can be observed in both countries, then he may break one of the two cascades. As the world becomes more of a global village, the cascades analysis predicts that such linkage can reverse local cascades. US "cultural imperialism" (in television, cinema, fast food, sneakers, and blue jeans) may be a case in point. Socially, it may be desirable to have separate groups that are only later combined, so that later individuals can aggregate the information of several cascades instead of just one.

The other extension is to consider varying costs of adoption. If costs of adoption are increasing, for example, then cascades of adoption can be broken. In work in progress (Hirshleifer and Welch, 1994a, b), Welch and I show that cascades are just a special case of a more general phenomenon which we call inertia. When an individual such as a corporate manager can observe previous decisions (of his predecessor) but not previous signals, the new manager is often biased in favor of continuing and even *escalating* the old policies. A new manager will rationally tend to invest in costly expansions of projects-in-place based on the likelihood that his predecessor had good reason for initiating the original project. We argue that failures of institutional memory (as when a manager is replaced) leads to such problems as sunk-cost biases (continuing investment in failing projects), retention of deadwood, the Peter Principle (promoting employees to their level of incompetence), and undervaluation of future opportunities for growth.

Notes

I thank Sushil Bikhchandani, Julian Franks, Jack Hirshleifer, Susanne Lohmann, Manuel Santos, Mariano Tommasi, and Ivo Welch for helpful information and comments.

1 After catching the attention of academic economists, his paper was profiled in a respected news magazine, *The Economist*. By popular demand, Becker published some further thoughts in a paper called "Son of Fish Market: ... A Further Note on Restaurant Pricing and Other Examples of Social Influence on Price," in honor of the restaurant that triggered his thinking on the topic.

2 But contrast Yogi Berra's remark about a once-popular restaurant: "no-one goes there anymore – it's too crowded."

3 There is, of course, a tradeoff here. A rational manager will balance the benefits of gaining higher revenues when the price is high against the risk of killing the goose that lays the golden eggs.

4 Banerjee (1992), Chamley and Gale (1992), and Lohmann (1992a) provide related theories of imitation.

5 But for forces that operate to overcome idiosyncratic outcomes, see Liebowitz and Margolis (1990).

6 People observe decisions of others when lining up behind political candidates through opinion polls, bumper stickers, and the endorsements of loudmouths at cocktail parties.

7 Some relevant articles and books are Akerlof (1976, 1980), Kuran (1989, 1991), and Coleman (1987). See also my own work with Eric Rasmusen (Hirshleifer and Rasmusen, 1989) on enforcing cooperation through ostracism.

8 In Kuran's model of revolution, a small spark can cause a prairie fire, because – owing to sanctions on deviants or on a direct desire to conform – people hide their true beliefs. In Eastern Europe, for example, many people who opposed the communist regime remained quiet. Only when public opposition attained a critical mass did change occur. Kuran's prairie fires are sudden and sweeping but occur only in rare circumstances in which society happens to be at the edge of change.

9 Becker's model can also be viewed as a payoff interaction theory.

10 Clarence, by the way, is a sophisticated smoker. Carefully weighing the probabilities, he knows full well that there is a chance that Betsy also observed an L signal, so that Clarence really ought not to smoke. But he can't be sure, so

he makes an overall judgment based on his information and the actions of his predecessors. This often leads him to a different action than if he had known not just Betsy's action, but her *information* and that of predecessors.

11 It is quite possible that many of these farmers observed mainly whether their neighbors adopted rather than the entire sequence of previous decision makers. Cascades can still arise in settings where only some of previous decisions are observable. Cascades can also arise when people see only a summary of previous actions; for example, someone deciding which of two types of car to buy may look at reports on total sales.

12 Suppose that the signal accuracy is 60 percent, so that when adopting is preferable, 60 percent of the time an *H* signal is observed. Then about one third of the time the wrong cascade occurs. Even if the signal accuracy is 70 percent, about one fifth of the time the wrong cascade occurs.

13 According to the theory of *psychohistory* in Isaac Asimov's *Foundation* science fiction series, the random behaviors of individuals average out to mass behaviors that are almost perfectly predictable in the long run. Thus, the mathematician Hari Seldon was able to forecast events in the decline of the Galactic empire over a period of thousands of years. The cascades theory, if correct, dashes the hopes of developing accurate psychohistory.

14 A more precise signal has a higher probability of *H* when adopting is superior, and a higher probability of *L* when rejecting is superior.

15 A fruitful extension of cascades theory would be to study information flows in organizations. If subordinates have useful but noisy information, then an upward flow of project recommendations may preserve their information much more effectively than a decision process that moves downward through the hierarchy.

16 Bandura (1977) states that "in situations in which people are uncertain about the wisdom of modeled courses of action, they must rely on such cues as general appearances, speech, style, age, symbols of socioeconomic success, and signs of expertise as indicators of past successes."

17 Early medical reports that oat bran lowers cholesterol levels led to sudden popularity of oat bran products. Newer studies contradicted the efficacy of oat bran, and the fad collapsed. A recent study has suggested that oat bran is moderately effective after all (*Consumer Reports Health Letter*, April 1991, p. 31).

18 Dugatkin refers to several studies of female mating choices in fishes indicating that females prefer males that already have broods from prior matings.

19 Routine tonsillectomy, the surgical removal of tonsils, seems to be another remarkably unfounded practice. According to Taylor, its adoption was not associated with any definitive supporting evidence, such as controlled studies. An English panel asserted that tonsillectomy was being "performed as a routine prophylactic ritual for no particular reason and with no particular result." Also notable are the extreme differences in tonsillectomy frequencies in different countries and regions. The routine tonsillectomy of millions of children was not without cost, since some children were injured and died as a result. As with hysterectomy, the rate of tonsillectomy has declined in recent years.

20 The Bible tells us that "For whosoever hath, to him shall be given, and he shall have abundance; but whosoever hath not, from him shall be taken away even that he hath."

21 As Michael Ghiselin has put it, "The mere fact of eminence provides a cheap substitute for inquiring as to the basis upon which that eminence rests. The main reason why a scholar gets an honorary degree is that somebody else has already given him an honorary degree."

22 These studies suggest that imitation is important. However, the finding that the profitability of competitors helps explain own-investment behavior suggests that firms may be observing each other's profits, not just their actions. This suggests that the situation is more like the model with public information releases than the basic cascades model. This is not too surprising. We don't really think that investment decisions, once made, last forever.

23 According to Pakenham (1979, p. 133), "There were times in the wars of the nineteenth and earlier centuries when a general had to sacrifice his life to rally the troops." He describes the disproportionately high English officer casualties in the Boer War.

24 In this model, since each person makes a single decision in strict sequence, fads are defined as shifts in behavior between early and later individuals. However, as Chamley and Gale (1992) and Lohmann (1992a) have shown, the cascades concept extends to settings in which a given individual chooses when to switch from one behavior to another.

References

Ainlay, Stephen C., Gaylene Becker, and Lerita M. Coleman. 1986. *The Dilemma of Difference: A Multidisciplinary View of Stigma*, New York: Plenum Press.

Akerlof, George A. 1976. "The Economics of Caste and of the Rat Race and Other Woeful Tales," *Quarterly Journal of Economics*, 90 (4) (November): 599–617.
1980. "A Theory of Social Custom, of which Unemployment May Be One Consequence," *Quarterly Journal of Economics*, 94 (June): 749–75.

Anderson, Lisa. 1994. "Information Cascades: A Logistic Model of Laboratory Data," Working Paper, University of Virginia.

Anderson, Lisa and Charles Holt. 1993. "Information Cascades in the Laboratory," Working Paper, University of Virginia.

Arthur, Bryan. 1989. "Competing Technologies, Increasing Returns, and Lock-in by Historical Events," *The Economic Journal*, 99 (March): 116–31.

Asch, Salomon E. 1952. *Social Psychology*, Englewood Cliffs, NJ: Prentice Hall.

Bandura, Albert. 1977. *Social Learning Theory*, Englewood Cliffs, NJ: Prentice Hall.

Banerjee, Abhijit. 1992. "A Simple Model of Herd Behavior," *Quarterly Journal of Economics*, 107 (August): 797–818.

Bartels, Larry M. 1988. *Presidential Primaries and the Dynamics of Public Choice*, Princeton, NJ: Princeton University Press.

Becker, Gary S. 1991. "A Note on Restaurant Pricing and Other Examples of Social Influences on Price," *Journal of Political Economy*, 99 (October): 1109–16.

　　1992. "Son of Fish Market: A Further Note on Restaurant Pricing and Other Examples of Social Influence on Price," University of Chicago, Department of Economics Working Paper, May.

Bikhchandani, Sushil, David Hirshleifer, and Ivo Welch. 1992. "A Theory of Fads, Fashion, Custom, and Cultural Change in Informational Cascades," *Journal of Political Economy*, 100(5) (October): 992–1026.

Burnum, John F. 1987. *New England Journal of Medicine*, 317(19) (November): 1220–2.

Chamley, Cristophe and Douglas, Gale. 1992. "Information Revelation and Strategic Delay in Irreversible Decisions," Preliminary Draft, Boston University, July.

Chen, Yehning. 1993. "Payoff Externality, Information Externality, and Banking Panics," UCLA Anderson Graduate School of Management, October.

Coleman, James S. 1987. "Norms as Social Capital," in Gerard Radnitzky and Peter Bernholz (eds.), *Economic Imperialism: The Economic Approach Applied Outside the Field of Economics*, New York: Paragon House.

Corb, Howard M. 1993. "The Nature of Bank Runs," Graduate School of Business, Stanford University.

du Picq, Charles Ardant. 1921. *Battle Studies: Ancient and Modern Battle*, New York: Macmillan Press.

Dugatkin, Lee A. 1922. "Sexual Selection and Imitation: Females Copy the Mate Choice of Others," *American Naturalist*, 139: 1384–9.

Dugatkin, Lee A. and Jean-Guy J. Godin. 1992. "Reversal of Female Mate Choice by Copying in the Guppy *Poecilia reticulata*," *Proceedings of the Royal Society of London*, Series B.

　　1993. "Female Copying in the Guppy *Poecilia reticulata*: Age-Dependent Effects," *Behavioral Ecology*, 4: 289–92.

Foresi, Silverio and Jianping, Mei. 1991. "Do Firms 'Keep up with the Joneses'?: Evidence on Cross-Sectional Variations in Investment," NYU Salomon Center Working Paper S-91-41, June.

　　1992. "Interaction in Investment Among Japanese Rival Firms," NYU mimeo, August.

Galef Jr., Bennet G. 1976. "Social Transmission of Acquired Behavior: A Discussion of Tradition and Social Learning in Vertebrates," *Advances in the Study of Behavior*, 6: 77–100.

Ghiselin, Michael. 1989. "Intellectual Compromise: the bottom line," New York: Paragon House.

Gibson, Robert M., Jack W. Bradbury, and Sandra L. Vehrencamp. 1992. "Mate Choice in Lekking Sage Grouse Revisited: The Roles of Vocal Display, Female Site Fidelity, and Copying," *Behavioral Ecology*, 2: 165–80.

Hinde, R. A. and J. Fisher. 1952. "Further Observations on the Opening of Milk Bottles by Birds," *British Birds*, 44: 393–6.

Hirshleifer, David and Eric Rasmusen. 1989. "Cooperation in a Repeated Prisoners' Dilemma with Ostracism," *Journal of Economic Behavior and Organization*, 12 (August): 87–106.

Hirshleifer, David and Ivo Welch. 1993a. "Institutional Memory, Inertia, and Investment Decisions."

1993b "Institutional Memory, Escalation, and Investment Decisions."

Jones, Stephen R.G. 1984. *The Economics of Conformism*, Oxford: Basil Blackwell.

Kawai, M. 1965. "Newly Acquired Pre-Cultural Behavior of the Natural Troop of Japanese Monkeys on Koshima Inlet," *Primates*, 6 (August): 1–30.

Keegan, John. 1987. *The Mask of Command*, New York: Elisabeth Sifton Books-Viking, pp. 13–91.

Kuran, Timur. 1989. "Sparks and Prairie Fires: A Theory of Unanticipated Political Revolution," *Public Choice*, 61 (April): 41–74.

1991. "Now out of Never: The Element of Surprise in the East European Revolution of 1989," *World Politics*, 44 (October): 7–48.

Lee, In Ho. 1992. "Market Crashes and Informational Cascades," UCLA Economics Department, September.

Liebowitz, Stanley J. and Stephen E. Margolis. 1990. "The Fable of the Keys," *Journal of Law and Economics*, 33 (April): 1–25.

Lohmann, Susanne. 1992a. "Rationality, Revolution and Revolt: The Dynamics of Informational Cascades," Graduate School of Business Research Paper No. 1213, Stanford University, October.

1992b. "The Dynamics of Regime Collapse: A Case Study of the Leipzig Monday Demonstrations," Graduate School of Business Research Paper No. 1225, Stanford University, October.

Merton, Robert K. 1973. *The Sociology of Science: Theoretical and Empirical Investigations*, Chicago: University of Chicago Press.

Pakenham, Thomas. 1979. *The Boer War*, New York: Random House.

Pomiankowski, Andrew. 1990. "How to Find the Top Male," *Nature*, 347 (October): 616–17.

Robin, Eugene D. 1984. *Matters of Life and Death: Risks vs. Benefits of Medical Care*, New York: Freeman and Co.

Rogers, Everett M. 1983. *Diffusion of Innovation*, 3rd edition, New York: Free Press, Macmillan Publishers.

Rogers, Everett M. and F. Floyd. Shoemaker. 1971. *Communication of Innovations: A Cross-Cultural Approach*, 2nd edition, New York: Macmillan Press.

Ryan, Bryce and Neal C. Gross. 1943. "The Diffusion of Hybrid Seed Corn in Two Iowa Communities," *Rural Sociology*, 8 (March): 15–24.

Schelling, Thomas C. 1978. *Micromotives and Macrobehavior*, New York: Norton Publishers.

Stamps, J.A. 1988. "Conspecific Attraction and Aggregation in Territorial Species," *American Naturalist*, 131 (March): 329–47.

Taylor, Richard. 1979. *Medicine out of Control*, Melbourne: Sun Books.

Welch, Ivo. 1992. "Sequential Sales, Learning and Cascades," *The Journal of Finance*, 47.

13 Public health and economic epidemiology[1]

Tomas Philipson

1 Introduction

The public control of infectious disease is often argued to be one of the main achievements of modern medicine and public health. Recently, the surging AIDS epidemic as well as measles and treatment-resistant tuberculosis epidemics have again made such control a concern in many developed countries including the United States. Moreover, the enormous mortality and morbidity caused by infectious disease in developing nations has always put this public health problem at the forefront of public policy. The importance of this topic is demonstrated by the fact that infectious disease is currently the number-one cause of mortality in the world.

Epidemiology is commonly defined as the study of the occurrence of diseases, whether infectious or not, across populations, areas, and times. *Economic epidemiology* studies the same class of phenomena, but differs from other approaches by attempting to determine the underlying forces leading to the transmittive choices made by individuals in the population where the disease is located. This article discusses the contribution this approach has made so far over the main existing approach, mathematical epidemiology, in explaining actual disease behavior and the effects that alternative public health measures may have in their attempts to limit the spread of infectious diseases.

The analysis of infectious disease joins the many other areas, including law and sociology, that the imperial science of economics, led in part by Gary Becker, has attempted to develop beyond their existing paradigms. However, with infectious disease analysis, economics attempts to improve one of the natural sciences, as opposed to one of the other social sciences. I believe that epidemiology is an area where social science may successfully compete with and even outperform the natural sciences by providing theories of greater explanatory power which will thereby be more useful in assessing the effects and desirability of existing efforts to control the spread of disease.

This chapter discusses, informally and qualitatively, a few questions asked in the study of infectious disease and the differences between the answers obtained by economists and epidemiologists. The epidemiological answers are exemplified in Bailey (1975), Anderson and May (1991), and Brandeau and Kaplan (1994). For the economic answers I will draw almost exclusively on the work contained in Philipson and Posner (1993) in the case of AIDS and Philipson (1994) for the remaining topics. The discussion will focus on three general questions:

1 How do economic and biological epidemiology differ in their predictions of disease occurrence?
2 How do their predictions about the effects of public health measures differ?
3 How do they define the loss inflicted upon society by a disease and determine what rules should govern attempts to eliminate the harm caused by a disease (e.g., by prevention or treatment)?

This chapter discusses partial answers to these three questions. Naturally, a single chapter cannot claim to cover everything that has been and is being done in this rapidly expanding area of research.

2 Differences in predictions about disease occurrence

According to the economic theory of infectious disease, differential disease prevalence across population groups is determined by differences in protection costs relative to infection costs. This theory is economic in the sense that individuals choose between exposure and protection based on the incentives involved – the likelihood of complications from infection (the "cost" of infection) relative to the disutility of protection (the "cost" of protection). The cost of protection may take many forms – for instance, lost learning or earnings from not attending school or work or, in the case of sexually transmitted diseases (STDs), lost pleasure from safe instead of risky sex. Such costs are usually not, but may be, monetary. Observe that if protection were "free" (i.e., without cost) there would be no disease since, *ceteris paribus*, no one prefers having a disease to not having it, and so free protection would always be demanded. One major reason for the positive prevalence of infectious diseases is, therefore, the disutility of protection – that is, that people are unwilling to pay the full "cost" of protection.

In general, when an activity is rare, the economist tries to explain this by looking for costs that outweigh the benefits of the activity (and, conversely, for benefits that outweigh the costs when an activity is common). Thus we expect the prevalence of an infectious disease to be higher the more the cost of protection exceeds the cost of infection. For example, protection against many airborne diseases such as colds or chicken pox requires complete isolation, whereas infection entails only a few days in bed. For these diseases, the cost of protection is very high relative to the cost of infection which leads us to predict that such diseases will have high prevalence relative to, say, fatal diseases.

Biological epidemiological models of the spread of infectious diseases correspond to the economic epidemiological model of disease spread restricted to the special case of *inelastic* transmissive behavior – that is, transmissive behavior which does not respond to surrounding incentives to alter behavior. These incentives may include different disease prevalence levels (defined to be the fraction of infected people in the population), or modes of transmission. In such models, the interaction pattern between individuals is the key determinant of the changes over time in the spread of a disease. In particular, the more meetings between infected and susceptible individuals, the higher the number of new cases of the disease.

2.1 The effect of prevalence on the hazard rate of infection

Economic and biological epidemiology make different predictions about the effect the prevalence of disease has on the hazard rate into infectivity (defined to be the fraction of susceptible individuals infected in a given time period). For example, if a population consists of 1,000 individuals of which fifty are infected then the prevalence is 5 percent. If these fifty individuals infect ten new individuals, the hazard rate into infectivity is 10/950. Prevalence is thus a measure of the infected stock, and hazard a measure of the flow into the infected stock.

Figure 13.1 illustrates the different models' predictions about the effect of prevalence on hazard rate. The horizontal axis measures the prevalence of a disease, and the vertical axis the fraction of still-susceptible individuals who become infected as a function of this prevalence (the so-called hazard function).

In a biological model with random matching, the proportion of susceptible individuals who will meet some infected person is equal to the proportion of infected individuals in the population – that is, hazard rate equals prevalence. Therefore, the biological model predicts an increasing relationship between the infectivity hazard rate and the prevalence level.

This relationship holds in the economic model only if demand for protection does not respond to a rise in prevalence – that is, only in the special case of inelastic (or unchanging) demand for protection given any level of prevalence. If it does respond to a change in prevalence – if the demand for protection is prevalence elastic (or prevalence responsive) – the effect of higher prevalence on the hazard rate into infectivity is not continually increasing. This is because as prevalence increases, so does

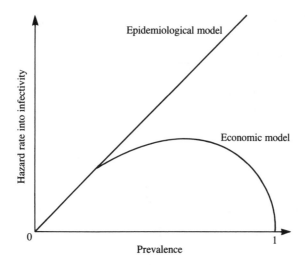

Figure 13.1 Effect of prevalence on hazard rate into infectivity predicted by the two models

demand for protection by susceptible individuals; since the price of exposed behavior has increased due to increased prevalence, the relative price of protection has decreased.

Figure 13.2 illustrates the prevalence pattern in AIDS data from the Centers for Disease Control (CDC). It shows that the AIDS population – that is, the cumulative number of AIDS cases to date minus the cumulative number of AIDS deaths to date – is stabilizing. It has also been documented (Philipson, 1993) that the hazard rate into infectivity for AIDS is decreasing over time – that is, the fraction of previously uninfected individuals becoming infected is decreasing as the prevalence of the disease increases. This negative effect of prevalence on infectivity hazard rates supports the economic model over standard biological models.

2.2 The effect of prevalence on matching patterns

In the case of STDs such as AIDS, the reduction in the hazard rate over time may result from the formation of partnerships in response to the epidemic. In the economic model of sexually transmitted disease, unprotected sex between two individuals is interpreted as a "trade" in the sense of being a mutually beneficial activity. As is true for other economic markets (e.g., car insurance markets with accident risk), traders generally are heterogeneous in their quality status, here interpreted as their HIV-infection status.

In treating this issue, biological epidemiology again assumes inelastic

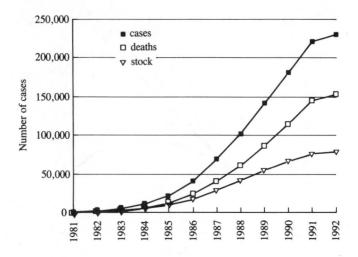

Figure 13.2 Prevalence pattern of AIDS

behavior – that an increasing epidemic does not alter the partner choices of individuals. The economic model, however, in following the analogy with insurance markets, assumes partner selection to be elastic. In other words, insurance companies will change the profile of their portfolios given different general levels of accident risk.

Consider an environment which contains different classes of individuals whose risk of HIV infection is known, where risk is defined as the percentage of the class infected by the AIDS virus. Such classes may be subpopulations stratified by gender, appearance, weight, race, or other observable demographic characteristics. Given this environment, determining who will engage in sexual activity with whom, and what type of activity they will engage in, determines the probable spread of the disease. Specifically, it determines the likelihood of the demand for unprotected sex by a pair of individuals, one of whom is infected, one of whom is not. This is necessary for new cases of the disease as one cannot get the disease from someone who does not have it, and we assume "safe" sex is truly safe.

Engaging in unprotected activity with members of different risk classes exposes an individual to different risks. The individual may be willing to assume such risks if they are small given the benefit of unprotected sexual activity relative to protected activity. In other words someone who derives a large benefit from unprotected sex is more likely to assume risk than use a condom or abstain. The opposite is true for someone who derives low benefits from unprotected sex.

These risks act like prices, where the risk level of an individual act is the price of unprotected sexual activity with that individual. And, as in most markets, the higher the price, the lower the demand. Other things constant, the risk class of the individual is inversely related to the desirability of engaging in unprotected sexual activity with that individual. In this sense, the risk class of an individual is a measure of quality in the sexual market: the larger the risk, the lower the quality.

One prediction concerning partnership formation among individuals of differential quality is that high-quality individuals will engage in activity among themselves and low-quality individuals will engage in activity among themselves, an implication of the "assortative mating" prediction used in the study of marriage markets initiated by Gary Becker (1991). In other words, low-risk individuals engage with other low-risk individuals, and high-risk individuals with other high-risk individuals. Hence, the economic theory predicts less growth in disease prevalence than when individuals are randomly assigned to each other without choice and engage in risky behavior regardless of their partner. This is so because disease growth is due to risky behavior between HIV-negative and HIV-positive individuals, and the economic theory concludes that the market is biased away from such interactions.

In the extreme case when everyone knows every other individual's infection status, the prediction is that non-infected individuals will engage in sexual activity only with non-infected individuals and infected individuals only with infected individuals. This is because equilibrium levels of interaction will be determined by the non-infected individuals. Here, the market solution minimizes the growth of the disease, and thus yields much lower growth rates than those predicted by biological epidemiology.

This is illustrated by the effect of prevalence on the *dependence ratio* which measures the degree to which partnership formation depends on infection status. This dependency is measured by the fraction of infected individuals who engage in different forms of partnership with other infected individuals relative to the fraction of *susceptible* individuals who engage in different forms of partnership with infected individuals. Under random matching with respect to HIV status (i.e., partnership formation independent of HIV status), this ratio is unity. This is the case of the inelastic epidemiological model. However, in the economic model, increasing prevalence provides increasing incentive for susceptible individuals to stay with other susceptible individuals. Infected individuals, on the other hand, have no incentive to seek protection and thereby keep interacting with individuals whose infection probability rises over time. Hence, the dependence ratio is increasing in the economic model. In other words, as the epidemic grows, the HIV status of a person is more likely to be the same as the HIV status of her or his partner. Such predictions can be tested by use of several available partner surveys.

So far we have not mentioned the effect of the asymptomatic nature of the HIV virus – that is, that a person may be infected without any symptoms observable to his partner. If we regard symptomatic disease as providing perfect information about the "quality" of individuals, asymptomatic disease corresponds to the case of incomplete quality information. The effects of such information problems on the volume of trade in economic markets were first studied by George Akerlof (1970). He showed that there may be an inefficiently low volume of trade in markets involving incomplete information about quality, because even mutually beneficial trades, which would be made with perfect information, are avoided for fear of trading with a low-quality trader. This may be relevant for HIV risk, which may cause pairs of *susceptible* individuals to not engage in mutually beneficial unprotected sex for fear of infection. For STDs, in general, positive disease growth may be the result of imperfect information, and, indeed, most public health interventions in STD control are information based (e.g., screening, partner notification, education, confidentiality legislation, surveillance reporting to the population). The effect of changes in the allocation of information ("who knows what when") is ideally suited to economic analysis and cannot be addressed in a purely epidemiological framework which cannot incorporate the demand for information because it cannot incorporate purposeful behavior in its models.

2.3 The effect of immunity on the prevalence of a disease

Biological and economic epidemiology also disagree in explaining the empirically observed age structure of such immunity-bearing infectious diseases as chicken pox, measles, rubella, and mumps (often called child diseases due to the low average age of infection). For many such diseases there now exist vaccines, starting with the polio virus vaccine of Jonas Salk in the late fifties. Before vaccination was available, cohort studies of immunity-bearing diseases invariably showed a rapidly increasing number of seropositive individuals (individuals that have ever been infected, i.e. are currently infected or immune) as age increased, nearing 95 percent by the late teens. Figure 13.3 illustrates this in the case of measles during the 1940s and 1950s.

This pattern is the same for all low-cost (or low mortality or morbidity) child diseases such as mumps, rubella, and chicken pox. The pattern is not the same, in particular the cohort prevalence never escalates to nearly universal seropositivity, for more severe diseases such as polio and diph-

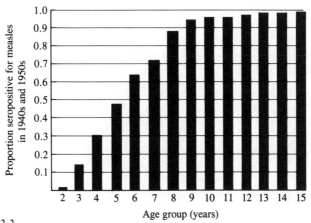

Figure 13.3
Source: Anderson and May, 1991, p. 47.

theria. Also, the last 5 percent of the cohort often escapes infection for the remainder of their lives so that the growth rate of cohort prevalence goes to zero after the cohort has exited their late teens.

Economic theory explains universal seropositivity by arguing that infection must be a *good*, that is, something an individual would be willing to pay for – people want infection. At first this claim seems absurd. However, biological epidemiological models in which infection is, implicitly or explicitly, a "bad" are forced to explain these cohort patterns by assuming an almost universal failure of protection. On the other hand, economics explains it as the universal success of individuals in infecting themselves!

To understand the incentives involved with these child diseases, observe that infection confers immunity. Therefore, infection may be interpreted as a *purchase* of immunity, that is, a cost undertaken for the benefit of immunity. The age structure of a disease therefore corresponds to the timing of this purchase so that if a disease is a child disease this means that the purchase is "front loaded" in age. The economist explains such front loading by citing two factors – the benefit of life-long immunity and the fact that the price of immunity, the cost of infection, is increasing with age. For example, the older one is when one contracts these immunity-bearing diseases, the higher is the case fatality rate (i.e., the fraction of those infected that die). Both factors make early infection preferable to later infection, that is, make the diseases child diseases. More important, people may be willing to "pay" for their children to be infected when vaccines are unavailable as witnessed in the common practice of having siblings sleep in the same room when one of them has the disease. This "get-it-over-with"

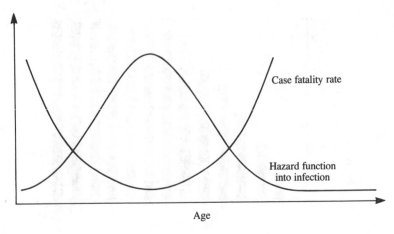

Figure 13.4

attitude among parents toward child diseases reflects the benefit of immunity and the rising cost of infection with age. Indeed, since vaccination and inoculation exactly induce a mild form of the disease aimed at spurring natural immunity, a purchase of vaccination is the same qualitative behavior as purchases of immunity through mild-form child infections. In essence, the incentives that drive early vaccination also drive early infection when vaccines are not available.

That the fraction of the cohort infected stops growing in the late teens is also easily explained through the incentives involved in the purchase of immunity through infection. Since it is in the late teens that the steep increase in infection cost takes place, demand for protection by individuals not yet immune also increases in these years. Put simply, if you are still susceptible to chicken pox and in your thirties and your friends' child is infected, you think twice about attending their party.

The economic theory of the age structure of immunity-bearing diseases implies that if the case fatality rate (the percentage of infected that die) is a U-shaped function of age, then rational exposure implies that the hazard rate into infection (fraction of the susceptible cohort that gets infected) is an inverted U-shaped function as illustrated in figure 13.4.

Thus in the early years a low percentage of those who are still at risk of infection become infected because of the danger of the disease. Once the case fatality rate goes down, the hazard rate goes up again.

Both of these predicted age-dependent patterns – for case fatality and hazard rates – hold for many actual diseases. Several studies document hazard rates into infection and show that the propensity to become infected displays the inverted U-shaped form discussed above. This implication is

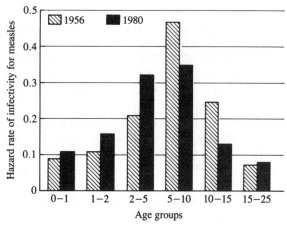

Figure 13.5
Source: Anderson and May, 1991, p. 165.

different from that resulting from a theory of genetic, and hence abehavioral, differences in susceptibility to disease among individuals. For example, figure 13.5 illustrates the standard patterns of hazard rates for measles for a cohort in England and Wales in pre-vaccination years (Anderson and May, 1991).

Epidemiologists explain such patterns in the age structure of disease through school mixing patterns – that is, since infected children are more likely to meet susceptible children when they are in school, the hazard rate increases in early school age. This amounts to saying that there is no *age effect* (so-called duration dependence) on the propensity to get infected across ages. Instead, it is argued that what drives these patterns is the fact that mixing patterns change with age. Although future studies must settle empirically whether such duration dependence exists, it is clear that school mixing patterns cannot be the whole answer since they are the same for both immunity-bearing diseases and non-immunity-bearing diseases, which, in fact, have drastically different age structures. Also, such a theory is incapable of explaining why not *all* diseases are child diseases. Parents let their children go to school even if a disease is around when the cost of infection is low and purchase of immunity through infection is desired. Parents react far more strongly when there are no benefits of infection, as was witnessed during the controversies over whether to allow children with AIDS attend public schools.

So far we have discussed the age structure of disease, that is, the timing of the purchase of immunity, but epidemiology and economics also make different predictions about the effect of immunity on the overall prevalence of disease. In epidemiological models, the only effect of immunity is to lower the average time of infection, which in turn has a *negative* effect on prevalence since the infected have less time to spread the disease through exogenously assumed interaction. However, in the economic model, the effect is clearly positive since immunity is valued because exposed behavior is preferred to protected behavior, holding the health status of an individual constant.

Finally, the economic approach suggests questions beyond those raised in traditional epidemiology. Since infection is a good, one might expect better-educated people to be better at making their purchases early, and, indeed, some suggestive evidence exists showing this positive education effect on infectivity. Note that if health is measured in terms of susceptibility, this contrasts with a frequently discussed positive education effect on health.

3 The effects of public health measures

In predicting the effects of public health measures on disease occurrence, the economic approach differs from the biological mainly in assuming that there is demand in the *private* sector for disease prevention which may or may not be advanced by efforts undertaken in the *public* health sector. It is difficult to determine the effects of private-sector demand for disease control – and, in particular, its interaction with publicly provided interventions – without a choice-based theory. Consequently, standard epidemiological models, which assume *zero* private demand for disease control, overestimate the effect of public intervention. In particular, they do so by not discounting interventions that may be preempted by private demand for protection or interventions that may be counteracted by a feedback effect from private demand for exposure given a control measure. Thus, epidemiological models tend to credit reductions in disease prevalence only to public interventions – a fundamental difference with the economic model.

This section illustrates this basic but important point by two simple examples – public-sector vaccinations and publicly supported HIV testing. However, the general idea illustrated, the lower effect of public control of disease when allowing for private control, naturally extends to almost any comparison between epidemiological and economic models regarding the effect of public health policies on the spread of infectious disease.

3.1 The effect of public vaccinations

As discussed above, immunity can be purchased through infection or vaccination, and therefore the allocation of demand between the two different methods of purchasing immunity is determined by their relative prices, interpreted as the physical and time inconveniencies, complications, and/or hazards involved with infection relative to those received due to vaccination. For example, today more people suffer complications from the polio vaccine than from the natural disease. If immunity is purchased through vaccination, the individual pays the cost of the vaccination to avoid going through full infection to reach immunity. If immunity is purchased through infection, the individual pays the cost of infection to avoid the cost of vaccination. Vaccination is thus simply one of two ways of purchasing immunity. The individual demand for vaccination therefore responds to changes in disease occurrence, changes in the costs of infection versus those of vaccination (e.g., through cure or vaccine development), and changes in the cost of avoidance, since these factors change the relative prices of the two methods of purchasing immunity.

The demand for protection in the case of vaccine-preventable diseases is easier to measure, through vaccine demand, than the demand for protection against HIV, where safe sex is harder to observe. However, the same basic positive effect of prevalence on the demand for protection is predicted for vaccine-preventable diseases as well as for AIDS. In other words, the elasticity of vaccine demand with respect to disease prevalence (i.e., how much the demand for vaccines responds to new infections) is positive.

This positive elasticity has important implications for the predicted effects of health-care expenditures on prevention and treatment suggested by epidemiological and economic models. Much health-care discussion about vaccination frequently concerns how many dollars are saved in treatment expenditure by each dollar spent on vaccination. Since prevention expenditure is made solely on vaccine demanders, and treatment expenditure is made solely on non-demanders, the way in which vaccine demand responds to increasing prevalence will determine the relative sizes of the two expenditure categories. The important measure of the ratio between these two types of expenditure is the number of vaccinations each new infection leads to on average. In biological models there is no such private response in vaccine demand to an outbreak, so this number is zero. By contrast, in the economic model, the response is positive. For example, if during a measles outbreak of 1,000 cases, the number of vaccinations increases by 10,000, the average number of vaccinations caused by each infection is ten. The larger the number of vaccinations caused by the average infection, the larger the expenditure on prevention versus treatment by the private sector, and the fewer the dollars saved on treatment by an extra dollar spent on vaccination.

This positive response of vaccine demand also implies that mandatory public vaccination programs "crowd out" the private demand for immunity purchased through vaccination, in the sense that some individuals not included in the public program would vaccinate in the absence but not in the presence of the program. This is because the risk to individuals not included in the program is lower than if there were no program. Individuals outside of the program are guaranteed not to be infected by those who might have infected them if there were no public program. The public program crowds out the vaccinations in this sense: the people *outside* the program reduce their private demand due to a lower prevalence of the disease.

This may have four important implications: (1) Any estimation of the private demand for vaccination made in the presence of mandatory public programs and restricted to people *outside* the programs is downward biased. The low pick-up rates of many vaccines that occur outside the vaccination systems of the public sector (in particular, public schools) is in fact due to this system, and is not the reason the system is needed, as is generally argued. (2) The crowding-out effect implies that the "production function" for preventive public health (i.e., number of infections saved as a function of expenditure on preventive medicine) exhibits decreasing returns to scale. This occurs because the higher the level of prevention, the lower the incentive for non-preventers to prevent, and thus the more the marginal person must be subsidized to engage in preventive behavior. (3) Partial mandatory vaccinations may have little effect on total demand for vaccination and therefore on the resulting disease prevalence. The responsiveness in vaccine demand with respect to disease prevalence may thereby limit the ability of public programs to eradicate vaccine-preventable diseases since as soon as the disease starts disappearing the demand for protection against it goes down. (4) There may be a low overall effect on health-care expenditures of new mandatory programs such as requiring vaccinations for participation in public programs other than schooling (e.g., AFDC or WIC). Since total health-care expenditure, on treatment and prevention, is directly determined by the aggregate demand for vaccines, the resulting effect on expenditures may be small as well.

3.2 Public subsidization of testing

One of the keystones of AIDS prevention strategy in the United States and abroad is the provision of publicly funded antibody testing and counseling services for individuals at risk of acquiring or transmitting the human immunodeficiency virus (HIV) which causes AIDS. Virtually all fiscal institutions that have responded to the epidemic, whether national or sub-national, have included HIV testing in their prevention efforts. Since the licensing of the HIV antibody test in 1985, the total private demand for publicly provided tests in the United States has increased steadily, from 79,000 in the first year to 1.3 million in 1990.

Economists ask what determines the demand for HIV testing, and what effect does such testing have on the epidemic? Answering these questions is an important prerequisite, along with an understanding of relative efficacies, for any sensible allocation of resources among alternative interventions to prevent the growth of AIDS. It is also important because the economic model leads to different answers than the epidemiological model, which *assumes* that testing has a negative effect on the fraction of infected individuals that transmits the virus.

As discussed above, we interpret sex between two individuals as an economic transaction in the sense of being (*ex ante*) an activity beneficial to both parties involved. The problem of AIDS can be viewed as a problem of quality uncertainty among traders. In such a market, HIV testing is a device by which traders can learn their quality status. Before entering any form of partnership, an individual may take a test to determine his infection status. We assume that the partners of the tested individual observe his test result. This is plausible because when sexual partners have an ongoing relationship, it is difficult as a practical matter for one partner to conceal from the other the shock of a positive test. This, along with the more obvious point that reducing the number of sexual partners reduces the probability of infection, may be a reason for the reported growth in monogamous homosexual relationships in the wake of the AIDS epidemic.

The demand for testing in such a society of self-interested individuals (i.e., of persons who are not altruists in the sense in which economists use the term) comes from individuals who cannot enter partnerships without a negative test, but can with one. In other words, the demand results from individuals who will not engage in unprotected sex with each other before checking their infection status – the test is used as a safety precaution before engaging in risky sex. Given this motive for testing, the demand for testing is predicted to be increasing with disease prevalence, because the more likely an individual is to be infected, the more likely his partner is to require a test before engaging in risky sex. Thus, one prediction of the economic model is that tests are more frequent in regions with higher disease prevalence. For instance, the demand for testing should be higher in New York or San Francisco than in the Midwest.

The surprising implication of such analysis of demand for tests is that a voluntary testing program will not decrease the spread of the epidemic in a society of self-interested individuals. In other words, the growth of the disease is larger when testing is feasible than when it is not, even though the opportunity set of traders is larger in the latter case.

This result may seem to imply that more choices make individuals worse off. But that interpretation would overlook the difference between *ex ante* and *ex post* efficiency. *Ex ante* efficiency minimizes risk, given certain behavior patterns, which may or may not result in transmission of the virus, while *ex post* efficiency requires minimizing transmission. HIV testing allows individuals to reduce risk, given behavior patterns, hence increasing the volume of trades and not necessarily reducing transmission.

4 The welfare loss of infectious disease and optimal research priorities

This section analyzes the economic welfare loss caused by infectious diseases, compares it to common public health measures of the loss, and compares the optimal research expenditures across diseases implied by the two measures. As opposed to the positive questions addressed in the two preceding sections, this section is exclusively concerned with normative issues. In other words, here, we are interested in determining what *should be* done, according to economic measures of well-being, instead of explaining what *is* done.

The central idea of our analysis is to interpret exposure to infection as a good, as before, and the expected cost of infection as a "random tax" on this good. The tax is random in the sense that not all individuals who consume the good (i.e., expose themselves to disease) are taxed (by becoming sick). Such disease taxes may be different for different population groups, for instance, the random tax imposed by rubella on susceptible pregnant versus non-pregnant women. Under this tax interpretation of disease, protection against a disease is what economists refer to as a "distortion." This means that, like any other tax, the disease may lead individuals to behave in a way they dislike, in the sense that they would not have behaved that way if it were not for the disease. An example of such distortion is vaccination. In the face of infection, people are led to disliked behavior (e.g., being vaccinated) which they would have forgone without the disease. As with all taxes, this type of cost imposed by a disease, i.e., vaccination, is taken seriously by economists in evaluating tax changes, and has led most economists to evaluate the cost of a tax not only by the revenues collected by the public treasury but also by how much disliked behavior people engage in to avoid paying the tax. To illustrate this, suppose a million dollar per gallon gasoline tax is imposed. This would probably make you stop driving, and so the government would collect no tax revenue from you. However, this tax would still impose a cost on you by making you engage in undesirable behavior – perhaps using less convenient forms of transportation or moving closer to work. This cost is in excess of the revenues collected on the tax and is therefore called the *excess burden* of the tax.

The main difference between the economic evaluation of the loss imposed by a disease and that of public health measures, such as the aggregate "cost of illness," lies in recognizing this excess burden of the tax-interpreted disease. We want to emphasize the similarity between the welfare effects of standard commodity taxation and the welfare effects of disease. A standard tax imposes a burden in excess of the revenues collected by the public treasury if costly tax avoidance behavior occurs. Similarly, a disease imposes an excess burden beyond the case reports documented by the public health authority if costly disease avoidance occurs. We know that this so-called excess burden exists because there are distortions in vaccine purchases given the cost (i.e., tax) of a disease. Reducing this excess burden is an important function of economics. However, most public health authorities (e.g., the World Health Organization (WHO) and the Centers for Disease Control and Prevention (CDC)) are explicitly "revenue-focused" and ignore the excess burden of a disease. The case of polio illustrates this point: there are currently no infections in the United States but each child has to be vaccinated. According to a revenue-focused measure of welfare loss, polio induces zero loss in welfare although enormous expenditures of time and money are devoted to its prevention!

The most recent deadly disease, AIDS, can also illustrate these points. This case differs from vaccine-preventable diseases because the excess burden, unvalued safe sex, is harder to observe empirically. Here, the excess burden exists because most young adults value sex but may abstain for fear of infection. The burden may be extra high because of the asymptomatic nature of HIV infection, which may lead even uninfected pairs to avoid any form of partnership with each other.

4.1 The welfare loss of disease and the Laffer curve of public health

As above, interpret exposed behavior as a commodity being taxed randomly by disease. Then the demand for vaccines can be interpreted as consumption that is distorted from the most desirable type of behavior – exposure without fear of infection. The burden that this type of distorted behavior produces will be the *excess burden* of the disease – that is, the cost the disease places on a population beyond that of infections. This excess burden, the total demand for vaccines in the case of vaccine-preventable diseases, and the prevalence of a disease are, of course, negatively related: The more protection, the less disease. Therefore, the prevalence effect of an

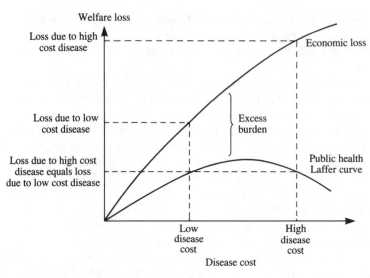

Figure 13.6 Disease cost and welfare losses

increase in the total cost of infection is negative, since the costlier a disease, the greater the demand for vaccine, and thereby the lower the disease prevalence.

Suppose we take a cohort of individuals, say all individuals born in 1962, and look at the loss of welfare imposed on them by a disease. The total loss is made up of two parts: the infections which the disease leads to and the excess burden of costly disease avoidance. The first term of the economic loss is made up by the excess burden of individuals who, given the disease tax, do not demand exposure. The second term is made up by the individuals who still demand exposure – that is, the individuals who eventually make up the disease case revenue (the public health measure of loss). The relation between the two welfare measures, the economic loss and the public health loss, is illustrated in figure 13.6.

The figure shows the two measures of welfare loss as a function of the total disease cost. The top curve is the economic loss and the bottom curve is the public health Laffer curve. The public health measure denoted makes up the "Laffer curve" of infectious disease in the sense of being the quantity demanded of the taxed good times the tax. This measure of loss may also be interpreted as an aggregate "cost of illness" measure. Two diseases are illustrated with low and high total disease costs, respectively. The important point is that welfare loss is increasing in the cost of the disease due to the excess burden. This continuous increase does not hold for the Laffer curve of public health. The aggregate cost of illness is the same for both diseases but the economic welfare loss is larger for the higher-cost disease due to its larger excess burden, perhaps as measured by sales of vaccines.

The figure also indicates when the two measures of welfare loss coincide. This occurs when the disease is completely harmless. In other words, the difference between the two losses, the excess burden of infectious disease, approaches zero only when the disease is harmless, its total cost of infection being zero. The total cost of infection may approach zero either by a lowered per unit time cost or a shortened duration of infection, both of which may be the result of new health-care technology through treatments. The two measures are only equal when the efforts of public health are irrelevant.

4.2 Optimal medical research expenditure and Ramsey taxation

Medical research expenditure may reduce the cost of infection by shortening the duration of infection or lowering the per unit time cost of infection; both decrease the total cost of infection, the cost paid when randomly taxed by the disease. Thus, in the economic model, research expenditures are interpreted as reducing the random disease tax.

Optimizing research expenditures across diseases with the objective of welfare loss minimization is analogous to lifting a set of taxes on a set of commodities – here, the commodities are exposure to the different diseases. This problem is analogous to a taxation problem first studied by Ramsey, which asks how to raise a given revenue through taxes without leading individuals to change their behavior in an undesirable fashion.

Applying these insights to our case, we obtain the result that taxes should be reduced – that is, the most research expenditure should be made on the disease with the largest excess burden. This implies that, *ceteris paribus*, the *smaller* a disease's effect, the more research expenditure should be allocated on reducing its cost of infection (due to its larger excess burden).

In the economic model, the expected benefit of a set of research expenditures comes from the chance of eliminating the welfare losses caused by the different diseases. Hence, a given expenditure pattern across diseases is optimal only if the marginal reductions in expected welfare losses across diseases are equal – if they are not equal, money could be better allocated by taking dollars away from low margins and spending them on high margins. Under diminishing research returns, it follows that the larger the welfare loss reduction would be upon finding a cure, the larger research expenditure should be. Therefore, since the welfare loss is decreasing in prevalence, this implies that more common diseases should get less research money.

This result can be applied to AIDS research funding. As one would expect, AIDS has lower prevalence than such lower-cost diseases as syphilis and chlamydia (see Philipson and Posner, 1993). Many individuals, including health economists, have argued that research expenditure on AIDS is excessive, given the small number of cases compared to other, more common diseases. This, however, ignores what the low prevalence of the disease tells us, namely the existence of a relatively large excess burden which *prevents* the number of case reports from increasing.

Note

1 I thank Gary Becker, Pierre-Yves Geoffard, Johan Linden, James Heckman, and Richard Posner for discussions on these and related topics. As goes without saying, I have been in intellectual, as well as financial, debt to Gary Becker ever since he brought me to the Department as a post-doc.

References

Akerlof, George. 1970. "The Market for 'Lemons': Quality, Uncertainty, and the Market Mechanism," *Quarterly Journal of Economics*, 84: 488–500.

Anderson, R., and R. May. 1991. *Infectious Disease of Humans; Dynamics and Control*, Oxford University Press.

Becker, G. 1991. *A Treatise on The Family*, Harvard University Press.

Bailey, N. T. 1975. *The Mathematical Theory of Infectious Diseases and Its Applications*, London: Griffin.

Brandeau, M., and Kaplan, E. 1994. *Modelling the AIDS Epidemic*, Raven Press.

Philipson, T. and R. A. Posner. 1993. *Private Choices and Public Health: An Economic Interpretation of the AIDS Epidemic*, Harvard University Press.

Philipson, T. 1994. "Economic Epidemiology," manuscript, Department of Economics, Universty of Chicago.

Index